Patrick Hein

How the Japanese Became
Foreign to Themselves

Patrick Hein

How the Japanese Became Foreign to Themselves

The Impact of Globalization on the Private and Public Spheres in Japan

LIT

Umschlagfotos:

Hannah Arendt, © Käte Fuerst, Ramat Ha-Sharon, Israel
Inazo Nitobe, © City of Towada, Japan, Nitobe Memorial Hall

Bibliographic information published by the Deutsche Nationalbibliothek
The Deutsche Nationalbibliothek lists this publication in the Deutsche
Nationalbibliografie; detailed bibliographic data are available in the Internet at
http://dnb.d-nb.de.

ISBN 978-3-643-10085-6

A catalogue record for this book is available from the British Library

©LIT VERLAG Dr. W. Hopf Berlin 2009
Fresnostr. 2 D-48159 Münster
Tel. +49 (0) 2 51-620 32 22 Fax +49 (0) 2 51-922 60 99
e-Mail: lit@lit-verlag.de http://www.lit-verlag.de

Distribution:
In Germany: LIT Verlag Fresnostr. 2, D-48159 Münster
Tel. +49 (0) 2 51-620 32 22, Fax +49 (0) 2 51-922 60 99, e-Mail: vertrieb@lit-verlag.de

In Austria: Medienlogistik Pichler-ÖBZ GmbH & Co KG
IZ-NÖ, Süd, Straße 1, Objekt 34, A-2355 Wiener Neudorf
Tel. +43 (0) 22 36-63 53 52 90, Fax +43 (0) 22 36-63 53 52 43, e-Mail: mlo@medien-logistik.at

In Switzerland: B + M Buch- und Medienvertriebs AG
Hochstr. 357, CH-8200 Schaffhausen
Tel. +41 (0) 52-643 54 85, Fax +41 (0) 52-643 54 35, e-Mail: order@buch-medien.ch

Distributed in the UK by: Global Book Marketing, 99B Wallis Rd, London, E9 5LN
Phone: +44 (0) 20 8533 5800 – Fax: +44 (0) 1600 775 663
http://www.centralbooks.co.uk/html

Distributed in North America by:

Transaction Publishers
New Brunswick (U.S.A.) and London (U.K.)

Transaction Publishers
Rutgers University
35 Berrue Circle
Piscataway, NJ 08854

Phone: +1 (732) 445 - 2280
Fax: + 1 (732) 445 - 3138
for orders (U. S. only):
toll free (888) 999 - 6778
e-mail: orders@transactionpub.com

For my parents Genevieve and Aloyse Hein

Chapter One.

A different perspective on globalization

The chapter questions the limitation of the vita activa to working and consuming and insists that the political public sphere needs to be maintained and enlarged in order to defend democracy and its open spirit against the champions of radical neoliberal globalization and private interests. The chapter acknowledges the importance of Hannah Arendt's political philosophy for today, builds a bridge between her framework and similar concepts of Japanese thinkers, identifies and compares distinctive shared political traditions of the West (Hellenic) and East (Samurai) and questions some myths and the shortcomings of globalization in Japan by presenting case examples and reflecting on current paradigm shifts in political culture under the impact of globalization.

Introduction

Many authoritative and engaging books have been published on globalization but few have highlighted the political, social, psychological and ecological implications in a historical comparative perspective and few have analyzed the reactions of various social actors such as civic groups, women, foreigners, mental health counselors, the media, social institutions, cultural and religious agents to the transformations induced by globalization. Japan as a local target of globalization has been chosen because studies on the topic have been rare for this country and rather focused on economic or financial aspects. The main theme of this study revolves about several topics structured into the following major subjects of interest.

- Significance of globalization within the theoretical framework of the political theory of Hannah Arendt
- Greek and Samurai shared wisdom and values that help coping with current globalization challenges
- Historical dimensions and milestones of westernization and modernization during and after the Meiji Restoration
- Changing identities and what it means to be Japanese in a global setting
- The social, cultural, mental, educational and environmental implications of globalization
- Extent to which globalization has generated and influenced changes in political culture
- Preserving the distinctiveness and learning from the wisdom of Japanese culture

Globalization and the affluent society have produced more ruins, waste of

energy and resources as well as garbage than any other period of Japanese history and this phenomenon contrasts vastly with pre modern times. This is not a
study for or against globalization but a book that wants to shed light on social
change and the risks of cultural transformation caused by radial economic global
transformations and uncontrolled human interference. According to a statement
of the International Labor Organization (ILO) World Commission on the Social
Dimension of Globalization

> "problems (we have) identified are not due to globalization as such but to deficiencies in its go-
> vernance. Global markets have grown rapidly without the parallel development of economic and
> social institutions necessary for their smooth and equitable functioning"(Source:
> www.ilo.org/public/english/wcsdg/docs/synope.pdf).

In other words what lacks is the commitment to balance and match the positive implications of globalization like increased trade, intercultural interaction
and human exchanges with the needs for social awareness, justice, equality,
mental health care and multicultural sensitivity. The working thesis of this book
is that the dominant economic globalization has mostly benefited big business,
bureaucrats and foreign investors and contrary to the recommendations of ILO
has not created a fair and well balanced world community creating equal opportunities for everybody. Globalization is to a certain extent manageable and con-
trollable. People have choices and the freedom and power to do things differently and the civic society trend towards gender equality, improved care for
children, a healthy family environment, resource conservation, sound immigration and integration policies, ethical corporate governance, respect for human
rights, fair distribution of national wealth and respect for the aged serves as a
benchmark for public political resistance against the status quo.

The focus on industrial growth has made Japan economically affluent but
socially and psychologically the country has paid a high prize: a general sentiment of meaninglessness and "empty affluence" (McCormack, 2001) among the
young and older people, a "fatherless society" (Mitscherlich, 1963) of physically
and symbolically absent fathers, who fail to play a role model for their families
at home, a high suicide rate correlated to high education levels, scores of depressed, stressed and burned out teachers, law enforcement officers who fail to
respect the law, the rise of lethal violence–defined as homicide and suicide combined–and the loss of self respect, a steep rise of mental, personality disorders
and eating disorders, aggressive and anti-social behaviors, respect less treatment
of the old aged and a deep gender cleavage in society. This rather pessimistic
picture depicts the distressed state of current Japan but in no way this should
predict the chances for social change and improvements in the future. Recent
research (Nakamura and Watanabe-Muraoka, 2006) has revealed that the
younger generation is more open to globalization talk then their parents used to
be and shows greater awareness for global social responsibility and this is a positive sign of encouragement and hope. More Japanese than ever take up the

challenge of 'thinking global, act local', study, live and work abroad, learn foreign languages, marry with foreigners and most importantly change and adjust
their mindset and way of thinking, behaviors and attitudes towards increased levels of multicultural awareness and ethnic diversity acceptance (Lee et al, 2006).

The root cause of the problem

Back in 2002 a research fellow from a renowned policy think tank Yutaka
Ohama published an article in the weekly conservative magazine Seiron and asserted that globalization would destroy Japan and that it would be a fatal error to
follow blindly the example of the United States. According to Ohama, a system
of competition for competition's sake formed in America due to historical factors,
such as the country's abundance of resources, ability to maintain its population,
and wealth of opportunities. In Japan, meanwhile, top priority was placed on
ensuring institutional stability, and systems were formed that placed the principle of coexistence above that of competition. He concluded that even if Japan
were to adopt U.S. style competition for competition's sake, it would not be able
to achieve prosperity. Apart from the fact that the article reflects a deeply rooted
hate-love relationship with its most important ally America it is noteworthy that
the underlying message given to the readers is that modernity and secular rationalization of the Western developed world threatens Japanese pure identity and a
value system striving for peaceful coexistence instead of identifying itself with
the alleged Western style brutal competition and coldhearted individualism. It is
also noteworthy that Ohama thinks that the Japanese government bears its part
of guilt on the shoulder for not taking more distance to the U.S. and trying to
pursue more self determined and autonomous policies. Similar attempts to claim
back national pride by relying on national policies, cultures and traditions and
escaping from America's intrusion have been made in the past by the Tokyo
right wing Governor Shintaro Ishihara and recently by the university professor
Masahiko Fujiwara (2007). Unfortunately those defensive anti-western attempts
do not offer any constructive insight or answers to the fundamental question of
what kind of nation Japan should become. In a special contribution to the Japan
Times at the beginning of the year 2008 former Prime Minister Yasuhiro Nakasone made the public indifference responsible for the stalemate and inertia in
Japanese politics apart from the lack of vision of current leaders. The issue he
raised is of extreme importance because politics in Japan has always been delegated to a selfish hereditary class whose self belief it was and still is to belong to
a special greed with no need of consultation with or connection to ordinary
people. This study will try to retrace the historical dimensions of the exclusion
of the public citizen from the political sphere and argue that the extreme and exclusive focus on economic globalization has worsened the gap between those
who benefit fully from it such as shareholders, business leaders and the political
hereditary class and those who are the losers–among them housewives, working
mothers, divorced women, the disabled, foreign workers, freeters and
part-timers, the mentally ill and abused children abandoned and confined to suf-

fering in privacy. The exclusion of the citizen from active participation in public affairs and his protective private sphere that is put at risk by disrupted family structures, low biological reproduction and social exclusion is not the reason for political inertia as falsely claimed by Yasuhiro Nakasone but rather the result of a development that is relatively new and dating back to the Meiji era. It will be shown that newly emerged decentralized NGOs and bottom up political movements have gained significant public strength and reputation by challenging a political establishment lacking vision and a system following blindly the global economic dogma of change without purpose. Citizens tend to believe more and more that NPOs are efficient and contribute more than traditional state agencies, labor unions or political parties to improving social services, quality of life or international cooperation.

Numerous authoritative, critical and thoughtful works have highlighted the impact of globalization on and from Japan from various perspectives and explored the meaning of the positive and negative consequences of Japan's globalization over the long term. Several works that have highlighted current issues of globalization and how they are impacting modern Japanese society in either complementing, contrasting or contradictory ways are Alomes (2005), Clammer (2001), Eades et al (2000), Hook (2001 & 2006), Schaede et al (2003), Itoh (2000), Morris-Suzuki et al (2008), Tamotsu (2002 & 2004), Yoda et al (2006) to name just a few. The multidisciplinary approach chosen for this study is borrowing from and relying on scientific and empirical research results from various science disciplines such as political science, history, economics, law, religion, clinical psychology, philosophy, anthropology, sociology, criminology and the humanities as this multifaceted approach allows for a broader, general view and is a very rewarding way to gain new insights and a better understanding of the otherness and the unknown. The historical comparison of the traditions of the ancient Greek polis city-state with medieval Samurai thinking will demonstrate that the alleged strict divisions between East and West are socially constructed artifacts and in this sense the topic of what is means to be Japanese will be expanded to what it means to be an engaged and active public citizen from a globally unifying perspective rooted in the shared traditions and traditional values of Samurai medieval Japan and the Hellenic polis.

This study assumes that individuals have a certain control over their destiny and can influence to a certain degree what they want to become. People may be restricted by environmental factors such as education, socioeconomic status, access to information, legal status and human rights and genetic or hereditary factors that go beyond their control or restrict them but at the same time they are free to choose and take autonomous decisions under such given circumstances. In his deeply moving book 'Man's search for meaning' (2006) based on his personal experiences in Auschwitz Dr. Viktor Frankl, who developed the logo therapy, wrote that even if submitted to the most inhuman, cruel treatment people could survive if they would see a meaningful sense in their suffering, have a dream for the future or set a teleological goal which would transcend their current suffering or apparent meaningless existence. The suffering caused by the current globalization has been induced by economic means and its external symptoms are mental health problems, violence, child abuse, homicide and suicide rates that have been steadily growing despite high statistical affluence, education and earnings levels. Citizens are told to comply and conform to others in public, restrict themselves to a routine life, refrain from getting involved in public affairs or treat their opinion as a purely private matter, and maintain a low self esteem and profile in public.

What it means to be a Japanese is not only defined by becoming or being a Japanese (Hendry, 1986)–something which suggests that it is beyond our control how we think and act in the future–but by what happens when transcending existing structures, cultural stereotypes, social barriers or legal restrictions. A recent study by Nakamura and Watanabe-Muraoka (2006) has shown that young female Japanese score high on the scale of global social responsibility (GSR). GSR is a parameter to measure a scope of acting that transcends national borders and gives new meaning to mankind as a whole. Could it be that global social responsibility transcends traditional cultural bonds and cultural stereotype patterns of behaving like Japanese? What it means to be Japanese is not a static concept but submitted to and influenced by the trend towards a multicultural and diverse society. The growing number of alienated and mentally stressed Japanese returnees poses a challenge and opportunity to the society as a whole. This study hopes to contribute to how a future multicultural Japanese citizen could look like and to help define his identity by exploring the joint cultural heritage of East and West.

The mainstream perception of globalization

Western academic thinking tends to favor knowledge production and highly abstract thinking. It is interesting to note that most Anglo Saxon contributions on globalization operate with systemic concepts such as power balances, economic development assumptions or Western cultural hegemony concepts such as Max Weber's protestant ethic. It is implicitly assumed that most societies strive to follow the Anglo Saxon way of cultural and economic development which is very questionable. The world is viewed as nothing but a huge market place where private companies supported by state institutions and investment agencies compete for producing, marketing or selling goods or knowhow to other countries. Top Japanese officials have been largely supporting this purely economical and technological view of globalization. The Ministry of Trade and Industry (MITI) and the external trade arm 'JETRO' have been promoting 'Invest in Japan' campaigns and assisting foreign companies into entering the market and eliminating obstacles such as skilled labor, quality and inspection standards, high business costs, real estate purchase, M&A activities, tax issues, difficulty of

capital participation and acquisition of management control in Japanese companies, complexity of distribution channels, legal restrictions, administrative procedures, lack of public low interest loan or subsidies or insufficient infrastructure. So called trainee visiting programs have been set up by the Ministry of
Foreign Affairs to secure the supply of cheap labor for companies and farmers.
The ultimate goal of globalization in the view of the government is to open
markets in a controlled way so that Japanese and foreign companies can mutually benefit from the consumption power and cash in profits. As a result globalization has caused a big irreversible shift in the country's infrastructure: the
high quality Made in Japan label representing superior craftsmanship has gradually been phased out and industrial manufacturing facilities have been gradually
shifted and outsourced to neighboring China. The extreme demand for cheap
labor and low cost products has nurtured a new poverty and domestic social injustice. The Asahi Shimbun in its morning edition of 28 September 2007 reported that more than ten million individuals were living with less than 2 Million yen income per year. The number of households who depend on welfare has
exceeded one million in 2005. More than 200 000 elderly patients in their 70s
who cannot afford paying their medical bill have been excluded permanently
form the legal medical insurance coverage. One of the dilemmas and antagonisms of modernity is that economic inequality, social injustice and material poverty have increased despite the general raise of national monetary national income, institutionalized welfare programs, affluence and increased ownership in
society. Is it just a problem of unjust distribution that could have been solved by
applying Keynes monetary redistribution policies or taking fiscal government
spending measures or is the root cause of the social gap between rich and poor,
men and women, qualified and unqualified uncontrollable and unsolvable? The
quest for cheap goods and cheap labor or the cheaper the better thinking expressed in the Japanese slogan *yasukereba ii desu* (what matters is that it is
cheap) has been the religion of the average Japanese consumer over the past 50
years. The price that had to be paid for this ideology has been huge: rise of unstable employment terms, disruption of social relations, food safety scandals,
food self supply insufficiency and social exclusion.

Globalization per se does not mean that there is only one single desirable
standard of development. The recent popularity of Japanese arts, cuisine, lifestyle, architecture, hybrid cars, animee, movies and sumo sports in the world
shows that globalization can be a two way process of mutual learning and
change. It is not the intent of this book to look at Japanese globalization trends
departing from Japan to the world but to focus on the external globalization impact on local thinking and culture in Japan. It is also not the intent of this book
to proof that Western style globalization has caused more harm than benefits to
the Japanese but it is rather the intent of this study to shed light on the many
shortcomings of unilateral economic globalization trends.

The present study also hopes to show that the radical social, environmental and socioeconomic transformations have been willingly supported and implemented by the government and private industry leaders of Japan. Many of the shortcomings have been self made and are not a result of external pressure or *gaiatsu*. Why have the Japanese become foreign to themselves and why do they not respect their own cultural heritage and traditions? The poor state of national politics symbolizes the lack of visionary leadership among all those who prefer to be conforming to and follow the trends passively rather than proactively create the future and be concerned about fellow citizens, the environment, peace preservation, equality and social justice. There is no doubt that the current globalization standard in operation has changed the traditional face of Japan in many negative ways and the Japanese themselves have to determine if the incurred changes represent what they really want or not. Recent surveys might suggest that many people do not perceive the changes and developments as an improvement of their lives: in a recent survey more than two-thirds of Japanese are worried about their lives–a record high, according to a news report. An annual Cabinet Office survey conducted in July 2007 found 69.5% of respondents were worried or felt uneasy about their everyday lives. The figure was the highest on record for the survey, conducted annually since 1958. Anxiety about life after retirement topped the list, followed by health concerns. Nearly three-quarters of all respondents said the government should reform the social security system, and more than half said measures should be taken to deal with the rapidly aging society.

The three areas of concern mentioned in the survey: life after retirement, health and social security are all related in a way to money and material or physical existence. One might argue that there is no apparent reason to feel uneasy as Japanese citizens enjoy the highest economic affluence since World War II, a statistically high standard of living, personal freedom to do whatever they like and to go wherever they want. However suicide rates tell a different story. The number of those who have lost a purpose in their life despite high economic affluence and despite high education levels tops annually thirty thousand and the number of those who engage in irrational and unpredictable anti-social behavior is growing as well. In the age of digital high technology, GPS systems, emails, text messages and mobile phones the ability of face to face communication, to perceive, feel, think and reflect has declined rapidly. Due to the high level of commercialization of all aspects of social life people suffer from an apparent existential malaise that prevents them from thinking, distancing themselves from self destructive consumption patterns and from reducing their over dependency on material and physical consumption. The materialistic and economic malaise and the perceived meaninglessness of existence are common among the highly industrialized nations.

The dramatic social changes to which the world as a whole has been submitted have been reflected in the groundbreaking monumental studies of global thinkers and scholars such as the philosopher Hannah Arendt (1958), the ecology science pioneer Lewis Mumford (1958) and the psychiatrist Viktor Frankl (2006). Frankl, Arendt and Mumford published their works in the 40s and 50s under the deep impression and shock of the aftermath of Auschwitz, the Hiroshima and Nagasaki atomic bombings and the mass destruction this had made possible. In the meantime new threatening or ethical issues such as global warming, water shortage, religious intolerance, cloning, euthanasia, gender identity disorders and life threatening infectious diseases have been added to the list of global matters of concern.

Yet despite the obvious global threats and despite the necessity to think and behave in a global way and come up with urgent and feasible solutions to prevent war, environmental destruction and human exploitation many opinion leaders in Japan seem to not have really grasped what is at stake and this is surprising when taking into account the considerable integration level of the country in the international community as reflected for example in its longstanding United Nations presence. In October 2008 for example Japan was elected as a non-permanent member of the United Nations Security Council (UNSC) at the elections held during the 63rd Session of the UN General Assembly to serve another two-year term in the United Nations Security Council starting from January 2009. With this election, Japan has assumed non-permanent membership in the Security Council for the tenth time, the most frequent among all the members of the UN.

To show its readiness to face the challenges of globalization the government has invested massive efforts in promoting information exchange and research on current globalization issues including education, sustainability or cultural heritage. The study of the impact of globalization on local communities, social relations, family and on the private sphere in particular seems to have however been low on the agenda. Unfortunately in none of the official globalization conferences conducted the social dimension has been given sufficient attention despite the tremendous impact of globalization on the social and private spheres of citizens. The government sponsored joint United Nations University(UNU) and UNESCO series of joint globalization conferences started in 2003 with the UNU/UNESCO International Conference Globalization with a Human Face - Benefiting all, that was held in Tokyo from 30-31 July 2003; the UNU/UNESCO International Conference on Globalization and Intangible Cultural Heritage: Opportunities, Threats and Challenges held from 26-27 August 2004, also in Tokyo; the UNU / UNESCO International Conference Sustaining the Future. Globalization and Education for Sustainable Development held from 28-29 June 2005 at Nagoya University, Nagoya, Japan; and the UNU / UNESCO International Conference on Science and Technology in the Era of Globalization organized from 23- 24 August 2006 in Yokohama and Pathways Towards a Shared Future: Changing Roles of Higher Education in a Globalized World from 29 to 30 august 2007 again in Tokyo and the UNU / UNESCO International Conference on Globalization and Languages: Building on Our Rich Heritage on 27 & 28 August 2008 in Tokyo. To support some of the arguments stated in this study statistics from internationally recognized and authoritative organizations such as ILO, UNESCO, OECD or the WHO have been included where appropriate.

This study on globalization aims to analyze and highlight the historical relationship between the private and public spheres. The statement that in Japan there is no distinction between private and public, that both have been completely separated or that private and public have a completely different meaning than in the West or the assumption that the public sphere has monopolized every aspect of life to the disadvantage of the private sphere indicates a need for clarification and conceptualization of the historic comparative evolution of both spheres. It is argued in this study that the issues raised by globalization have been caused by a decline of political activity or better the lack of equal citizen participation in public affairs in a world totally governed by private societal economic and business interests and by business friendly state administrations. The renowned political philosopher Hannah Arendt (1958 & 2005 & 2007) considers the disparity and loss of the public and private spheres in the modern world as major root cause for the societal problems of today. Even though the fundamental approach is rooted in the tradition of European history and thought, her conclusions can nevertheless be applied to Eastern or Asian societies as well for two reasons: the first reason is that the formal Western model of political rule and government has made its way through other cultures in the wake of economic globalization; the second reason is that many of the concepts and values thought to be exclusively Western can also be found in Eastern cultures. This is true for Japan as well as this study will show.

What distinguishes Arendt from many other authors who worked on the same subject is her profound knowledge of world history especially the ancient Hellenic and Roman civilizations and her sharp deep analytical intellect when it comes to elucidate the historical events and facts of transformations that concern mankind as a whole. She is one of the very few scholars who undertook the enormous task of understanding and explaining the changing meanings of private, public and political from its origins in the Greek city-state to modern bureaucratic rule. Before starting to compare Japan with the rest of the world and before drawing conclusions it seems useful to reflect on the terminology used in this study and seek a common understanding as a base to start from. Social scientists often wrongly assume that their readers know what they mean. When comparing different cultural contexts it matters however even more not only to be precise, objective and critical but to offer clear-cut definitions of the words used. One of the distinguished merits of Hannah Arendt is to have explained and interpreted the linguistic and historic origins of common language words such as politics, private and public.

Her masterwork 'The human condition' (1958) known also as 'Vita activa' in the German print edition underlies the historical framework for equal political participation among free citizens. Based on her observations of political life in the ancient Greek city state she analyses the political preconditions necessary to establish a free social order and defines politics in its original Greek meaning as the equal opportunity for every citizen to deal with public affairs in a civilized way by using words and arguments and not by using coercion or violence. The difficulty in understanding the Greek meaning of politics lies in the fact that the modern mind considers politics as a means to an end such as classless society or justice whereas the Greek consider being political as an end in itself. The best definition of Greek politics is given by Arendt herself:

> "The point is (...), rather, that we know from experience that no one can adequately grasp the objective world in its full reality all on his own, because the world always shows and reveals itself to him from only one perspective, which corresponds to his standpoint in the world and is determined by it. If someone wants to see and experience the world as it "really" is he can do so only by understanding it as something that is shared by many people, lies between them, separates and links them, showing itself differently to each and comprehensible only to the extent that many people can talk about it and exchange their opinions and perspectives with one another, over against one another"(Arendt, 2005, p128).

Action and speech are the two outstanding political activities. Politics is in the Greek sense more process than contents and its outcome is therefore not only unpredictable but also irrelevant. More important than the decision is the ability to incorporate the viewpoints of others into one's own viewpoint. Being political requires a deep sense of passive ability to listen and empathize. For Arendt equal political participation is valued not because it may lead to agreement or to a shared conception of the good, or finding the truth, but because it enables each citizen to exercise his or her powers of agency, to develop the capacities for judgment and to obtain by voluntary and concerted action some measure of political freedom.

Rule over others in the public sphere is anti political according to Arendt. She rejects politics in the traditional meaning as defining the relationship between those who rule and those who are ruled as it has been the common understanding among Western philosophers from Plato to Montesquieu, Hegel and Marx. According to her the Greek democracy excluded rule over others and resembles therefore closely to the modern concept of direct democracy–citizens conduct public affairs by themselves–as opposed to representative democracy where sovereignty of the citizens is exercised on behalf of them by and delegated to professional lawmakers subjected to strict party discipline.

By investigating human interaction within the Greek city state Arendt finds evidence for her theory that politics in its original meaning has been very much related to the concept of public or positive freedom. Freedom from the private sphere enables citizens to seek political freedom among their equals for the sake

of life itself, appreciation, fame or immortality. The paradox of this public freedom was however often violent rule over others in the private sphere. The great
public achievement of the Greek polis citizens was that they never ruled over
others even though their rule in the private sphere was absolute. Arendt has asserted that real democracy can only function in small numbers and only where
precedence is given to action and debate over purely conformist behaving and
opinion less functioning. Wherever overpopulation and mass gatherings of
people occur democracy cannot survive. Therefore real democracy best works
on a local decentralized level like the one of the Greek polis. According to
Arendt the Greek polis–despite all its negative outcomes such as subjugation of
women, barbarian foreigners and slaves, homosexuality, war and violence–was
the most ever free and equal political system in the history of mankind. Arendt's
defense and re-discovery of the authentic political has been criticized as being
naïve and utopian but ultimately utopian comes from the Greek *u topos* which
literally translated does not mean impossible as many falsely believe but simply
not yet existing or possible but not realized yet. Arendt can be considered as the
forefather of modern civic society and equal civic participation and free citizen
involvement into public affairs. She defines equality not in the modern egalitarian western meaning expressed in the famous slogan of the French revolution
'liberty, equality, fraternity' but as political equality amidst economic inequality.
The unequal's are those who have no access to the political sphere–for example
in historic terms the slaves and the women–whereas the equals are those who
share the same political rights. Equality in the political sphere presumes inequality in the economic private sphere. In modern theory formal egalitarian concepts and political equality are often confused.

The Stanford online encyclopedia of philosophy maintains that

> "monetary equality can strike one as a misguided ideal for the different reason that it does not
> deal in what is of fundamental importance. The value of purchasing power, equal or unequal,
> depends on the value of what is for sale. Imagine that the economy of a society is organized so it
> produces only trivial knick-knacks. Freedom to purchase trivia is a trivial freedom, and render-
> ing it equal does not significantly improve matters. (Critics of consumerism and consumer cul-
> ture are moved by the idea that in actual modern societies, the economy, responsive to consumer
> demand, is responsive to demands for what is not very worthwhile and ignores many truly im-
> portant human goods that either happens to be not for sale or that by their nature are not suitable
> for sale on a market)" (Source http://plato.stanford.edu/ entries/ egalitarianism/).

The quest for public, positive freedom might be ultimately the most important and desirable of these intangible and invisible human goods. The Western
model of globalization relies on the private freedom to consume and on formal
passive equality restricted to working, voting and being submitted to the rule of
law.

As already mentioned formal equality allows or restricts everybody to have
the same passive or functional right to work, consume and vote. In Greek socie-

ty politics used to be a sphere of public freedom and reflected the equal interaction of the most able and brightest or the morally best and wisest as opposed to modern times where the freedom to consume in an egalitarian mass society erases all distinctive traits. Arendt has been criticized for her model of an elitist or aristocratic democracy type but what she imagined was a kind of communitarian self administration of the wise, pacifist, emancipated and educated people on a smaller scale. For Arendt the existence of the political defined as absence of rule is a precondition to achieve positive freedom. Without a thriving political space real freedom is not possible. Arendt asserts that modern mass society is hindering and obstructing equal political interaction, the unity of speech and acting, critical thinking and judgment. She defines modern mass society as a form of co-dependency for the sake of making a mere living, where the pursuit of material revenue and income overshadow the search for meaning and freedom and where private activities that merely focus on physiological and biological needs have gained precedence over public political participation.

Despite democratization attempts during the U.S. occupation and liberalization efforts similar to those that have gradually changed the political landscape in post Nazi Germany the political culture in Japan has not achieved the same degree of maturity, common sense and wisdom as in postwar Germany. Rarely do common citizens engage spontaneously or directly in public political debates or discussions and the disdain for political participation and politicians in general has been considerable. There is also a looming tendency among people in Japan to either turn a blind eye on unpleasant matters or avoid their own responsibilities and shift all the blame on others. The government encourages people to keep their explicit opinion–*honne* in Japanese–private and conform to the *tatemae* principle of pretending and masking for the sake of harmony and peace in public. As in other advanced countries freedom exists if at all only in the private sphere. For Arendt however the private sphere is politically a sphere of privation or de-privation.

The Latin word for private *deprivere* means to prevent someone from participating in public affairs. An exclusive private person does not exist in a political sense. According to Arendt and other scholars like Lewis Mumford the supremacy of working and consuming has brought the world to the verge of collapse and annihilation. The environmental and social consequences of globalization are universal and do not differentiate between East and West or communist and capitalist systems. The economic miracle that took off after the war with the restoration of the former *zaibatsu* conglomerates under the form of industrial *keiretsu*, reached a peak in the 60s and in the 70s when the first oil shock struck the nation, the enormous environmental damage resulting from the continuous overuse and waste of natural resources for the sake of industrial development became obvious in Western and in communist blocs alike(Strunkel et al, 1976; Schreurs, 2004). Japan the export nation number one had paid a huge prize in terms of irreversible damage done to its environment, cultural assets and local landscapes.

Expansion of private society interests into the public sphere

According to Arendt the private pre-political sphere with its emphasis on private property, satisfaction of physiological and other biological needs expanded after the 17th century gradually into a privatized borderless capitalist system characterized by mass production of goods, ownership without property, dependence on social welfare and bureaucratic regulation undermining political pluralism and public participation. The transformation from the *communitas* or *Gemeinschaft* to the *societas* of same-minded private citizens who expanded their private particular interests into the public sphere peaked in the development of the cities, urbanization and the modern sovereign nation state defined by his sovereignty, a single currency, fixed borders and a standing military force.

During the transition to capitalism, modern mass consumption and central nation state, a functioning consumer market and a regulatory bureaucracy have prevailed over the nurturing of a political sphere and its ideal of the politically active and involved citizen who takes pride and care of political affairs by himself. In his book 'The affluent society' (1958) the economist John Kenneth Galbraith claimed that the modern assumption of capitalism–increasing the output and producing growth–had been formulated in a pre-modern age of scarcity and ended therefore in overproduction and over affluence with the consumer being coerced into consuming the surplus. In order to be able to take time off and engage in politics and public affairs the citizen has to be free from private worries and interests. The private sphere and right to private property need to be protected from the state interference and society. One of the biggest antagonisms of the modern capitalist society and the state is according to Arendt that it takes away property from private hands to build roads and tunnels for the alleged benefit of society. The disappearance of private property goes hand in hand with the spread of anonymous ownership and shareholding. For Arendt the paradoxes of capitalism make it unworthy and incredible. The capitalist sacred principle of competition is derailed by continuous attempts to create non competitive monopolies and cartels or going deliberately bankrupt as the U.S. Chapter Eleven procedure demonstrates. The bailing out or nationalization of bankrupt private companies by public taxpayers money is another enigma of uncontrolled capitalism that can be summed up as: privatize the profits and socialize the losses or private affluence versus public poverty.

For Arendt a society of privatized interests is undemocratic and apolitical because it is based on principles in which economic interests and institutions dominate with no room left for the citizen to take political action or participate in the public realm. Politics conceived as modern welfare state or public welfare is not the beginning of politics but its end in Arendt's theory. Public social welfare aims at separating and isolating the mentally and physically weak, the disabled, the homeless, street children, bullied juveniles, the abandoned elderly and all those whose distinctive character has become their factual non-participation in public life.

Social justice is defined as the ideal, unachievable principle that all persons are entitled to basic human needs, regardless of superficial differences such as economic disparity, class, gender, race, ethnicity, citizenship, religion, age, sexual orientation, disability, or health. This includes the eradication of poverty and illiteracy, the establishment of sound environmental policy, and equality of opportunity for healthy personal and social development. In Arendt's thinking the social or better societal sphere is undemocratic because it is the extension of private, purely consumptive and profit interests into the political public sphere and prevents the individual from realizing its full human potential.

Recently there has been a trend in Japan to disregard the ideal of social justice as yardstick for social progress and replace it with the ideology of self-responsibility (Hook, 2007) or 'take care of yourself' which has become the dominant neoliberal dogma in a fully globalized market where social inequality and poverty amidst overflowing affluence have reached unprecedented levels. The after war consensus of lifetime employment and seniority based pay has been abandoned for the sake of shareholder interests and investor profitability gains. State agencies supposed to support the socially weak pursue anti-social policies and the bureaucracy itself restricts citizen access to basic social care and services. The area most affected by a loss of purpose and accountability is probably the public service. It is noteworthy that applicants who apply for a job in the civil service feel attracted to it not because they are proud to be part of a greater vision serving the public good, social justice, or other public ideals but because it is an economically safe lifetime job. The loss of purpose of one's public mission and service to the general public affects all civil servants including once highly valued government jobs such as policeman or teacher.

The state

State is defined as the bureaucracy, the judicial system and the executive branch of the government. Quite often it is taken for granted that parliament is part of the established institutional state system. This misconception does not reflect the intention and tradition of parliamentary representative democracy complemented by modern elements of direct democracy. Historically parliament has always been considered as a separate body from other state institutions as it is the only democratically elected, legitimate direct people body. Unfortunately the spirit of parliamentary democracy has been corrupted by money and vested interests both on a local level in city parliaments and even more on the national level. The original idea of a public forum or space where elected politicians bound by a fixed term and mandate, deliberate public affairs in an equal spirit and are accountable to their conscience and voters only has been substituted by centralized party discipline, lobbyism and the interference of bureaucrats into the legislative process with most bills submitted for vote being drafted by the civil servants themselves. A member of parliament exercises his free but limited mandate similar to a liberal profession. The regular and continuous renewal of lawmakers and exchange of membership is critical to maintaining the spirit of parliamentary democracy. The composition of the parliament is meant to reflect a representative picture of the whole society. It should represent the whole range of professions and reflect the gender distribution. Every mature and legal public citizen has a right to active as well as passive voting. Passive voting means that one can become a representative of a local constituency for a limited term of usually four years in most Western democracies. To secure his financial independence the representative was originally entitled to a symbolic and honorific compensation. The word itself is meaningful in that it suggests that the task of the office holder is not a permanent fulltime job but an honorific temporary engagement. In Western parliaments the representatives are in principle accountable to their own conscience in the first place and theoretically blind loyalty either to the voter or the party without careful consideration of personal conscience would be against the spirit of representative democracy. Unfortunately in reality most ballots are strictly dictated by party discipline and as a result individually motivated decisions based on personal ethical convictions or conscience occurs very seldom in parliamentary institutions. The element of faithfulness towards one's own individual conscience seems to be universally accepted even if political reality often contradicts the principles of respect for autonomy, inner freedom and individual consciousness. The original spirit of parliamentary democracy has been distorted by modern party politics and bureaucratic institutionalization. The formalism symbolized by the rule of the majority principle has substituted the ideal of free impartial, debate among equals accountable to their conscience. The reality is that politicians nowadays do not represent the diversity of society but have either a background in civil service or their status is equalized to a civil servant rank. The honorary based compensation system has been replaced with a pay scale based on civil servant seniority and qualification levels. As a matter of fact highly paid professional representatives have become integral part of the institution they were supposed to reform, decentralize and liberalize. In several countries attempts have been under way to supplement and complement representative democracy with elements of direct democracy. Contrary to legally binding plebiscites, consultative referendums–surveys without any legally binding character–do not reflect the true purpose of direct democracy but are often used to support and backup government policies and decisions. Direct democracy can only work if the right to information and perhaps even more the right to balanced and objective information is guaranteed by the constitution. Most representatives would rather hesitate to delegate their power–even for limited decision-making–to citizens because they would never trust the citizen's maturity of judgment.

The benefits of direct democracy cannot be measured by looking at the results but rather at the liberating political process of involving informed and responsible citizens instead of taking anonymous decisions on their behalf without even consulting them. Direct democracy works best on a local or regional level and it makes no sense to have nationally elected representative lawmakers decide on local issues. Issues related to the environment or energy that can be solved locally should be addressed locally. There should be no taboo themes and every subject of public interest should be debated by the assembly. Direct democracy can correct the shortcomings of representative democracy without necessarily substituting it. Centralization, urbanization, anonymity, passivity, indifference and reliance on state bureaucracy do not constitute a positive environment for the nurturing of civil participation, plurality and diversity. Arendt herself rejected modern party politics and opted for direct democracy. She had been inspired by the short lived anarchistic–anarchy being defined as order without rulers–council republic of Weimar in 1919 and had worked out herself an utopian political council concept for the Israeli-Palestinian unification in her later years.

The state is composed of the bureaucracy who essentially protects its own vested and hidden interests, reacts more than it acts and fails to serve citizens in a spirit of transparency, benevolence and accountability. As a result of social transformations the state took away the monopoly of violence from private citizens, centralized criminal justice and legalized social relations to regulate the interests of the competing society members and to protect the nation state against internal or external enemies. In the Greek polis the household chief had the right to kill his private slaves and his often violent authority exercised in the private sphere was absolute. The modern nation state has the prerogative for law enforcement, punishment, surveillance of citizens with security cameras, for gathering and storing their personal data and intervening militarily to secure its self declared national interests, peace or humanitarian goals.

Arendt has described the social transformation process from a decentralized community of traditional farmers, artisans and craftsmen grouped into the category of *homo faber* to the modern centralized passive working for consuming commercial mass society and has insisted that the political public sphere needs to be maintained in order to defend democracy and its open spirit against the modern rule of anonymous bureaucratic institutions. Without a stable political sphere of freedom from rule or government real positive freedom is not possible. A democratic political culture allows autonomous citizens to broadly and directly discuss, debate and speak out anything on their mind in public without fear, protest in a non-violent way, engage in litigation through independent courts, and question the legitimacy of political acts or laws. Not being able to discuss topics of general concern in public is contrary to a mature political culture and not being allowed to engage in non-violent passive protest against decisions that have a disastrous or life threatening existential impact on mankind is a violation of basic rights.

Self-interest and civil participation

Self interest will be defined as private economic profit seeking or personal gain contrary to the not for profit public good and public benefit. Public interest or national interest as such does not exist. Civic engagement, civility and civil courage are the public virtues of the mature and independent global citizen. Civil society can be defined as a social sphere that occurs in groups outside the state, the market, and the family. NGOs and NPOs form part of the so called third sector besides the market and the state. The purpose of any democratic NGOs is to defend the public good against the irresponsibility, resistance or indifference of the state or society as a whole. The role of NGOs and social movements is that of acting as citizen lobbies, often on a volunteer basis. They are social movements in so far as they may engage in a one stop public protest against some specific injustice or lobby for some affirmative action in some specific field and disperse after goal fulfillment. A Japanese NGO who had sought compensation and guilt acknowledgment for a blood contamination scandal disbanded after achieving its goals.

NGOs are part of society in the sense that they are composed of private ordinary members of society. They are political in the sense that they constitute an alternative public sphere either opposed to what the state does or complementing or rectifying what the state does or omits to do and they may evolve into a political representative party on a parliamentary institutional level if they estimate that it is necessary to codify and legislate their political roadmaps, manifests or long-term visions. They are gendered in the sense that their backbone is often made up of women who prefer a more flat, human communication or human relations oriented and equality based approach towards politics than men who prefer a more vertical, domineering and institutional approach. They are global in the sense that they are influenced by international norms and developments that translate into enhanced local activities. They are independent in the sense that citizens, rather than being dependent on the state or the family, freely choose to become involved by defining themselves how the common good should look like and contributing to it proactively with their own, often limited, means in terms of staffing and finances. The question if the state absorbs the civil sector or co-opts it to take over part of the state's responsibilities is a futile debate that may even be arrogant as it takes not into account how the recipients think about receiving volunteer aid. Nakano who interviewed the care receivers reports that the civil sector has changed the predominant thinking of growth, work and consumption into a new paradigm of post materialist val-

ues:"Recipients placed moral, social and human values ahead of material consumption and productivity" (Nakano, 2003, p. 163) and suggests that this constitutes a new way in which people articulate their relations with society outside
family, the company and the state.The inner motivation that drives the civil sector should not be underestimated: active citizens feel dignified, proud and honor
by doing what they do. Finally civil groups are per definition voluntary in the
sense that people gather and disperse by free agreement. Even in a collectivist or
group oriented society coercion or pressure alone cannot induce a desired civil
behavior over the long-term. Serving the community for free and voluntarily
outside of family responsibilities and the workplace is basically an honorable
activity. The German wording for volunteer work is *Ehrenamt* or literally honorific office a combination of the words office entailing public importance and
honor entailing that public involvement is a matter of individual honor not related to money. Helping people without receiving money is yet another key definition of civil sector activities. Recently private business organizations such as
Keidanren that encourage their members to donate part of their profits for pre-
dominantly foreign aid projects have started to support NPOs in Japan. Nakano
is suspicious of such attempts because they submit the civil sector to private for
profit benchmark thinking and criteria and because they discourage NPOs from
acting in a spirit of compassion, spontaneity and flexibility. From the perspective of Hannah Arendt's political theory of the public and private the civil sphere
might be defined as a pre-institutional public political voluntary network that
acts as counterbalance against vertical state rule and differentiates from society
in that it does not pursue private for profit interests. Plurality and participation
are its key elements.

Legal versus legitimate

In the Greek city state law was meant to setting boundaries to protect the
civil political sphere and political activity and this is not to be confused with the
modern meaning of law as a controlling and regulation tool restricting public liberties. The Meiji Samurai statesman Saigo Takamori regarded external formal
laws as irrelevant and unnecessary insofar the inner moral laws dictating the
right code of conduct were respected. The modern concept of rule of the law and
lawful government as a means to limit absolute power led to a complete negation of political activity and participation. Today rule and law have actually become one and the ruler only administers and obeys the laws he himself created.
Political activity in modern terms is limited to producing laws, legal ordinances
and legislative acts that regulate the public and even private life of citizens. The
modern right of equality before the law responding to a sense of justice is not to
be confused with the Greek idea of the legally or constitutionally protected equal
legal right to free political speech and participation.

It is assumed that no government however tyrannical it may be can survive without maintaining a minimum of legitimacy in the eyes of the ruled. To be perceived as legitimate a government needs tacit approval and acceptance of its citizens. Terror and violence cannot guarantee or secure long term legitimacy. Even totalitarian or authoritarian regimes need to recur to media manipulation and information control, censorship, brainwashing, indoctrination and propaganda or personality cult to maintain legitimacy and cannot rely on constant physical terror and violence alone. In democratic regimes legitimacy is achieved through affluence, consumerism, welfare, media intrusion or other more subtle manipulative means.

Power, from the Latin to make possible, is regarded as a positive force contrary to ruling (Habermas, 1983). Where citizens gather to pursue a voluntary political act and disperse after the goal has been achieved power has been exerted in a positive way. Power does not exist as per se and is not permanent. It disappears when people disperse and does not require permanent institutions. Permanent institutionalization of power by one or several parties relying on the state bureaucracy is called ruling or governing.

Change without purpose in Japan

The malaise about the ongoing global changes, the purposelessness of those changes and the cultural diffusion has been described by the eminent head of the agency of cultural affairs Professor Aoki Tamotsu:

> "In contrast, however, the present great wave of change, to which the term globalization is applied, is distinct due to the absence of any clear agent or goal. In every part of the world, including Asia, numerous forms of very rapid change can be seen, such as the spread of information technology, the expansion of economic markets, the diffusion of the consumer economy and consumer culture, the spread of mass entertainment, the homogenization of lifestyles, the domination of fast food, and the standardization of urban landscapes, especially the proliferation of high-rise buildings. At the same time, we see the opening-up of the digital divide and growing disparities of wealth and poverty, ethnic and racial discrimination, increasing levels of violence and crime, the rampant spread of terrorism, and the continuation of wars. The world is simply full of rapid and expanding processes of change, all in the name of globalization. Behind these phenomena one can discern the goal of attaining commercial hegemony through the sale of computers and other high-tech equipment. However, there seems to be no overall objective for which these changes are being pursued. No underlying principle or purpose can be found, and there seems to be almost no discussion about this either" (Tamotsu, 2004, p. 90).

Professor Tamotsu from the perspective of a country that has been Westernized and modernized late, speaks up against those who want to make people believe that globalization does not endanger cultural identity or diversity and laments that "culture in Japan has lost any overall coherent pattern by which it could be recognized as distinctively Japanese" (Tamotsu, 2004, p. 90). The exposure to the risk of cultural and human alienation through globalization is closely linked and connected to the monopolization of the public discourse in the hands of government and bureaucracy and the remolding of what originally constituted the privacy of an intimate and protective sphere towards atomization, isolation, lethargy, routine, consumption and loneliness.

What Arendt described as patterns of global conformity, loss of identity, cultural uniformity, emptiness, loss of intimacy and family values is reconfirmed by Professor Tamotsu in his pessimistic assessment on the impact globalization has had on Japan and concludes that "the end of globalization is in the end nothing" (Tamotsu, 2004, p.94). What is at stake is mankind itself: the destruction and waste of natural resources, the extinction of wildlife and natural reserves, unequal distribution and access to food and water, mega-urbanization and overcrowded cities, the worsening of life quality, the decline of traditional family bonds, finally the loss of the awareness of the preciousness for life itself.

A tentative definition of globalization

Globalization will be defined as increased international mutual exchange of commercial goods and trade, traveling and migration, financial streams and direct cross border investment, as well as exchange of ideas and intellectual property. The overwhelming literature refers to economic criteria when describing globalization. The non-commercial dimension of globalization will be called mutual cultural understanding and respect, tolerance, social justice, autonomy, freedom, fairness, equal opportunities, diversity and the right to be different from the mainstream. Western style globalization has been successful in establishing a global standard of values and concepts rooted in radical individualism, assimilation, fierce competitiveness, the winner takes it all thinking, focus on exclusive shareholder value and ownership, materialism, self enrichment, an anything goes liberalism and extreme rationalism. Japan's decision makers in business and government adapted this model as well and suited it to their own needs.

Western style globalization has been the dominant force in the past and the Western instilled way of affluence and mass consumption threatens human mankind more than ever. The supremacy of linear production and consumption patterns without consideration for the social cost and ecological damage, the disintegration of stable social relations and community networks, the growing disability to communicate verbally and face to face in the age of digital new multimedia communication tools, the cost and damage caused by immobility and car traffic, the decline of food self sufficiency ratios and eating disorders, illiteracy, new poverty, drug and alcohol abuse, youth violence, religious intolerance, mental health problems and dangerous infectious diseases have a lasting and sometimes irreversible impact and the risk to lose the ability to live a healthy, meaningful and fulfilled life might become very real for many.

The latest victim of Western style globalization is likely to be China who has replaced Japan as the industrial platform of the manufacturing world. China used to be a poor but relatively equal society. It is without doubt true that globalization has worsened social justice and equality among citizens in China and widened the gap between rich and poor. Among the latter the most vulnerable are the rural poor.

The joint tradition of East and West

Many studies have been published on the Samurai and the Greek polis but very few studies have actually compared the similarities and differences of both orders. The Greek city states were established in the 7th and 8th century B.C. Scholars generally agree that the ancient Greeks sought a form of self administration that would break the constraints of traditional aristocratic rule. It is agreed that the political body would support the individual and provide certain rights and liberties to him and expected him in return to fulfill certain obligations and duties to the community. This in turn, led to the end of aristocratic rule, which paved the way for democracy to be successful. Scholars agree that the new democratic institutions and councils established during this time led to the creation of the city states, because the people realized that smaller sized cities allowed for easier direct administration. The *agora* or market place was the central public space where free citizens interacted and socialized. The political process was inherited by the citizens themselves and political interaction was fully public, transparent and open.

The Samurai era expanded roughly from the 8th century to the late 19th century in Japan. The literature on the Samurai is abundant as well. Publications on two of the most inspirational and outstanding Samurai figures, Saigo Takamori (Ravina, 2004; Yates, 1995; Morris,1975) and Inazo Nitobe (Howes, 1995 & 2003 ; Burkman, 1990) are complemented by excellent Samurai studies from Ikegami (1995 & 2003), Friday (2004), Hillsborough (1999), Shiba (1998), Mishima (1978), Sato (1995), Jansen (1995) and Nitobe (2007). Preston (2003) and Wright (2005) have taken a comparative approach focusing on similarities between the Greek polis and the Samurai order. There is a need for more comparative studies with a focus on philosophical principles, ethical norms and sociological categories such as rule, power, legitimacy, plurality, freedom and others.

Karl Jaspers (1962) and Lewis Mumford (1956) have been among the first to highlight the joint cultural heritage of the East West axial philosophers Socrates and Confucius who had a similar impact and taught a similar way of living and practical ethics. Despite the geographical and historical different context that separates them, both philosophers rooted their beliefs in common ground. Both axial philosophers went the way of thought as Jaspers and Mumford highlight. They showed humanity the way of philosophy. Confucius by "concentrating upon the reflective study of books, he trusted the power of thought to subdue in the end, mere thoughtless power" (Mumford, 1956, p. 72). He was not for or against anything but supported what was right in a moral sense. This high moral sense can be achieved through education, cultivation of character, arts, etiquette and politeness. Socrates in a similar way goes the way of reason and human thought and by conversation, dialogue and questioning he compels other to think thereby "transcend the world without negating it" (Jaspers, 1962, p.92). For both knowledge acquisition is not for the sake of knowing but for the sake of self-betterment.

The key hypothesis is that from a historical and comparative perspective the basic features and characteristics of what it meant to be Japanese and what constitutes the distinctive traits of Japanese identity does not radically differ from the classical Hellenic tradition inspired by the glorious and distinguished life within the political structure of the polis. The Hellenic civilization regarded as the cradle of European political thought resembles Samurai ethics in early medieval Japan at the peak of Samurai authority and influence in many ways. Similar to the citizens of the polis the Samurai landowners reigned with absolute authority over their private sphere and had great freedom within the boundaries of their fief. Initially they were allowed to use their sword for the purpose of war fare, self defense, acts of vendetta or suicide, but under Tokugawa rule the use of the sword was restricted as well as their status curtailed. One of the ideas forwarded in this study is that in a comparative historical perspective a horizontal equal public sphere was already present in the hierarchical order of medieval Samurai society before Tokugawa and later on Meiji rulers enforced Westernization and modernization introduced Western formal concepts of social order such as a bureaucracy, parliament, national criminal jurisdiction and imposed radical changes on the domestic systems creating a new social inequality and rising gap between the few at the top and the mass of unequal nameless subjects.

The similarities between the spiritual foundations of the polis and the Samurai order cannot overshadow the fact that neither of those orders represented an ideal world or the best of worlds. As mentioned women, slaves and foreigners were excluded from the public realm and did not enjoy equal status. Both the Samurai and the Greek polis order were subsequently disbanded by strong forces of modernization, commercialization and Westernization. It is noteworthy that both the great Greek thinkers such as Plato or Socrates and great Samurai medieval thinkers and Confucian teachers such as Sato Issai have lost their spiritual inspiration and ethical foothold on history and contemporary society. The decline of the classical education tradition that has affected Europe with classical Greek and Latin having been deleted from school curricula and Japan where classical Chinese philosophy and Confucian moral education principles lost their influence has left an empty space. The existential vacuum of the modern subject has been well described in literary masterworks such as 'Kokoro' by Nobel Prize winner Natsume Soseki and portrayed in movies such as 'Ikiru' by film director Akira Kurosawa. The painful soul searching for self-identity and overflowing sadness distinguishes both artistic works. What unites both works is the search

for an answer to an existential malaise in the wake of deep social transformations caused by war and rapid economic modernization.

Individual conscientiousness as common fundament

According to Inazo Nitobe (2007) all Samurai behavior is ultimately rooted
in what he calls *kokoro* and which is equivalent to conscience:"we know right
and wrong by this (PH: *kokoro*), called conscience, and which makes no errors"
(Nitobe, 2007, p.11). The word *kokoro* appears in many word combinations and
one of the strongest expressions is probably the saying *kokoro wo sute-
ru*–literally to throw away one's conscience meaning to be socially indifferent to
others. Arendt quotes Aristotle who in a similar way said:

> "The measure for everybody is virtue and the good man" (Arendt, 2005, p.24) and continues
> that "the standard is what men are themselves when they act, and not something which is exter-
> nal like the laws or superhuman like the ideas" (Arendt, 2005, p.24).

The requirement for a strong individual, personal conscientiousness independent of external pressure and laws is shared by both traditions.

As Nitobe puts it knowledge acquisition had for Samurai no value as such.
Knowledge was related to action. Samurai warriors intuitively knew what was
right to do without necessarily knowing why and without having to justify their
acts to anybody. Not doing what was right to do or doing the wrong thing was
considered disgraceful. Socrates reflects a similar insight when he says that "the
awareness that man is a thinking and acting being in one–someone, namely,
whose thoughts invariably and unavoidably accompany his acts–is what im-
proves men and citizens" (Arendt, 2005, p.23). To stick to the path of morality
was not only expected from the subjects but also from the rulers and in that
sense rule could never become absolute but was subject to fair and just behavior
of the ruler himself. Ansart (2007, p.144) for example notes that loyalty was
conditioned to the good behavior of the *daimyo* land lord and this requirement to
good rule was codified in the ruling Tokugawa house codes.

Wright (2005) suggests in her excellent comparison of Soseki's novel 'Kokoro' with the texts of Plato on Socrates that the death of Socrates and suicide of
'Kokoro's' main character called *Sensei* (teacher) offer analogous examples of
suffering, isolation and loneliness in a world that does not honor anymore individual autonomy, self worth, virtue or honor. She regards 'Kokoro' as a critique
of the economic, cultural and social transformations induced by Meiji Restoration and stresses several elements of congruence between the Samurai ethics
displayed by the main protagonist Sensei and Socratian thinking. The story of
Sensei's moral failure is the story of a man who betrays at the end his best friend
identified only by his initial 'K' who symbolically represents the dishonored and
nameless modern subject. For Wright both "Socrates and Sensei's failure
represents a broader failure of their respective cultures" (Wright, 2005, p.66).

Sensei by abandoning his best friend K, abandons his conscience and Socrates by leaving behind his students when choosing to die betrays his followers. Both choose death as a way out of misery and disgrace over honor. In both cases death can be viewed as a form of induced self-punishment rather than a mode of self-sacrifice for a noble or honorable cause. Socrates inverts his commitment to individual honor above death by not resisting or trying to defend his individual honor when facing a meaningless death disguised as judicial suicide. For Sensei his life without honor leaves him no way out of his dilemma but death. A real Samurai or Greek warrior would have resorted to the last means of voluntary death only to protest a great injustice. Now death suddenly becomes the lesser evil compared to saving or defending one's individual autonomy rooted in honor. There is no room for dying for a great cause in both scenarios: for Wright both "exemplify the paradox of freedom: life is often more tragic than death" (Wright, 2005, p.75). The world's highest suicide rates in a society cut off from its own roots, disrespectful of its traditions and spiritual foundations seems to support this conclusion.

Virtue and honor

When speaking of a moral virtue or an excellence of character, the emphasis is not on mere distinctiveness or individuality, but on the combination of qualities that make an individual the sort of ethically admirable person he is in practical terms. The virtue as inner moral guiding principles represented a cornerstone of Samurai education. The study of the Confucian Five Classics and Four Books formed the basis of Samurai practical ethics.

Arête is the Greek word for unique excellence especially moral virtue. Socrates supposed that *arête* can be equated with knowledge of the good and held that doing good follows directly from knowing what is good. The unity of thinking, knowing the good and action are constitutive elements of both the Greek and Samurai heritage.

Hannah Arendt (2007) refers to the influential writings and insights of 18th century French political philosopher Montesquieu when she reiterates that the three criteria that underlie all political life can be classified into virtue derived from equality, honor derived from distinction and finally fear derived from coercion and terror in a despotic state. This is in line with the modern interpretation in that ethics and integrity are internal elements whereas fame, approval, admiration and popularity are the visible output of cultivation of one's own character. As long as the abovementioned criteria are taken for granted or legitimate in the eyes of the rulers or the ruled the political system will survive. Once this belief or common understanding breaks down the political system ceases to exist and will come to an end either by peaceful means or not.

That happened precisely when the Samurai were economically gradually absorbed by the merchant class which led to the loss of their once high status and high self esteem. The new merchant criteria that took precedence over morality, honor and virtue were routine, contractual trust and material self-interest. The consensus among the classes had eventually faltered away: what was once considered as honorable and virtuous behavior was considered now as treacherous and criminal. The poor treatment given to the authentic Samurai leader Saigo Takamori after his resignation from the Meiji cabinet exemplifies the breakdown of the traditional morality consensus: in his Satsuma (Kagoshima) home domain he continued to be admired as an immensely popular hero and respected dignitary but the newly established rulers in Tokyo viewed him as nothing but a criminal and traitor. Most former Samurai warriors were gradually co-opted into the new dominant system and given a new sense of purpose as civil servants under Meiji.

Timê is the Greek term for honor, esteem, or dignity. For Plato, a timocratic society or person is governed by concern for public dignity or reputation. Honor is often put as opposite to death. In ancient Sparta, a warrior was expected to return from a battle either with his shield or on his shield–implying that victory or death were the only honorable options. Fleeing a battle was a shameful act and punished. For the Greeks *timê* meant honors bestowed by others. The word *timê* means the good opinion of others and the display of it in prizes, awards, and political offices. This concept excludes an individual's personal honor resulting from the act of fidelity to one's ethical norms. For the Greeks the word honor always implies something external. Nitobe takes a similar stance when he recognizes that in Samurai history "only a few men realized that honor exists within each person" (Nitobe, 2007, p.38) while most identified honor with gaining outward derived fame on the battlefield.

Virtue and honor constitute the two key constituents of both the Samurai and Greek political order. Even though virtue, equality, honor and distinction played a vital role in both the Greek and Samurai orders their degree of influence varied. Within the more hierarchical Confucian framework a relative sense of equality could only become reality among friends whereas within the Greek order equality was the constitutive part of public life. On the other side it might be mentioned that the Samurai were hypersensitive to honor whereas in the ethical systems of the Greek honor was not the highest ranked good.

Honorable competition and honorable collaboration

It is Ikegami's (1995) merit to have refocused the twofold double-faced and inter-relational aspect of honor in Samurai thinking. The starting point and question that intrigues her is to figure out how Samurai could manage to regulate and appease their strong internal sense of honor by adjusting it to new external standards of behavior. She comes to the conclusion that "honor mediates between individual aspirations and judgments of society" (Ikegami, 2007, p.213) and in the case of Japan this evolution "appeared to offer an effective analytical tool for articulating the distinctive trajectory of Japan's passage to modernity" (Ikegami, 2007, p.213). Sources of transitions of samurai honor as cultural concepts are identified by Ikegami as "control through the refocusing of the expressions, loci, and sources" (Ikegami, 1995, p.342).

The expressions shifted from autonomous violent acts to technically organized warfare, and then to the eventual expression of honor in a civilizing and pacifying environment through emphasis on the Samurai's moral character. The second shift, on the locus of honor, involved a shift from a personal to organizational nature. The Kamakura period, during which a close personal master and vassal relationship was formed, transferred the political authority from the aristocracy to the military caste. One component of honor, loyalty, was reinterpreted during the so-called *Sengoku* era of the warring domains at the turn of the 16th century when betrayals were rationalized if for the purpose of achieving glorious victory. By the Tokugawa period, the locus shifted eventually to the collective organizational honor of the samurai class, to the master's family, to the domain, and by the end of the period, to the emperor, to facilitate the Meiji Restoration.

The third shift was changing the source of honor from the performance, action, and valor of the Kamakura and *Sengoku* warring state periods to that of the Edo period. When regional warlords vied for hegemony, the new fighting philosophy permitted a certain amount of self-determinism and some horizontal alliances that still glorified strength. Tokugawa ascendancy brought a total pacification and consolidation policy, and introduced a highly hierarchical bureaucratic samurai class, creating an inevitable "cultural dilemma" (Ikegami, 1995, p.155). This cultural dilemma valorized the collective honor of domesticated Samurai, but privileged ranking and uniform principles of government had to be reconciled in a fashion that could either safeguard pride in lineage and class or maintain the hidden love for the master as advocated in the Samurai piece 'Hagakure'.

Despite defending their moral code for centuries amidst ongoing social, economic, military and cultural changes both the Greek and Samurai orders disappeared with the formation of a unified nation-state monopolizing the right to rule, the right to exercise violence, the right to set up criminal jurisdiction, the right to public education, the right to issue laws, to issue a national currency, to build a public transportation infrastructure, to unify the military service and to establish a standardized tax administration. Neither the city states in Greece nor the Samurai domains were able to overcome their differences, join together or unite in a permanent alliance against the new shaping order or work out a consistent foreign policy.

In the Japanese case Ravina (2004) notes that Saigo Takamori's native domain of Satsuma (Kagoshima) had been aware of the intentions of the new Meiji rulers to unify the country if necessary by force and engaged therefore in a sweeping effort to modernize its administration, its military and its governance of the countryside to improve its financial solvency and overall ability to stay independent. Although the emperor commended these measures they were problematic for the central government because "if Satsuma could create a modern state within the boundaries of a traditional domain, then perhaps local autonomy was a viable alternative to initiatives from Tokyo" (Ravina, 2004, p.163). The introduction of the centrally controlled prefectural system led ultimately to the defeat of the local independence model. Equality, virtue, distinction and honor as common bond and destiny of the warrior class had lost their raison d'être in a society that valued scientific objectivity, conformity, control and rationality more than individuality, selflessness or subjectivity. In the verge of transformation from Tokugawa society and disbanding of the Samurai class to the secular Meiji rule moral Samurai virtue was substituted by Meiji obedience, harmony, conformism, uniformity, standardization, ritual and habit.

Phren and *hara*

In Greek *phren* designates originally the diaphragm, also more loosely the adjacent intestines, and hence that part of the mind which is or seems to be located in those regions. Thus it becomes a synonym for fear, joy, and grief; but also for the seat of the mental faculties, thought or will. The meaning of *phren* is kept alive in terms related to mental illness such as schizophrenia. In similar ways the Japanese identify the *hara* or lower abdomen as the center of human activity and not the brain as seat of the intellect or heart as seat of the emotions and feelings. This is revealed in the following idioms: *hara o kimeru* meaning to make up one's mind; *hara o watte hanasu* meaning to have a heart to heart talk; or *hito no hara o yomu* meaning to read someone else's mind. The most famous Samurai word *hara-kiri* relates to this concept too.

Shame

When discussing the notion of shame it is often referred to the book 'Chrysanthemum and the sword' by Ruth Benedict (1989) to reiterate the dual separation and incompatibility of Eastern shame culture versus Western guilt culture whereby the shame culture is enforced by external sanctions whereas the guilt culture is introverted. Shame is not only caused from reactions to public opinion but is also the result of inner conflicts of the self. The same is true for guilt: it is not only correlated to internalized sin feelings but also externally to public opinion and judgment of society. Psychologically, guilt has been thought to be a more advanced emotion than shame. In a study by Ikegami (2003) the notion of shame in Samurai behavior appears in a new more differentiated light against the backdrop of the ancient Greek shame culture. Ikegami argues that the stereotype assumption of Eastern shame culture versus Western guilt culture is overly simple and inaccurate as well. She exemplified the moral dilemma of the Samurai figure Yoshida Shoin, who secretly tried to board a foreign ship despite a Shogunate edict forbidding any contact with foreigners, torn between his external duties towards the authorities and internal sense of autonomy and doing what he deemed to be morally right even if this was considered a crime in legal terms. He was not publicly ashamed of his illegal action because he knew that is was morally right to ignore the edict for the sake of the greater noble cause of studying the intentions of the enemy in order to protect the nation against a possible future invasion by Western forces. When he did what he did he was in full agreement with his conscience and not the least ashamed. In Ikegami's words "it is the moral integrity of the person rather than society that defines shame" (Ikegami, 2003, p.1357).With psychological insight Ikegami refutes the shortsighted thinking of Benedict assuming one undivided and static self that is either ashamed or feels guilt. Freud already mentioned three distinct selves the biological self, the social self and the ideal self. In modern psychology personality development is viewed as a mutual interaction between individual and environment, whereby the environment shapes the individual and the individual interacts with his surroundings. During this process the individual regulates his self in alignment with changing circumstances without compromising on personal core convictions and inherent principles. Ikegami argues that "shame in the Samurai honor culture actually exemplified an overlap and relatively fluid interaction between the external and internal dimensions of the self" (Ikegami, 2003, p.1370).

In Samurai society social status was not gained through birth or hereditary privileges but had to be merited by constant acts and efforts incorporating practical Confucian ethics. When confronted with a dilemma the Samurai had to weight principles against each other. In Yoshida's case he chooses to be loyal to his internal conscience rather than feeling ashamed or resentful of his public act of disobedience. He preferred to die in an honorable way rather than to continue living in a world of moral wrongdoing or be loyal to a morally wrong ruler. Ikegami defined this key element of Samurai pragmatic behavior as honorific individualism. In a more general sense it may be called ethical individualism.

Superiority, excellence, honor and fame

Hannah Arendt's concept of excellent, superior citizens taking charge of public affairs has been sometimes misunderstood as an aristocratic or elitist concept excluding the majority of common citizens from political participation. Arendt was aware of the historical limitations of the polis democracy in that it left untouched the practices of slavery, war or gender discrimination. However she gave credit to the positive elements of superiority; an excellence that allowed a small group of men to nurture an independent personality and become distinct individuals. Distinction is one–the other one being equality–of the two core criteria of political action in Arendt's theory (2007). She argues that in monarchies and in all hierarchical forms of government superior distinction and honor are perceived as stronger elements than equality which is more characteristic of republics. Her observation that individual distinction is a constitutive element within any hierarchical society–including thereby implicitly the Confucian or Asian model–indicates the importance of being better than others not with regard to strength or brute force but with regard to moral behavior, justice seeking, honorability and compassion.

In Greek and Samurai traditions the concept of superiority is not to be taken literally. The Greek passion for fame opens the door to immortality. Arendt defines this quest for fame as aristocratic in the sense of trying to be or show your best to others. For Confucius only a virtuous, fair, impartial, humble and compassionate person is qualified to receive the attribute superior. As Jaspers (1962) points out in his book on the great axial philosophers the superior man is a man of pragmatic ethics combined with action. Compared to the inferior man the superior man does not pursue any material self-interest or personal gains: "The superior is concerned with justice, the inferior man with profit" (Jaspers, 1962, p.48). He knows what is right to do "The superior man is not for against anything in the world. He supports only what is right" (Jaspers, 1962, p.51). Superiority may be resumed as inner strength or moral steadiness independent of the changing *Zeitgeist* or the moods of times. Superiority is not revolutionary and does not seek to change the pre-established existing order. It is rather a method or way of internal growth and moral refinement. This is also the reason why such importance is given to proper ethical education of the young.

The power of (male) friendship

The Tokugawa shogunate relied on Neo Confucian orthodoxy after it seized control of the country from around 1600 putting an end to instability. Neo Confucianism based on the teachings of Chu Hsi (1130-1200) stressed the static order of the universe and human relations are thought to be vertical such as those between parent and child, teacher and disciple or lord and vassal. The Tokugawa rulers strictly prevented any formation of political horizontal alliances. The only exception to the strict vertical structure was the equal relationship among friends. Choosing the right friend was of capital importance. Confucius himself stressed that one should not accept somebody as friend who is not one's equal. The Samurai had to be constantly aware of their relations towards those above them such as master, authorities, emperor and below them–the serfs, the slaves, the subordinates–and under such circumstances had either to rely on their inner guiding virtues or on the opinion and advice of very close friends when considering issues of social order, morality or right behavior. Real and true friendship was highly valued: the goal of friendship was not to share irrelevant intimate private or secret information about oneself to others as is the case nowadays but to maintain a lifelong strong alliance between equals built upon strongly shared convictions aimed at better serving the master, emperor or shogun. In his study on the Samurai ethic in the work 'Hagakure' Mishima (1978) maintains that friendship involves a high level of sincerity and that true friendship will reveal itself only in times of crisis and troubles. Arendt adds a human touch to the importance of friendship when she notes that the opposite of equality is loneliness and the "ruler of a rural household had no equals unless he went to war" (Arendt, 2007, p 950).

Male friendship has been a dominant theme since the Heian period. Male relationships play a powerful role in the oldest novel of the world 'The tale of Genji'. The lifelong bond and friendship between Saigo Takamori and the Meiji politician Okubo is so strong that it will play a decisive role in the destitution of the last Tokugawa shogun Yoshinobu (Ravina, 2004; Shiba 1998) and put the effective end to the *daimyo* system. In 'Hagakure' Yukio Mishima (1978) maintains that friendship requires the highest degree of mutual trust and loyalty. In a world of excessively exposed masculinity, virility and disdain for women male friendship risked to derail into male love, pederasty and open homoerotic feelings. In Samurai and Greek society male relationships were a common and accepted practice among the warriors and true spiritual bonds of loyalty and faithfulness were believed to exist only between males.

Saigo Takamori's political legacy

Thanks to Mark Ravina's (2004) excellent study on the legacy and political significance of Saigo Takamori we have been able to re-experience how true Samurai ship really looked like at the end of the 19th century in the most critical period of Japanese history when Western imperialism and internal struggles dominated political life. A poor man attached to strong individual guiding principles who felt his deep loyalty to the person of the Meiji emperor not in an imaginary sense as obedience to a distant symbol but in a real sense, Saigo may be considered the last living example and archetype of Samurai behavior. Considered by many to be one of the first truly visionary and global minded statesmen of Japan he died in 1877 under the gunfire of Yamagata Aritomo's government troops because he refused to give up his identity and pride as a representative of the Samurai class and blindly support the moral wrongdoings of the new Meiji government such as the imperialist attack on Korea. After his death he became a legend and has since been enshrined and worshipped as a quasi deity in his home city of Kagoshima.

What made him so popular then and today was his deep conviction that political power was not a perpetual end in itself but a timely means to be used for achieving the public good for all. In that sense he was powerful but selfless and did not seek any kind of privileges of self-interest of material, social or military nature. Once his public goals were achieved he took distance and returned to normal life as a private being. He loved the simple frugal life of farming, teaching children and spending time with his many friends. Having been trained in Chinese classics and Confucian ethics he insisted that a government must comply with the highest moral standards and serve benevolence and the public good so that people are guided by loyalty, filial piety, humanity and love. For him the new tools of modern government such as national laws, public education, administrative regulation, and tax sovereignty were necessary but incomplete means to achieve autonomy, stability, peace and independence. What counted most to him was to cultivate the Confucian virtues and be a role model to others. Saigo opposed hereditary or birth privileges and had himself a deep social sense of compassion and empathy despite his belonging to the ruling class. Saigo is one of the few Japanese statesmen who had a worldly perspective on things.

He did not simply copy the Western model but remained critically distant to it. Based on his personal experience of forced exile to a remote island in south Japan Saigo expressed his view that Western prisons were of higher moral standing than Japanese prisons because they aimed at reeducating and reintegrating offenders into society instead of just seeking punishment. Regarding economic underdevelopment he opposed the Western thinking of seeking pure profit instead of promoting long-term policies aimed at improving life quality. Being loyal to his conscience and the emperor he fought the Tokugawa shogunate and played a key role in orchestrating the downfall of the last shogun Yoshinobu Tokugawa, who, backed by the French, was only interested in his own survival at any prize amidst the background of civil war and instability. Saigo was aware of the foreign interests but he was also aware that not all foreigners were barbarians as stated in the famous slogan *sonno, joi*, literally honor the emperor, expel the foreigners, of the militant Mito school that supported the shogunate and felt encouraged by the 1863 edict of the shogunate to expel all the foreigners from the Japanese territory. Saigo saw the British as potential allies to put an end to the shogunate (Satow, 2000) unify the country and restore peace without giving in to the foreign pressure and was one of the first politicians at that time to advocate for foreigners to be allowed to take legal residence in Japan and marry with Japanese. He never voiced xenophobia against the West but warned of learning the wrong things from the West.

When the new Meiji rulers took over government control and restored the emperor Saigo supported the changes initially because he felt loyal to person of the emperor regarded as earthly representative of the gods. He soon became suspicious of the intentions of the new rulers, among them many of his former friends such as Okubo and questioned the legitimacy of centralizing the country, destroying the *daimyo* system and annexing foreign countries such as Taiwan or Korea. What was most unacceptable to him was that the new government did not respect virtues, follow the highest moral standards or respect established traditions (Ravina, 2004). Feeling estranged and alienated his conclusion could only be to die for a noble cause: saving the honor of a tradition the Samurai had embodied for many generations.

For him the Meiji rulers were worse than foreigners because they did not serve the people, rejected the old traditions and enforced an artificial new model on Japan that only represented the form of Western thinking but lacked the content and spirit of the West and negated traditional Japan. He could not forgive this crime to his former friends who had sacrificed the culture and traditions of his country for the sake of modernization and bureaucratic nation-state building.

The deep humanity of Samurai spirit

In 1899 Nitobe wrote a beautiful literary masterpiece 'Bushido', literally the way of the Samurai warrior. Nitobe, himself a Samurai native from Morioka, has been representing together with Sadako Ogata, former UN High Commissioner for Refugees and Yasushi Akashi, UN diplomat, the global face of Japan and has been involved in a multitude of agricultural, social, educational, political and diplomatic activities.

Among Nitobe's achievements were his involvement in the growth of sugar-cane in Taiwan to improve the economy of the island which was under Japanese colonial control; the professorship in colonial policy at the University of Tokyo; the founding of the Ochanomizu women university and the International Committee for Intellectual Cooperation, which after World War II developed into UNESCO; the diplomatic service as undersecretary general of the League of Nations; and the post-retirement assumption of the chairmanship of the Japanese branch of the Institute of Pacific Relations. One of his greatest achievements as statesman and politician has been the solving of the Aland island conflict between Sweden and Finland by applying the philosophy and principles of 'Bushido' (Hara et al, 2007). To commemorate this outstanding global minded statesman and role model the International House of Japan launched a seminar series called the 'Nitobe Juku' in 2008. The Nitobe school aims at training young professionals from various fields to contribute to the realization of a better international and multicultural society.

Despite what one might think 'Bushido' is not at all a book on military warfare but rather a thoughtful, concise attempt to explain traditional Japanese values and life philosophy to the Western mind in a way that does not offend or repeat stereotypes. The meaning of Nitobe's message for today must be viewed from the perspective of 19th century Japan: the Meiji restorators identified themselves and competed at the same time with a West looking down on them and the rising influence of a merchant and military class desperately trying not only to distance itself from the past but to reinterpret it and suit it to its needs. In this atmosphere of change for the sake of change, reevaluation of the past and transition to something proclaimed to be more scientific, rational, objective, Western and modern Nitobe stuck to his native and authentic values and principles. The following quotation reflects his thinking well:

> "What is important is to try to develop insights and wisdom rather than mere knowledge, respect someone's character rather than his learning, and nurture men of character rather than mere talents" (Source: http://www.newworldencyclopedia.org/entry/Nitobe_Inazo).

Nitobe not only hailed the noble, civic, philanthropic and humanistic spirit in theoretical terms but embodied it himself and he was in that respect a true samurai. He followed his own strong principles and that distinguished him from most of the politicians that followed him thereafter. Nobody else in Japan managed to achieve a similar high level of international recognition and respect at the beginning of the 20th century. 'Bushido' has been unduly criticized as idealizing the harsh reality of Samurai world and even preparing the thinking ground for Japanese colonialism in Asia. Nothing could be more far away from Nitobe's intentions. Despite some nostalgic and romanticist shortcomings, Nitobe's book constitutes an attempt to demonstrate that the roots of Japan have more in common with the classic Western tradition especially that of the Hellenic civilization as Westerners and Japanese alike might have thought. He tried to explain and prevent misconceptions the West had about Japan by highlighting common grounds and seeking mutual understanding and overcoming divisions (Burkman, 1990; Howes, 1995 & 2003). Nitobe tried to build a bridge where others started to construct barriers by distancing themselves from shared universal human values and principles to pursue the rule and submission of Asia. Whereas Nitobe's work succeeds in synthesizing the positive elements of the Western and Japanese cultural heritage others contented themselves with copying and remodeling the form of Western political thinking without grasping its spiritual content.

Nitobe was the unity of word and action and a true politician as per Arendt's definition. His life story is the embodiment of Samurai beliefs and value system of being principled, seeking glory, being peace loving, being loyal to one's conscience first, seeking honor, showing compassion, complete sincerity, being honest and just. The famous seven Samurai principles mentioned in 'Bushido' namely justice, courage, benevolence, politeness, veracity, honor, and loyalty were later abandoned and replaced by a strong state and strong army ideology to suit the needs and interests of the ruling merchant and military classes. One of his greatest achievements as statesman is the resolution of the Aland conflict between Finland and Sweden in 1921 at the peak of his involvement as undersecretary of the League of Nations in Geneva.

Samurai principles at work: the Aland conflict

At a conference sponsored in 2006 to celebrate half a century of diplomatic relations between Russia and Japan participants evaluated the Aland conflict resolution model as example for resolving the unsolved conflict of the so-called Northern Territories issues between both countries. The extraordinary framework for solving the Aland conflict not only in a peaceful but also mutually beneficial way reflects a deep human concern:

> "The Aland settlement was a human solution in the sense that the resident's interests were somehow respected in the unique arrangement, even though the Finnish and Swedish governments had conflicting interests" (Hara, 2007, p.10).

Seen from a purely national viewpoint it seems that Finland benefited more than Sweden from its close ties with Japan. When the League of Nations met in Geneva to discuss whether Aland Islands should belong to Finland or Sweden, Kunio Yanagita who had been an official at the Ministry of Agriculture was a member of the Japanese delegation, whose support to Finland, according to the first finish envoy to Japan Ramstedt, was crucial when the organization in 1921 made its decision over sovereignty in Finland's favor.

From a perspective grounded in principles of sincerity, benevolence or justice the question of formal territorial or military sovereignty became however secondary. What mattered most for the Alanders, who previously had sought reunification with Sweden, was to have their political autonomy, physical safety, civil rights, cultural identity and economic status maintained. The islanders accepted the legitimacy of the intra-government agreement because they felt that it reflected their legitimate bottom up wishes and needs such as demilitarized neutrality and autonomy. The military safeguards helped Aland to maintain its integrity as a neutral and independent zone within a highly sensitive geostrategic area full of past military tensions.

The settlement went beyond traditional diplomacy by proclaiming a right to cultural diversity and issuing safeguards for political consultation:

> "The new guarantees to be inserted in the autonomy law should specially aim at the preservation of the Swedish language in the schools, at the maintenance of the landed property in the hands of the Islanders, at the restriction, within reasonable limits, of the exercise of the franchise by new comers, and at ensuring the appointment of a Governor who will possess the confidence of the population".(Source:http://www.intstudies.cam.ac.uk/centre/cps/ documents_ aland_ resolution.html)

The before mentioned stipulation not only helps to prevent conflicts from escalating but also guarantees a shared power balance. The Alanders have a right to reject the nomination of a chosen Governor and propose five alternative candidates by themselves and can in this way influence Finland's choice of Governor for the island. The Aland settlement constitutes a unique and successful attempt of resolving a conflict by taking into account the long-term interests of all stakeholders and parties involved. Aland showed the world that there was a chance for an outcome with many winners and no losers. By clinging exclusively to short-term legalistic territorial sovereignty prerogatives the dragging border conflicts between Japan and its neighbors Russia, China and Korea have failed to produce so far any mutually acceptable and satisfying results and in that sense the Aland solution may serve as a lesson for future oriented multilateral human security centered proposals.

Nitobe's ceaseless efforts to uphold authenticity and cultural identity have been depicted as pre-modern, feudal or old-fashioned at best. Yet despite the disdain for the deeply humanistic Samurai culture and traditions by Western and Japanese scholars alike recent efforts have been made to give back to the Samurai the honor they deserve. The tragedy of Nitobe was that no decision maker gave him credit or made any attempts to reflect on his teachings or learn from his lectures. He was punished and humiliated by the Japanese government for having criticized off records the Japanese army he considered the most dangerous element besides the threat of international communism (Howes, 2003). Nitobe is known for his relentless efforts to offer basic educational opportunities to disadvantaged and weak social groups such as orphans or women. He founded and headed several schools and universities across the country. His proactive promotion of women education has been highly acknowledged.

The neoconservative reaction to globalization: wrong answers to the right question

In the early 90s a book titled 'The Japan that can say no' (to the West) raised ear brows and caused uproar in the West not only because of its content but because it had been written by a person considered to be one of the most outspoken politicians in Japan and a representative of the baby boomer generation born after the war who sacrificed themselves for the economic growth of their country. It is critical to understand the logic and thinking behind the Japanese intellectual rightist mainstream. According to their logic the only answer to globalization is saying no to learning–positive things–from the West, saying no to social change in Japan and returning to a nostalgic pre-war nationalism and maintain the values of the glorious past be it called national pride and unity, strong army, racial purity or emperor worship. The nostalgic trend for movies on *kamikaze* fighters and heroic war ships is dangerous. Neoconservatives do not see cultural globalization and international mutual exchange as something positive but as a threat and danger. The current debate on amending article 9 of the Japanese constitution and rearmament has more to do with upbeat nationalism to counter the imagined threats posed by North Korea, growing China military strength or international terrorism then with support for global peace and human security. It is simply a step back to Japan's nationalistic prewar condition. The conservative elderly males constitute the hard core of regression and revision. They are gender biased, nationalist, racist, speak hardly any foreign languages, are arrogant, elitist, money and status oriented and if they face major setbacks or resistance they escape responsibility by blaming others or committing suicide. In the after-war several ministers have committed suicide because they could not bear to be brought to justice for their criminal acts of bribery, corruption or financial scandals. For Samurai it would have been unthinkable to die for a cause which is not worth to die for or trying to escape personal responsibility for having caused public trouble or guilt ridden acts of public distrust. How can Japan preserve its valuable uniqueness, traditions and culture in a world threatened by Western style modernity, hegemony and uniformity? The answer to globalization cannot be closing the eyes to reality, nostalgia, more law and order or turning the clock back. The reality of ongoing social changes and globalization such as the rising number of mixed marriages and mixed children, the rising influx of refugees seeking a place to stay, the illegal over-stayers and immigrants, the schools established by foreign institutions and governments, illegal human cross border trafficking, the rising number of Japanese having lived abroad and experiencing a reverse culture shock and the rising number of foreigners staying long term speak for themselves. Complex problems need complex solutions but what leading politicians offer as solution under the slogan "let's build a beautiful Japan" is too simplistic and naïve. The main theme of creating a beautiful country refers to a Japan that values culture, tradition, nature and history, and is free but disciplined, full of energy for future growth and blessed with leadership that is trusted, respected and loved by the international community. Many of the alleged authentic traditions and values in the neoconservative discourse have been artificially created in the wake of the Meiji restoration to fit the contemporary mainstream thinking of political correctness and endorse the self image of today's political establishment (Vlastos, 1997).

Myths and traditions that have been invented to support the globalization of Japan

Many of the concepts that describe what it means to be Japanese suggest that they have either existed since long ago or cannot be really fully understood in their cultural context and objective meaning by outsiders i.e. non-Japanese. Other authors (Weng-Shing et al, 2005) have highlighted the distinctions between Eastern cultures and Western cultures without suggesting however that Western and Eastern character traits, attitudes, beliefs, behaviors, cognitions and values are to seen as mutually exclusive or antagonistic. After all East and West are metaphors for the two divided selves of human mankind and a holistic approach will reconcile both. Identity is not fixed and permanent. Cultural concepts or stereotypes of what it means to be Japanese tend to evolve and are shaped by human interaction: one is not born Japanese but one becomes or is made Japanese by being socialized in a certain way. One can influence and even transcend the cultural framework or footprint. The cultural footprint is impacted when emigration leads to a change of living environment or when children grow up in mixed environments. Often the center-periphery cleavage enables those in remote local areas to eventually preserve their own distinctive subjective reality, attitudes, beliefs, rituals and values distinct from the top down constructed reality of the center. The way the Japanese define themselves has been greatly influenced by Meiji rulers when they abolished Samurai traditions and reinvented the Japanese national character to suit their needs. Some authors have established evidence for the theory that much what we consider to be authentic Japanese traditions were invented retroactively to justify the new political and economic order after Meiji rulers took over (Vlastos, 1997). The myths of the gender equal society, monoculturalism and ethnic purity, the agricultural roots of Japanese society or deified emperorship have been systematically demystified (Amino, 2001 & 2003; Ueno 2001 & 2003; Dale 1998; Denoon, 2001; Lie, 2001; Lee, 2006).

In 'Bushido' Nitobe gives himself an example of invented tradition when he refers to the change in meaning of the term *giri* : the term meant originally 'righteous' but later on to suit the needs of the merchant class the meaning associated with *giri* was to become duty. Nitobe noted that under changed societal circumstances *giri* has been used for doing and justifying evil things such as the selling of a daughter as prostitute to pay off debts (Nitobe, 2007, p. 13).

On veracity Nitobe said "To sacrifice truth merely for the sake of politeness was regarded as an "empty form" (*kyo-rei*) and "deception by sweet words" (Nitobe, 2007, p. 31). Empty useless formalities like formal politeness create barriers instead of mutual understanding. The more formal and ritual–would it be more accurate to use the word dishonest–a society is, the easier it is for the state to achieve mass conformity and compliance.

Other formalistic concepts to describe the Japanese culture and tradition such as *keigo* (polite language), *wa* (harmony), *ie* (household), *tatemae and honne* (pretention and veracious opinion) or absolute equality reflect the impact of the alleged absence of horizontal 'bonds of civility' (Ikegami, 2005) in today's society. In a provocative study McVeigh (2002) traces the importance of *aisatsu* (greetings) in modern Japan and argues that ritual formal behavior has superposed or obscured the civic or public sphere on purpose. In his view "rituality and staged formalities take the place of a neutral public space" (McVeigh, 2002, p.130). The public realm is described as a place "where atomized individuals take their privacy with them and try their hardest to disregard others" (McVeigh, 2002, p. 132).

Invented tradition: national male blood purity

Blood ties and kinship that have once been defined as characteristic of archaic societies (Mumford, 1956) and keep to play a central role in Japanese interpersonal and gender relations until today. Japan is basically jus sanguineous, but with various restrictions depending on whether the mother or father is Japanese and whether a child is born within wedlock or outside of wedlock.

In a country that insists that all nationals have pure blood or are ethnically homogenous nationality will only be granted under strict conditions, immigration policy will be as restrictive as it can be and refugee seekers from outside will not be accepted. The Japanese nationality law requires anyone born in or after 1985 by a foreign and Japanese parent to choose citizenship by their 22nd birthday. Until then dual nationality is allowed. What happens in reality thereafter is that parents declare their mixed children as Japanese citizens but tacitly continue to keep a second passport for them even after they turn 22. De facto they continue to have two passports. On the other hand a Japanese who immigrates to the US and gives up his Japanese citizenship may be regarded–strangely enough–still as a Japanese from the perspective of officialdom. When the Nobel Prize for chemistry was awarded in 2008 the confusion of who is Japanese reached a level of unprecedented ridiculousness: first the government announced that the prize had been awarded to two Japanese and one naturalized Japanese American, but later it revised its announcement and suddenly mentioned that the prize had been awarded to three Japanese among them one with an American passport !

It is noteworthy that the *koseki* register still discriminates between foreign male husbands and foreign female brides. A foreign female bride is allowed to register after her marriage in the family register of her Japanese husband whereas a foreign man is not registered as husband and the Japanese bride continues to be registered as if she were unmarried under her maiden name. The Supreme Court ruled that illegitimate children borne out of wedlock between foreign women and male Japanese fathers are eligible for Japanese citizenship whereas this does not apply to the reverse case of Japanese mother, male foreign father.

The Japanese general term for impurity is *kegare* differentiating *ketsue-e* for blood impurity, *san-e* for childbirth impurity and *shi-e* for death impurity. The aversion against impurity is foremost an aversion against death and women. Ohnuki-Thierney asserts that "the symbolic opposition of purity and impurity has always been (...) the most important principle in Japanese culture, from ancient times to the 21st century" (Ohnuki-Tierney, 2005, p.221) with a male emperor and agrarian rice cult symbolizing purity and everything non-agrarian related to blood and death being classified as impure. In ancient history women were not considered impure but on the contrary closer to *kami* then men. In

Shinto only women were allowed up to a certain period in time to become high priestess of a shrine. It is also noteworthy to mention that pure blood ties used to be advantageous to women politically: there have been eight ruling empresses in Japanese history and they were all members of the imperial family on their fathers' side.

Experts agree that the symbolic meaning associated to purity underwent changes from positive to negative over time but offer disparate answers when it comes to dating these changes. Robertson (2007) argues that prior to the 17th century blood had already the negative association of death and impurity and whereas Ohnuki-Tierney (2005) guesses that the strong negative meaning associated with impurity became established around the 12th century Abe (2002) asserts this change to have happened during the 14th century. Regarding the reasons behind this change it may be related to the patriarchal transformation of society which affected also the position of women in society.

Ohnuki-Tierney (2005) notes that the stigmatization attributed to impure activities was institutionalized by the Tokugawa rulers in the 16th century. McCormack (2005) argues that the Meiji restoration instead of improving equality status of all social groups regardless of their occupation, gender or ancestry by reclassifying them all as commoners cemented segregation and prejudice against *burakumin* by shifting or reframing the ethnic stigma to a stigma of lower cultural standing and back warded mental development status.

Roberston (2002) retraces the early Meiji ambivalent blood discourse on justifying the conceived impurity and inferiority of female blood and its positive male component of superior life force to justify a nationalist theory of race and ethnicity aimed at delimiting the Japanese national pure body symbolically from non-Japanese elements. The blood ties had a strong gender bias at least until 1985 when having a Japanese blood parent alone was not sufficient to make one Japanese. What mattered was that the blood parent was male: children born of foreign fathers were given foreign citizenship because of the foreign blood of the father.

The Meiji rulers had made a wise choice in declaring formal Japanese paternity as sole factor for recognizing citizenship and nationality because pure blood ties among extended families and cemented by interfamilial marriages on a village level had become actually a big health concern at that time. For the 1920s Robertson estimates that 16% of all the marriages had been consanguineous. The fact that more than 40% of today's Japanese are believed to carry the same common blood type A is a rather curious reminder that blood is a carrier of cultural archaic bonds. It is believed that inbreed, consanguineous marriages practices frequent in rural isolated areas had been widely responsible for genetic defects among newborns and from a public health perspective the promotion of more distant kinship marriages between disparate individuals was meant to replace the health risks posed by traditional marriages between blood relatives. Roberston (2002) argues that the new Meiji national policy of eugenic marriages differed from the Tokugawa ideology in two important ways: the physical health and contribution of women to heredity was acknowledged and the extension of the scope of marriage was extended from closed and restricted preexisting rural inter-familial boundaries to more open national and even international boundaries under the presumption that Japanese would always marry other pure-blooded Japanese wherever they may live. Maybe one should also add that despite all the talk of equality and maternal health the attribute of superior purity continued exclusively to be reserved to males.

It is a woman's fundamental right that she is able to choose whether to give birth to a healthy or disabled child or not and how to give birth. The old eugenic protection law before 1996 aimed at population control by preventing the birth of "inferior descendants" and by making medical abortions available at clinics. Eugenics was not only nationalist and racist but also infringed on the dignity and basic rights of women. It was used to justify the controversial sterilization of women. The after war segregation against stigmatized Hansen disease patients has been widely mediatised. Unfortunately the spirit of the new maternal protection law of 1996 does not radically differ from the old law except that the "inferior descendant" wording has been removed.

The NPO *Shoshiren*, who has been very active in protecting the reproductive rights of women, has criticized the new act of 1996 in that it still contains the spirit of eugenic ideology and regards women's bodies as a means to control the size and quality of the population. The symbolic discrimination against women goes on and even today it is still a taboo for women to enter the sumo ring or climb some sacred mountains because of their alleged impurity and dirtiness. The ideology of pure blood versus mixed or impure blood is upheld among the political establishment as well. According to conservative nationalists the male line of emperor succession must be maintained because of the importance of keeping the blood of the emperor line free from any possible foreign impurity. Under the Imperial Household Law, only males can assume the throne. Since 1889, women have been barred from the throne regardless of blood ties to the emperor and male members who marry must get permission according to the Imperial Household Law.

Paradoxically despite the male supremacy the mother child relation is more valued and gets better protection than in Western countries because of strongly valued blood bonds between mother and child. In case of divorce custody is often automatically given to the mother and the father will never ever be able to see or contact his biological children again. Some of the negative ramifications of this situation are however child abuse and rapes committed against children by stepfathers when mothers remarry. Recently the abduction of mixed children by their divorced or separately living mother to Japan has received attention in the English spoken media because Japanese family courts do not consider this to be illegal from a cultural perspective and consequently do not feel it necessary to intervene. Sovereignty and nationality are the two constitutive legal elements of the traditional nation-state. Nationality and ethnicity are strongly connected and once a foreigner decides to naturalize he has to give up his former ethnical identity. Murphy-Shigematsu (2007) argues that in a globalized world nationality should be free from any ethnic or racial associations and that it is of critical importance to separate the concept of bottom up citizenship, which is basically a concept of civil society from the pro forma or official nationality status which he says is no more than a "legal artifact" (Murphy-Shigematsu, 2007, p.324). He highlights on the positive side that the government has been gradually granting rights to non-naturalized foreigners including local voting rights and mentions that many foreigners in Japan have freely chosen not to become naturalized Japanese because they are proud of their origins and culture. This fact requires separating the nationality issue from the citizenship issue. The point Murphy-Shigematsu makes that it is necessary to overcome the illusion that there are two categories of individuals: supposedly homogenous and pure Japanese defined by their nationality feature who represent the majority and the rest.

What he proposes is in fact a concept that overcomes the illusory nationality trap. It is called "coexistent citizenship" (Murphy-Shigematsu, 2007, p.323) which goes further than mere tolerance of practicing one's own culture in private, teaching what separates foreigners from Japanese at public schools, entails not only rights but also responsibilities as well and accepts and integrates multicultural differences and plurality of ethnic identities not only in between people or communities but within the self as well. He concludes that it is imperative

"to move beyond racial dichotomies and ethnic boundaries into a form of multicultural society in which individuals are free to choose and enjoy affiliations with many identity groups, rather than with just one" (Murphy-Shigematsu, 2007, p.322).

Invented tradition: the family unit *ie* as organization principle

Many well-known scholars such as Haruo Kawai (1999) or Chie Nakane (1970) have described the *ie* as key distinctive element and essence of Japanese culture to delimit themselves from Western concepts. In her study the sociologist Chizuko Ueno (2001) denounces this approach as being ahistorical as well as cementing male dominance in society and gives evidence for the politically motivated reinterpretation of the *ie* family system under the Meiji government.

Before Meiji the 90% of non-Samurai commoners had practiced matrilineal succession in the feudal era, yet ironically the actual tradition of the vast majority was dismissed as barbarian. The status of the upper-class Samurai women was not based on equality as acknowledged by Nitobe but nevertheless their role of raising and educating the children at home, working in agriculture and defending the honor of the family–if necessary by armed means–was respected and they were not looked down upon by their husbands. Needless to say those Samurai women had no equal political rights or public influence compared to male Samurai who were allowed to have a mistress or engage in acts of homosexuality or homoeroticism. One of the first acts of the Meiji rulers was to prohibit polygamy but this did not mean that things would improve for women.

After the Meiji takeover the purpose and meaning of the *ie* was completely overhauled and adjusted to the needs of the national state, military expansion and ascending economy. The regime sought to install a new social structure deemed more suited to the new Japan founded on the primacy of the lineal family as articulated in the family code of 1898. A patriarchal spirit remained enshrined in the civil code from then on. By linking the family to the state, the former was brought out more in public to be controlled by the latter. The family changed its status from former autonomous, horizontal, community based and economically independent unit of agricultural production to a dependant, vertical, separated and isolated formal organization principle whereby the male part was separated from the family to spend most of his time outside at work and the female part secluded to the private role of being a good housewife and wise mother living a boring life in total isolation.

The dependency status of women overall worsened and the commercialization of society has forced women to support low family income as cheap part-timers labor force or work as hostesses or engage in other activities to make a living. Especially single working mothers are hardly hit by these developments. The state has supported the male dominated status quo by squeezing around eleven million unemployed housewives as dependent spouses into the public pension system. The once vigorous Samurai family full of dignity and pride became a place for passive retreat, relaxation and consuming television programs. At most the housewives are allowed to engage in strictly non-political volunteer activities to support local city services (LeBlanc, 1999).

One cannot but wonder why volunteerism should be reserved to women and retired males only. The *muko-yoshi* system of adopting a husband into one's own family has been invented to ensure the continuation and economic survival of the *ie* in times of social turbulences. Without the aggressive industrialization, military expansion and centralization of administrative and economic functions these changes would never have occurred.

Invented tradition: state Shinto and emperor deification

Natural Shinto believes that people are good and pure by nature. Ancestor worship and filial piety or devotion to one's parents is one of the cornerstones of the way of the *kami*. Natural Shinto is not a religion in the sense of transcenden-talism of someone or something supernatural and belief in future resurrection but bound to immanent rituals and secular protective deities that live and exists among the humans, governs their daily lives and is fallible and innocent as hu-mans are. Natural Shinto is centered in the local community and the *matsuri* is its foremost expressive ritual (Moriarty,1972). *Matsuri* can be translated as food offering ceremony to the local deities. The ideological belief of being unique and separate from the rest of the world has been deeply rooted and closely asso-ciated with the concepts of emperorship and rice culture. Most Japanese will even insist nowadays that non-Japanese cannot grasp the unique and special re-lationship, character or symbolic meaning and importance of the emperorship system. Interestingly natural Shinto and rice culture had already existed for six centuries before the emperorship as institution emerged at the end of the 4th century (Ohnuki-Tierney, 2005). Even after its establishment due to the disparity of the territory and disparate rules some remote regions did not know about the existence of an emperor (Amino, 1978).The association and identification of the emperorship with rice and agriculture seems to have occurred with the gradual loss of economic influence among the fisheries, forest works and other primary industries. Government has always given priority to farming interests over mari-time protection: a recent example is the Ariake sea near Nagoya where rec-laimed farming land in a previous sea area led to the massive ecological erosion of marine fauna and flora. Amino maintains that despite its less prominent role compared to other agricultural products rice was to become a national symbol and became such important that it was valued as a currency and the emperor was considered to be a shaman whose role it was to ensure to communicate with the deities and ensure good rice crops and fertility. Shamanism is based on the pre-mise that the visible world is pervaded by invisible forces or spirits which affect the lives of the living. Shamans are mediums who establish a relation between the humans and deities. Shinto is widely believed to share matriarchal elements with shamanism. The emperor used his power to serve the benefit of the human community. He was the earthly descendant of the sun goddess Amaterasu but he was not a deity himself. Neither the emperor nor most of his people ever thought that the emperor was a god in the sense of being a supernatural supreme being. Some popular emperors attained the status of deity but only after their death. The attribute god has been attributed to some of the most popular emperors who passed away in the service for their country. To remember them Shinto shrines have been erected in their memory.

From the 6th century onwards it was accepted that the emperor was des-cended from the gods, was in contact with them, and often inspired by them. This didn't make him a god himself, but rather imposed on him the obligation of carrying out certain rituals and devotions in order to ensure that the gods looked after Japan properly and ensured its prosperity. From the 8th to the late 19th cen-tury the status of the emperor was more formal and symbolical than real: in po-litical terms he had no real power or military influence. A change occurred however when the Meiji rulers redefined Shinto to instill nationalist feelings and devotion to the emperor. To enforce the new ideology decentrally organized Shinto was put under control of the state. In 1871, all Shinto shrines throughout Japan were declared property of the central government, were assigned an official rank within a hierarchy and received a subsidy for their upkeep. Shrines were divided into twelve levels with the Ise Shrine dedicated to the sun goddess Amaterasu, and thus symbolic of the legitimacy of the imperial family at the top. Furthermore, all citizens were required to register as a parishioner of their local shrine, and each parishioner of a local shrine was automatically also a parishioner of the Ise Shrine. This was a major reverse from the Edo period, in which families were required to register with Buddhist temples, rather than Shinto shrines. In 1872, an office of Shinto worship was established to develop and promote new government-centered rites of worship, and all Shinto priests officially became government employees. Thus, from a legal perspective, state Shinto was not a ritual or religion anymore and its values came under the heading of moral indoctrination rather than ritual practice.

In 1889 the first constitution codified the new state ideology and deified the emperor for the first time in history. The military caste formally transferred absolute power to the emperor and declared him an inviolable god like deity who stands above all and everything. The ultra-nationalist and militaristic groups took advantage of the emperor's status and claimed to speak for the emperor. These groups then turned the tables on the parliamentarians by claiming that they, not the civil government, represented the imperial will. The parliamentarians, confronted with this perversion of their own policy, failed to unite against the militarists and nationalists. Instead, they compromised with the nationalists and militarists groups and the general populace took the nationalists' claims of devotion to the emperor at face value, further bolstering the popularity of the nationalists. The theory of imperial will became an underlying flaw in the government's democratic composition. After the war defeat the succeeding governments tried to uphold the public role of the emperor by keeping his activities under state control and suggesting to the world that the emperor essentially still represents Japan even if he is not a formal head of state.

As a matter of fact however in a legal and constitutional sense the Diet is the highest sovereign authority of Japan. In 1989 the government was accused to have violated the constitutional spirit when it chose to divide Hirohito's state funeral into official and religious components. Akihito's accession to the throne in November 1990 also had religious and secular components: the enthronement ceremony was secular; the great thanksgiving ceremony, traditionally, a communion between the new monarch and the gods in which the monarch himself became a deity, was religious. The government's decision to use public funds not only for the enthronement ceremony but also for the great thanksgiving ceremony, justified in terms of the public nature of both ceremonies, was seen by religious and opposition groups as a serious violation of article 20 of the constitution stipulating the strict separation from state and religion (Hein.P, 1990). This article has also been invoked to stop politicians from visiting the Yasukuni Shrine either in private or public.

The question if the emperor should continue to serve as a symbolic public, secular figure serving directly or indirectly state interests or if he should be a ceremonial, religious and spiritual private person focusing solely on Shinto devotions designed to preserve the good fortune of Japan, and the continuity of the imperial line is legitimate. The fact that even today school children believe that the aggression war against Asia was just and that it was right to sacrifice oneself for the sake of the emperor should induce every responsible citizen to rethink and reconsider the roles and responsibilities attributed to the emperor. Would it not be in the best interest of the emperor himself to give him the status of a private respected spiritual Shinto leader preserving the communitarian spirit of the culture and nation instead of being pushed into the role of a symbolic or whatever head of state for the sake of maintaining good foreign relations?

Invented tradition: *wa* as a top down social construct

It is a feature of the Japanese to refrain from annoying others or being aggressive and solve problems without recurring to open conflict. The saying *anmoku no ryokai* literally unspoken mutual agreement reflects a certain acceptance for trespassing commonsense rules. In the West police would be called to intervene in solving conflicts whereas in Japan both parties inherently accept the trespassing of rules. *Omoiyari* (empathy), *tatemae* (what one pretends to be) and *honne* (real opinion) are other concepts that are referred to explain social harmony in Japan. People prefer not to tell their real opinion because they do not want to hurt the feelings of the opposite or because they do not want to engage in a hurting argument. Japanese will usually be able to tell if a smile expresses sympathy or rather disagreement. If in disagreement they will say *komarimasu* (embarrassed) at most which is not a strong statement. This does not mean however that social conflict does not exist in Japan. A history of social movements and groups opposing government policies shows that citizens will take action and engage in social unrest to protect environmental interests, promote nuclear free activities or women's rights (Feldman, 2000; Ellis, 1984; Najita et al, 2005; Upham, 1987; Sasaki-Uemura, 2001).

Wa is one of the most representative and symbolical Japanese letters associated to the concept of peace. In the most accurate and authentic translation it could be described as peace of mind, calmness, serenity. In modern Japanese language the letter appears in words such as *chouwa* (harmony), *heiwa* (peace) or verbs such as *yawarageru* or *yawaragu* (to appease, calm down).

In 604 Prince Shotoku authored and laid down a document called 'The seventeen article constitution' that served as moral and ethical guideline to the rulers and the ruled. The emphasis of the document is not so much on the basic laws by which the country was to be governed, such as one might expect from a modern constitution, rather, it was a highly Confucian document that focused on the kinds of virtues and values that were to be expected of government officials and the emperor's subjects to ensure a smooth running state with the emperor at the top. The need to achieve harmony by conducting acts which are appropriate to one's relationships in a Confucian rooted vertical and hierarchical society goes back to Prince Shotoku's first constitution. The need for harmonious social relations does not require the negation of the individual self. On the contrary the key to maintaining harmony is the upholding of virtue as inner guiding principle for righteous conduct. Without nurturing virtues on a subjective or individual level social relationships with subordinates and superiors can not be fulfilled or harmonious.

The influence of Samurai thinking is best reflected in the concept of loyalty. For a real Samurai loyalty was foremost towards one's own conscience before anything else. The story of Yoshida Shodoin who decided to ignore a Tokugawa edict forbidding contact with foreigners by trying to secretly board one of Perry's ships to visit the foreign enemy by himself serves as famous example of Samurai self loyalty. The pre-Tokugawa Samurai practice of turning the back to a weak, unjust or unfair *daimyo* and joining a new lord serves as another example of autonomous, self-loyal action. For the Tokugawa shogunate such a conduct was considered suspicious and unacceptable. Under their rule it became a disgrace for a Samurai to abandon the lord they served. Ultimately, the Meiji government perverted the concept of loyalty and made an artificial construct out of an honorable feeling by using it to forge homogeneity and obedience among its subjects and demanding absolute loyalty to the emperor figure and the state. Loyalty and obedience are not the same and loyalty is not blind but must conform to one's conscience in the first place as Nitobe cautions:

"Alack the day when a state grows as powerful as to demand of its citizens the dictates of their conscience! Bushido did not require us to make our conscience the slave of any lord or king" (Nitobe, 2007, p 43).

The autonomy and dignity of the individual against all odds is at the center of Samurai thinking.

There are two translations of the Shotoku code of conduct available that differ slightly but in essence they convey the same messages rooted in Confucian philosophy: Harmony is a product of desirable virtues, there are differences and biases among people that can lead to conflicts, if matters are discussed and sorted out in a serene and friendly atmosphere conflicts can be prevented and truth can be revealed by itself in a natural way.

The first version states that

> "Harmony is to be valued, and an avoidance of wanton opposition to be honored. All men are influenced by class-feelings, and there are few who are intelligent. Hence there are some who disobey their lords and fathers, or who maintain feuds with the neighboring villages. But when those above are harmonious and those below are friendly, and there is concord in the discussion of business, right views of things spontaneously gain acceptance. Then what is there which cannot be accomplished!" (Source: http://en.wikisource.org/wiki/Seventeen-article_constitution)

The second version states that

> "Harmony should be valued and quarrels should be avoided. Everyone has his biases, and few men are far-sighted. Therefore some disobey their lords and fathers and keep up feuds with their neighbors. But when the superiors are in harmony with each other and the inferiors are friendly, then affairs are discussed quietly and the right view of matters prevails". (Source: http://www.sarudama.com/japanese_history/jushichijokenpo.shtml)

Even if the wording is differing the spirit of the two versions is similar: the key element for preserving harmony is avoiding conflicts and disagreements beforehand by discussing things out in a calm and respectful spirit. The spirit of the documents reflects Hannah Arendt's classic definition of politics in that objective truth does not exist per se and that conflicts or diverging opinions can be sorted out in a non-coercive and non-violent way. Listening to each other helps to preserve harmony. Nitobe noticed that "virtue and absolute power may strike the Western mind as being out of harmony" (Nitobe, 2007, p.19) and that only a "good and kind ruler" (Nitobe, 2007, p.18) will become unified and one with his people. He counterbalanced his statement however by insisting that only faithfulness to one's own conscience will prevent people from becoming blind followers of an unjust country, state, lord or king. Amicability, calmness, goodness, kindness, consciousness constitute some of the prerequisites of *wa*. In a study Ito refers to the changing ideological interpretations given to the Seventeen Articles before and after Meiji. The most obvious example of manipulation attempt of the authentic meaning of *wa* is found in the *kokutai no hongi* (1937) issued by the Ministry of Education, the gralesholder of moral education: "(…) cooperation by successive generations to maintain our nation" and the "sacred virtue of the emperor and the fidelity of his subjects have fused to create a beautiful harmony" (Ito, 1998, p. 46). Virtue and absolute authority of the emperor over his subjects become one. The key prerequisites of *wa* such as the involvement of the subjects, the discursive element to avoid or settle conflicts and find the solution, or the required goodness and kindness of the ruler and peaceful intentions of the state are completely left out and it is presumed that there is no bias or disagreement and that all the subjects obey blindly and conform to the orders of the emperor. Blind devotion, blind loyalty and blind obedience to the emperor are set as equivalent to social harmony.

Invented tradition: absolute equality

The myth of absolute equality among all Japanese has been maintained up to day to stress the racial and cultural difference with the West. In an essay the well known clinical psychologist and former head of the governmental agency for cultural affairs of Japan, Haruo Kawai noted that "a sense of absolute equality denies any individual differences" (Kawai, 1999, p.12) and the popular Japanese saying 'even more than poverty equality is important' underlines the alleged equality as distinctive fixed and eternal trait of the Japanese nation. Furthermore Kawai puts Japanese style equality in opposition to Western individuality.

Other mainstream sociologists and anthropologists such as cultural anthropologist Chie Nakane (1970) have maintained that whereas individuality is central to Western societies it is not in collectivist Eastern societies where relationships are predominant and the self exists and defines itself only in relation to others. Semi-governmental organizations follow the footsteps of the mainstream collectivist approach in their pamphlets and visitor brochures. Referring to the theory of Chie Nakane the guidebook 'Inside Out' distributed by the Foreign Press Center states for example that "Individuals who refuse to follow their elders or deviate from the instructions or intentions of the group are punished by losing their group membership and becoming ostracized" (FPC, 2008, p. 2).

The 'I' statement *ware-ware nihonjin*–literally we Japanese as a nation–serves as proof to underlie the alleged negation of individuality in the Japanese mind. Situational, inter-dependence and group oriented behaviors and other more modern concepts such as the group insider outsider *uchi / soto* dichotomy go in the same direction and refer to the group to which the individual belongs and not the individual himself. Japanese define themselves via others and put great importance on how others look at them. Japanese also score low on self-esteem which is an indicator for individuation. The worst that can happen to Japanese is being expelled from an *uchi* group.

Without going too much into detail it suffices to mention that historically the vertical principle seems more dominant in Japan then the equal principle, the patriarchal kinship principle of pure blood relations has been more positively regarded than alleged female impurity and passive intuitive dependence on others also called *amae* seems to have been given stronger preference then individual independence and autonomy. This study will seek to demonstrate that the attempted cultural negation of relative equality and ethical independence in Japanese history by political scientists, philosophers, psychologists, anthropologists or sociologists cannot be maintained and that repressed needs for equality and independence seeking have made their way back through civic political participation and gender liberation.

According to Arendt the survival of the private sphere and biological reproduction itself depend on preserving the private sphere including property rights.
Without protection a private sphere tends to become obsolete because there is no
safer zone to retreat or feel at home. The rapid economic development has
changed the landscape of Japan radically. After the war the effectiveness of the
emperor system as traditional symbol of national unity erased gradually and was
replaced with loyalty to the company, monetary gains and material affluence.
The male salary man who sacrificed himself for the sake of the company and left
behind his biological family became the driving force of the economic miracle
with all the social and consequences this encompassed. The private sphere underwent extremely tense familial and social disruptions during the economic
miracle period in the 50s, 60s and 70s when dispatched male salarymen lived
away from home in company dormitories, worked almost twenty four hours,
seven days a week and sacrificed their family life to the company and nation.
The human right and biological need to private property and privacy within a
safe protected my home zone of familial and community ties was rendered impossible and this is the reason why the private sphere has been given so low
recognition. The absence of a neat distinction between private and public is not
the reason but the result of a social transformation that denies the right to privacy and to private property in the name of absolute equality conceived as a kind
of nivellation in the name of same treatment for everybody.

Post-war Japan rebuilt the nation from scratch with everybody standing on
the same ground. As the economy grew quickly people felt they belonged to the
middle-class. The myth of absolute equality began to crumble after the bubble
burst during the 1990s and the word *kakusa*（格差）describing a supposedly fair
society full of inequalities, even in basic needs, made its appearance. The gap
between the new rich and the new poor, unfair tax burden and irresponsible tax
spending, missed equal gender and education opportunities can no longer be
overlooked. The most obvious symptom of the decline or loss of the private
sphere as center of familial bonds and biological reproduction is the current
childless society (Jolivet, 1997). The unsolved gender cleavage of male earner
versus female housewife has largely contributed to the contemporary social
deadlock. Any positive changes in the status quo of women who seek self determination risks to worsen things: a married working mother who divorces in
Japan risks to fall into poverty or be excluded socially.

As Samurai society preserved the hierarchical rank differences between
classes absolute equality was out of question. If at all equality existed only in
relative terms between peers or friends. The Samurai social structure was based
on strict meritocracy principles: ability, effort, skills were given priority over seniority, birth rights or privileges. Advancement in status or financial gains could
not be inherited by future generations. Without a horizontal alliance of equal

friends among the Samurai from the outer provinces in Kyushu–formerly known as Satsuma–and Yamaguchi–formerly known as Choshu–the downfall of the last Shogun Yoshinobu could not have been orchestrated and made possible. Individual attributes such as unconditional and personal loyalty to the emperor and weak bonds with the last Tokugawa ruler were decisive elements in leading the changes from Tokugawa to Meiji.

Nitobe believed that the Samurai sense of loyalty and equality was opposed to the concept of formal or absolute equality characteristic of a mass democracy. "In America our feeling for loyalty cannot be appreciated because all people are thought to be equal" (Nitobe, 2007, p 39). For Nitobe the wisdom of the Samurai spirit was aimed at containing the monetary, commercial and industrial interests of the new emerging classes and prevents them from destroying the principles of honorific autonomy, individual excellence, pride, self-esteem, merit and ability. The modern formal equality to vote, consume and work lacks virtue, spiritual purpose and content.

Trendy fashionable scholars such as Fujiwara (2007) but also acknowledged cultural experts such as Haruo Kawai (1999) seem to have mistaken the Samurai dimension of individually motivated relative equality for substantial or absolute egalitarism. The culture and wisdom of the Samurai could not have cared less about monetary income, selfish interests or people who did not care about social position or were not loyal to their conscience. Their lifestyle was ascetic, simple and frugal and their education was targeted at forming and strengthening the character and learning the required skills to become strong, wise and live a dignified, honorable life and engage in compassion for others. The noble virtues and values of the Samurai disappeared with the ascendance of the merchant class. The meritocratic model of political equality among the very few best and bright was replaced by a model of economic communist like egalitarism which was far away from individually conceived search for moral integrity and independence of the mind and judgment.

The Meiji period has been hailed by many as having set progressive "functional prerequisites of modern society such as efficacy, achievement and equality" (Eisenstadt, 1996, p. 431). However equality whether in social rights or equal opportunities was only granted to those who could afford it. The Meiji assembly continued to be an exclusive club of male nationalists. Women as well as commoners who could not afford to pay the census for example remained unequal's and were therefore initially totally excluded from the political sphere. Education policy was clearly designed to uphold a uniform morality centering on the Neo Confucian ideology of loyal subject, filial piety and faithful wife and wise mother. Only later on were commoners and women in general given universal voting rights. Even after they acquired the same voting rights than their male counterparts in 1945 women continued to remain politically unequal and voiceless. They are still today clearly underrepresented in the political and business world because there is no middle way in between childless career woman or getting married and having children. Compared to other countries Japan lacks behind when it comes to the number of educated working mothers active in politics or as members of the board of private companies. Strangely enough the only employer that offers lengthy child care leave and benefits and job security to working mothers in Japan is the public service.

Prior to World War II Japan had been at war with one country or another statistically once every ten years. The Meiji transformation of the public education system towards a basically non-meritocratic public egalitarian mass education system aimed at building up a uniform skill level among all regardless of individual abilities and preferences that was driven by military and industrial or technological needs. For Samurai it would have been unthinkable to set up an education system that produces a mass of willful and thoughtless subjects geared to serve blindly the imperialistic interests rather than following the path of individual character strength, maturity, and respect for human dignity, empathy and compassion for others. Likewise the introduction of formal mass education failed to produce peace minded visionary political leaders and wise rulers. The myth of the absolute loyalty to the emperor and state established by the Meiji rulers paved the way for imperialism and ended in a disaster. After the war the top down democratic constitutional framework implemented by the U.S. did not prevent the survival and establishment of an institutionalized class of pre-war politician turned bureaucrats engaged in money politics and nepotism. The public aim number one became rapid economic development. Only after the burst of the bubble economy a new community and network based grass root approach to politics started to gradually change the face of Japan and maybe "the teaching that virtue is the highest good" (Nitobe, 2007, p. 90) may find its way back after all and sound an end to the ideology of formal monetary or economic egalitarism.

The myth of the absence of a free pre-Meiji public sphere

Japanese scholars tend to use the private, public distinction to distance themselves from the West by suggesting that the idea of public sphere was imported from the West in the 19th century and Japanized even though not having been totally internalized or fully accepted. It seems to be a common misunderstanding among leading Japanese intellectuals that the public realm conceived as a free horizontal space had never existed in pre-Meiji times. The same is true for the privacy concept. It is believed that privacy in the sense of conceived individuality and independent self has never existed before Meiji and that the Japanese word for private, *watakushi*, is negatively correlated to egoism, selfishness, secrecy, partiality and therefore not only distinct from Western privacy but seen as something negative compared to the established concept of public described by the Chinese letter *ko* (公) in the Japanese terms for public rule or authority.

Ko appears also in the word combinations *omise,* literally shop, and designating officialdom; *okami,* literally those on high, or *oyake* a Neo Confucian synonym for public in the sense of absolute paternalistic authority over right less subjects of what continues until today to be the commonly shared understanding of the term public.

One of the leading after war political scientists Masao Maruyama mentioned that terms such as assembly, political representation, pluralism and public speaking were coined and popularized by the leading Meiji intellectual Yukichi Fukuzawa. It was supposed that until Meiji no notion or concept of public debate, separation of powers, and constitutional limitation of state authority had ever existed in Japan (Oe, 1999). It suffices to say here that the Western institutional forms introduced by Fukuzawa and hailed by Maruyama did in no way reflect the contents, spirit and values of representative or parliamentary democracy.

The official Neo Confucian ideology of strict vertical social stratification, obedience and denial of individual rights implemented by the Tokugawa regime did not fundamentally change under the new Meiji ruler ship. The ultimate goal of public rule was transferred from serving the master and heaven which were above criticism to obeying the will of the emperor equated to social harmony as such. The obligations owed by the subjects to the emperor and social harmony maintained absolute priority. The abolition of the four classes and opening up of public institutions to the commoners did not remediate in any way the deep vertical cleavage and antagonism between public coercion to harmony and private freedom.

Ishikawa et al (1996) and Kato (2002) offer evidence for the argument that horizontal civil society under Tokugawa rule had been much more developed than previously thought. Expanding on the Edo volunteer concept of free public service it has been mentioned that the Tokugawa central Edo government was very lean and small in numbers and that "the role of *okami* was no more than the superficial control, under which the vast majority of public affairs was handled with complete autonomy by local communities" (Kato, 2002, p 4) with reference to services such as police and safety control, firefighting, schools and public works. A special note should be given to the *terakoya* schools that led to Edo's reputation as having the highest literacy level in the world at that time. All public services were taken care of by unpaid neighborhood volunteers. This civil engagement seems to have been limited to the flourishing life in urban dwellings inhabited mostly by merchants or artisans. In the remote countryside where the majority of the population lived things looked certainly differently. Likewise, *chonaikai* (neighborhood associations) were a major feature of militarism in the prewar decades. These state-mandated and state-controlled initiatives prevented the development of an autonomous civil society. The membership was not voluntary and government shaped their activities through funding it. After the war the neighborhood associations lost their influence in the wake of massive urbanization, loss of community spirit and ageing of society. Their major role within the modern city is limited to organize annual citizen's sports events, earthquake drills, clean up public spots and rivers, conduct safety patrols, cooperate in holding local festivals and coordinate garbage collection. Funding occurs nowadays through donations by local business owners or by receivings funds through the selling of recycled citizen garbage to the municipalities.

As discussed already equal relationships between friends were tolerated by Confucianism and the friendship of equals was a powerful horizontal alliance that could be turned against unjust or immoral rulers as the toppling of the last shogun by Saigo and Okubo has shown. Friendship as a voluntary act was thus constructed as the one eternal bond whose function was to serve the emperor. Samurai warriors were guided by strict internal principles and virtues and possessed a very strong individual personality. In the public context they were empowered to pursue their subjective autonomy, conduct critical debate with their friends on an equal standing and make their own political judgments independently from public opinion and unconcerned by private interest or material desires. The only concern they had was to respect the way of righteousness and consciousness. As a private person the Samurai never engaged in secret or selfish activities as suggested by the negative meaning of *watakushi* but maintained and trained his mental self composure, subjected himself to total ascetics and enjoyed poetry, music, farming, hunting or fishing as a pastime. Friendship was a politically powerful public concept and it never came to his mind to share his inner secrets, feelings or ethical conflicts even with his most intimate friends. In modern society it has become a commonality to expose one's most intimate private feelings, secrets, desires, motivations and sometimes criminal intentions anonymously on public websites because it is considered to be a free, safe zone and because face to face communication is not required.

Kugai, muen, raku

Under Tokugawa the Buddhist religion and sects as well as Christian missionaries were seen as potentially dangerous to the established shogun order because they were supported by merchants and craftspeople in the towns. They were therefore strictly regulated and submitted to state control. Buddhist terms such as *kugai, muen* and *raku* describe people and places outside the realm of vertical public rule and reflect the huge influence Buddhism had on pre-Tokugawa medieval Japan. The historian Yoshihiko Amino (1971) has made himself a name by being one of the first to have investigated the sociolinguistic origin of the term *kugai* (公界); a Buddhist coined term referring to public spaces of liberty or describing someone without worldly ties such as outcasts and marginalized social groups. A *kugai* public space was what is called the commons in modern language: it was uncultivated land, riverbanks, sacred land and roadways not belonging to anyone. The social agents populating *kugai* were not the peasants but marginalized parts of society such as outcasts, actors, entertainers, mountain priests and others. According to Johnston (2005) *kugai* did restrict the influence of central vertical rule. He lists some examples that demonstrate the limitations on political power:

> "These included limitations on entry (*funyuken*), tax exemptions, guaranteed rights of free travel, places of peace where it was the custom to refrain from conflicts pursued in other places, locations that enforced liberation from serfdom and slavery, places where the suspension of debts was enforced, where punishment were limited solely to the individual responsible for an offence, and where authority was organized according to age and seniority" (Johnston ,2005, p.23).

In above context maybe the modern term of asylum or sacred refuge for the persecuted or outcasts may be better suited to understand the meaning of *kugai* from today's perspective.

For Amino *kugai* "signifies the embodiment of the Buddha mind in the world (...) and a complete openness (...) or commonality" (Amino, 2007, p 163). Later on the meaning of *ku* changed from 'public' to 'suffering' and was finally discarded from the official language and replaced by the word combination *kogi* (公儀) meaning public rule. Amino also mentions research done by noted ethnologist Tsuneichi Miyamoto that refers to *kugai* as public work done in local rural communities and describes it as *kyoudotai* (共同体). According to Miyamoto *kugai* seems to have been common practice all over Japan until recent times. More research is needed in determining to what extent the *kugai* world represented an attempt to actualize horizontal political or civil activities and in how far *kugai* may represent an alternative Japanese theory to the Western concept of equal public political participation.

Horizontal public bonds

Ikegami (2005) has offered separate evidence for the existence of horizontal bonds of civility in pre-modern Japan but again it seems unclear to what extent those informal artistic horizontal associations of socialization within the strict vertical Tokugawa hierarchy were related to politics conceived as participation into public affairs. Ikegami (2007) herself claims that these associations had a political impact but lacks to give empirical proof. Maybe it makes sense to differentiate between political public sphere and cultural public activities. Ikegami uses the word *paburikku ken* (public sphere) and not the word *koykyo ken* (common sphere) as the Japanese equivalent for the English wording public sphere to stress that there is more than one public space that allows for citizens to socialize and interact. Ikegami criticizes the Western approach of treating public as equivalent with political. According to her many public gatherings do not pursue political aims but reflect simply the wish to interact socially or pursue a similar pleasure or leisure activity. It appears that Ikegami attributes a special public meaning to cultural activities such as the tea ceremony or flower arrangement. The public sphere is set apart from the social order and is voluntarily attended by individuals from different social backgrounds. To participate in such circles enables the participants to escape their real identity and social status temporarily. The tea ceremony for example evolved over time from a more male dominated and private domestic activity to a more female dominated and out of home, semi-public activity. From the viewpoint of European antiquity equality can only exist outside the private household and accordingly Samurai women, who were not allowed to enter the free political space reserved exclusively to men, could not be considered free or equal in rights despite the high regard they received. How about the women using the medium of the tea ceremony to interact socially in public as discussed by Ikegami? Does their socializing constitute a public act? For Hannah Arendt the key requirement for being considered a public person is being able to move around freely in public and of acting and speaking in freedom. There is no in between. One is either confined to the private domestic sphere or one is a free person among equals. The tea ceremony allows women to leave their home temporarily and interact with other women in the restricted semi-public setting of a tea house or a private room in a temple.

The tea ceremony setting does however not empower women to move around freely as they wish, interact with others such as for example the male gender- as they like and speak up their minds about issues which are of a more general nature such as societal issues or current affair topics. The tea ceremony does not only not intend or contribute to change the social status quo of women but rather cements the established status quo of women despite the surrounding ongoing social changes towards gender equality and more gender freedom. Even today flower arrangement and tea ceremony are part of the education for well groomed and economic affluent future brides. The semi-public sphere of the tea ceremony is not meant to drastically alter the conservative framework of society. At most the tea ceremony enables women to escape the confinement from home and get distracted or experience rare moments of happiness by finding consolation with similar situated women in a semi-public setting.

The unequal distribution of land properties among individuals and the unequal distribution of its added value in form of crops or monetary income are central to understanding the categories of social disparity and social injustice in human history. Those who either control or hold themselves directly land or profit indirectly from land labored and rendered arable by others have always been part of the wealthy and dominant class in Japan such as the Samurai, Buddhist temples and sects, large individual private owners, the modern political class and even the state. It does not matter if the landholdings are in public or private hands. What matters is who controls the distribution of the added value produced directly or indirectly by land holdings. Ravina (2004) mentions a very interesting farming practice of publicly administered common landholding in the

Satsuma province at the end of the 19th century. The so-called *kadowari* land-holding practice refers to farming on commonly hold land by farmers with the local Samurai administration acting as the farmers' trustee. The principle of commonly held land reflected the moral principles of Samurai rule of governing for the long-term benefit of all even though in reality social harshness as such continued to persist under this system and the system was by no ways perfect. Saigo strongly resisted the Meiji land reform which in his view destroyed the principle of sharing the benefits of farming to all. To him commonly hold land would benefit the majority long-term more than offering or selling land on the market for profitable or short-term monetary gains. His concern was that the market principle hailed by Meiji restorators would eventually destroy the well-being of all, fairness, impartiality and community stability. The difference between Saigo and Meiji was that he had the common good of all in mind whereas Meiji rulers wanted to submit everything to the rule of the market principle. Even though there was no political equality for the farmers the Samurai ensured by their trusteeship that virtue and fairness were upheld as public moral principles. Compared to the ruthless market privatization, land transactions and private ownership, the commons approach was considered the lesser evil. Although the practice of commonly hold land escaped control of the central government it may be seen differently from the *kugai* or *muen* concept of Amino in that *muen* or *kugai* farmers either did not receive any fields for cultivation or held no arable land (Amino, 2007, p.167).

Amino traces the origins of capitalism in Japan back to the 14th century (Amino, 2001, p. 18) when commerce, circulation of money and urbanization came into conflict with a Samurai based economy based on agriculture, and exchange of loyalty and service to their lord for private landholdings. The 16th century constituted an important turning point when Japan was unified into peace by the Tokugawa shogunate. Not only were the Samurai separated from the land and required to live in castle towns but their status changed from independent warrior to dependant bureaucrat living on a stipend. The paradox that surrounded their status change was that they were still considered to be part of the ruling class of the country despite the loss of their economic powerbase formerly rooted in privately held land properties. Amino (2001) notes that the settlement of the non-agrarian population in the cities initiated the development of a commercialized society and worsened the life of the Samurai and their financial dependency from merchants and artisans. Controlling the money became the new powerbase of the merchant class but the Tokugawa rulers continued to look down on them and treat them with disdain. On the other side the Tokugawa rulers did nothing to relieve the Samurai retainers financially or give them a meaningful public role. The biggest paradox was in the words of Amino

"that the state ceaselessly advocated an agricultural fundamentalism grounded in Confucian ideology despite that it was completely dependent on commercial, financial and shipping networks, was precisely because it depended on taxes levied on the yield from the land- the land tax or nengu- for its basic taxes" (Amino, 2003, p.240) with all profits being being converted into rice as standard of taxation also known as *kokudaka* system. The antagonism of an economic model rooting on an outdated agricultural taxation principle within an essentially non-agrarian society where the free flow of goods and money symbolized new prosperity and wealth reflected the antagonism in social status between a higher ranked Samurai class relying on selfless service, the common good, guidance through moral principles and a socially low ranked merchant class relying on self-interest, contractual faith and legal commitments.

The formerly exchange of Samurai loyalty for landholdings in war times underwent a dramatic exchange of service for money in peace times. Ansart (2007) highlights this change of function of the concept of loyalty from initially being conceived as a selfless service to the *daimyo* ending up in becoming an empty or meaningless concept to serve the self-interests of the new dominant merchant society.

Seken, musi, ikai, shakai

The modern Japanese term for society means *shakai* (社会). Besides this term there exist other older terms denoting the influence of Buddhism. The secular world *seken* (世間), the denied self *musi* (無私) and the non-secular supernatural world *ikai* (異界). In their study Nakada et al (2005) regret that modern social science relies solely on the society concept and use a real homicide case to argue that by having put detailed private information on the victim's family in a newspaper what appears to be a violation of privacy in Western terms is acceptable for Japanese from the perspective of the *seken* belief appealing to morality and ethical behavior. Although very instructive and informative the article compares two completely different concepts namely Buddhist religious teachings that prize compassion, morality and gentleness towards others with secular, civil code based thinking of privacy and information protection. *Seken* means things such as world, society, the others or the public in very general terms. *Sekentai* (reputation) is the result of how others react or others see somebody. A Christian perspective would have taken probably the same *seken* approach to deal with the moral problem behind homicide by treasuring the importance of life, seeking pity and compassion for the victims and trying to understand the motives behind the crime and intentions of the perpetrator. Whereas *seken*, has a religious meaning designating private feelings and intimate compassion *shakai* designates a sociological concept used in social sciences to describe the expansion of originally private consumptive, materialistic patterns or self interest into the public political realm of equality, participation and pluralism. Hannah Arendt considered this process of modernization as universal but undemocratic in essence. The rapid transformation after the war of Japan to a private society of business interests dominated by steadily growing consumption patterns, mass production of goods, heavy industrialization, trade and boom of the service segment has formally substituted the natural and creative processes symbolized by the activities of the farmer, craftsman, artisan, fisherman and forest worker. The influence of Buddhist morality has been confined to the private, spiritual sphere where it continues to play an important role of communitarian integration and identity formation.

More recently NPOs and nationwide very unique volunteer circles represent bottom up attempts of horizontal equality, public and political bonds and civil excellence as well as plural activism that transcend the classic vertical, submissive features characteristic of the past characterized by the tradition of recognition for authority and negation of the masses where the state occupies the public realm while the subjects are permitted the pursuit of private gain, consumption and personal welfare within a strictly regulated legal framework. In this respect it is also quite interesting to note that many elderly Japanese mention with a certain sense of pride that they would not like to be dependent on the state for welfare support even if subject to material or financial hardship. In modern society citizens have become equally dependent on public pensions systems and welfare support and as such are the modern slaves of a system that reproduces economic inequality and financial dependency on state welfare institutions.

Japanese scholars stick to the myth of the non existence of a horizontal public equal sphere and give outside observers the impression that Japan is completely different and cannot be understood with Western yardsticks. The question whether Arendt's threefold distinction of the private, public and society is applicable to the Japanese model has been raised. Indeed some may argue that Arendt's thinking roots in the European or Anglo-Saxon cultural tradition and that she was not aware of the Asian model of organization. Arendt was indeed very much knowledgeable about Confucian thinking and even wrote the foreword for Karl Jasper's well-known book on the axial religions. In 'The human condition' only one sentence refers to the Asian type of despotism a well known stereotype of Marxist thinking. Arendt never wrote a book on Japan, few non Japanese studies by Japanese scholars on the Hannah Arendt reception in Japan are available (Chiba, 1995 & 2006; Tonaki, 2008) and few have been trying to apply Hannah Arendt's political theory of the public and private to the specific historical evolution of Japan (Kodama, 2003). Recent general studies in Japanese on Hannah Arendt include Terajima (2006) and Kawasaki (2006).

Despite the geographical, cultural and historical distance that separates Nitobe Inazo and Hannah Arendt, 'The human condition' and 'Bushido' defend similar values and concepts. Both content that the search for fame, glory and immortality or greatness was one of the major drivers of political action in both the Greek polis and the Samurai political order. Both the polis inhabitants and the Samurai had enough personal material security and properties to set time free for political activities. Both orders, the Greek city state and the Samurai *daimyo* territories were composed of independent, rather decentralized, local, smaller size administrative entities. Both orders distinguished and treated ordinary or common people according to their rank and status. Women had the same low public status in both orders. The Hellenic used slaves for their private use and the samurai lived from the labor force of the peasants. Both civilizations were peace loving and used force only to defend their honor or their loyalty obligations. Both valued education, philosophy and wisdom as highest public goods. Both had a high level of literacy and oration, maintained self-sufficient and ascetic lifestyles and categorically rejected imperialism or the annexation of foreign countries or territories. In both orders the peaceful politician was at the same time also a warrior, who had to be ready to defend the territory against invaders. In both systems the free inhabitants were supposed to excel and lead by example. In the Greek polis the free citizen was a native of the city state and received the right to be free by birth. Women, slaves and foreigners could not be free. The Samurai class was a strictly hierarchical and elite status oriented class as well. Women, outcasts, peasants and merchants were excluded from public duties and their given social status remained unchanged for long.

The public sphere as embodied by *zatsudan* village talk

As pointed out by Arendt the ultimate aim of any political undertaking is not to take a decision by votes or find the truth but allow for equal participation and exchange of views and opinions of all involved. Direct political participation works best in a decentralized, local setting of a small sized community where people can deal with public affairs by themselves. Tsuneichi Miyamoto's important book 'The forgotten Japanese' (Japanese 1971; english edition 2009) offers valuable insight into the process of community participation in remote locations. While working as a teacher at an elementary school in Osaka, he was interested in folklore and traveled around Japan in search of the country's lost elements of folklore. He continued to carry out field study in every corner of the islands of Japan throughout his life. According to Kazuo Sato, a professor at Chiba University in Japan, the observations about village talk Miyamoto made in the rural setting of Japan correspond to the model of political participation as described by Arendt.

In his book 'The forgotten Japanese' (2009) Miyamoto observed the chatting tradition of rural villagers. By calling them forgotten he insisted on the fact that old valued customs had been declared primitive or irrational as a consequence of establishing a new social order based on rational and logical arguing. *Zatsudan* means chat on general topics or in a wider more negative meaning idle talk. It is different from *sekenbanashi* defined in a more narrow sense as gossip talk about others. Miyamoto describes the habit to discuss problems or matters of concern by involving every member of the community into the discussion process and find a solution that satisfies everybody. The process is more important than the result itself whatever it may be. By stressing communication and free debate among equals the result or consensus to be achieved becomes secondary and less important. Involving everybody keeps the debate lively and interesting and reduces tensions. The members listen with empathy to each others, are allowed to state their opinion freely and issue their opposition to others. A key element of *zatsudan* is probably that everyone pays attention to what the other says without anybody dominating the meeting or imposing his opinion on others. *Zatsudan* comes close to Hannah Arendt's understanding of politics and democracy of emphatically listening to the opposite viewpoint first before trying to impose one's own opinion or trying to influence. There is no fixed agenda and members are free to talk about any subject. It is no coincidence that women are believed to be better skilled in *zatsudan* than their male counterparts because they seem to prefer equal cooperation over hierarchy and competition. Relying on personal subjective experiences to make a point or enforce an argument is valued as well. Here again it might be true that male members prefer to engage more into objective and theoretical factual like talking and thereby create a distance and gap with other members. Even silence is regarded as a statement of opinion and this may seem peculiar to Westerners. In Confucian thinking silence plays an important role in a meeting. It is accepted to voice opposition by being silent and such silent opinions of protest or disagreement are taken into account as well. Furthermore members are allowed to discuss matters as long as it may take and there are no deadlines until when to reach a conclusion if any. What matters is that members feel that they had enough time to express themselves fully to each other's and feel understood and taken seriously.

It must however be noted that above type of grass-roots democracy would soon find its limits in a centralized, bureaucratic and highly interest driven political apparatus represented for example by the national Diet of Japan as the practical prerequisites for a chatting grassroots democracy such as communitarian spirit, absence of self-interest, absence of speaking limits, absence of party discipline or pressure, absence of a fixed agenda, absence of consensus pressure, absence of the majority decision making rule and the full respect for and inclusion of minority opinions are not given. Miyamoto's contributions should be interpreted as a helpful insight into independent, rural, traditional community based ways of coexisting and cooperating that reflect a sense of autonomy, equality, mutual support and social awareness uncommon to what is going on on a central or prefectural level. It may be worthwhile to remember that chatting on the street among commoners or in public has been a common tradition to Japan and Mediterranean Europe. Unfortunately the decline of the public sphere has been going hand with the desertion and depopulation of local communities.

Fukuzawa's and Maruyama's dilemma

The political thinking of the pre-Meiji Samurai era and the resurgence of political thinking inspired by recent civic movements offer inspiration and hope that go far beyond the somehow tainted writings of Fukuzawa and Maruyama championed as the defenders of enlightment, Westernization and democracy in the West. A recent study has been trying to give a more critical and realistic picture of the limitations of both acclaimed thinkers (Sakamoto, 2001). Fukuzawa's contribution has been tainted by his positions on China and Asia. For Fukuzawa the dilemma was that he had to support Japanese imperialism in Asia to get the love and respect from the West and not be treated as a primitive tribe.

Maruyama's dilemma consisted in showing sympathy for the German rational fascism and underestimating the damage Japan had done to Asia. His contributions have been tainted from a gender critical perspective as well. Both denied parts of the Japanese tradition to find themselves in a political vacuum of absence of nation state for Fukuzawa and absence of independence from the U.S. for Maruyama.

The former Samurai pride that had been damaged by the emerging simultaneous inferiority complex against the West and superiority complex against other Asians gave rise to a delusion that Japan had a mission to fulfill to guide Asia by liberating it from Western imperialism. The change of tone and new policy became quite clear when looking at how the Korea question was perceived both by Saigo and the Meiji leaders (Ravina, 2004). Saigo who embodied the pure *bushido* spirit wanted to send troops to Korea to punish the Koreans for not acknowledging the dignity and inviolability of the emperor. It would never have come in his mind to annex or occupy Korea for any other reason than punishment and stay there indefinitely. The Meiji policy towards Korea reflected more bluntly the Western style colonial policy thinking than it reflected *bushido* wisdom. The Meiji aspirations were not to defend the honor of the emperor but to occupy, exploit and annex Korea and submit it to state Shinto and its godlike representative on earth.

The Tokugawa ideology of seclusion and expelling the barbarians was substituted by a new expansionist ideology with state Shinto replacing natural Shinto, Confucianism and Buddhism and proclaiming the godlikeness of the emperor, the *kokutai* ideology of 'one race, one language, one state' proclaiming the superiority of the Japanese race over other Asians and peaking in the forced Japanisation of Asia similar to the fascist Nazi Germanisation of Europe. The traditional order of the four classes with the Samurai at the top, then farmers, artisans and merchants was reversed and the military and merchants were co-opted to the top of the country. The Japanese as a nation tried to forget about and distance themselves as far as possible from the spirit of *bushido*.

No Meiji ideology? A critical discussion of Eisenstadt

Eisenstadt has maintained that the Meiji restoration can be distinguished from European revolutions because "no universalistic, transcendental, missionary ideology developed" and because there was no "pretention of saving mankind as a whole" (Eisenstadt, 1996, p 431). The Meiji restorators managed to achieve and maintain national unity by abolishing the shogunate and keeping Western powers off hands. But it did not stop there. Its representatives radically broke with traditional values. The West and its institutions were copied but there was no clear will or attempt to incorporate the political spirit of Western democracy. The Meiji restoration was not only inward-oriented to prevent a social revolution from the bottom but also outward oriented. It was universal in the sense of liberating Asia from the old backward Confucian order and makes it modern, it was transcendental in the sense of expanding state Shinto and the god like role of the emperor to the rest of Asia and missionary in the sense of demanding self sacrifice for the nation-state and the emperor.

It turned to xenophobic and anti-Western sentiments, the *Nihonjinron* ideology (Befu, 2001) of ethnic authenticity and shared identity to control opposition movements and pro democratic Western thinking internally and project its xenophobic sentiments on its Asian neighbors and later on the U.S. and its allies. The 'one state, one race and one language' ideology and the presumed superiority of the Japanese race were constructs or rather artifacts used later on to justify the liberation of Pan Asia from the West and the discrimination of Asians. The Meiji state used crude xenophobic instincts against the West to conquer Asia and oppress internal opposition. Anyone who dared to criticize the national consensus was rubberstamped as anti-Japanese or pro-Western. The nation-state was formed to protect the interests of the ruling elite and a quickly expanding industrial society represented by the pre-war *zaibatsu* known after the war as *keiretsu* or industrial conglomerates. The Meiji style enforced nation-state formation derailed into imperialism. Unless in China where a social revolution had occurred because the masses revolted against the aristocratic and feudal elites who had tied up with Western colonial interests the last shogun in Japan who had been heavily influenced and supported by the French, seeking to control Japan, was more or less coerced to resign and transfer power peacefully to the new Meiji government. The new leaders of government and society opened the country, transformed Japan along Western lines, whether through the adoption of Western-style constitutional government, the import of industrial technology, or the imported habit of meat-eating, a practice little known in Japan until the mid-19th century arrival of Westerners. The ultimate goal was the complete the metamorphosis of Japan into a Western style nation proving and convincing the world that Japan had achieved the status attainment of civilization and achievement of parity with Western powers.

Today, teachers and students of world history tend to accept the idea that the Japanese people, from government officials to the everyday citizen, turned Western without looking back and contentedly imported and implemented Western ways. Yet this understanding of Japan's reaction to the Western threat, while not entirely inaccurate, needs further examination. To begin with, Japan's self-conscious modernization was a form of anti-Western Westernization. Japanese embraced things Western out of fear and hate of the West as much as attraction and esteem. Moreover, Japan's adoption of things Western during the Meiji era was by no means uncritical and their evaluation of Western ideals and customs was never entirely admiring. The old traditional order had been abolished top down but the mold of the new Western style order that was created on paper but not in content remained faceless and weak.

The birth of parliamentarism

State and the public sphere are defined as the bureaucracy, the judicial system and government. It does not include parliament, the only democratically elected and legitimate citizen people body. Despite the dominance of private society and state interests the political sphere has been kept alive on a decentralized level in local city or prefectural parliaments where social movements and NGOs have made their appearance and try to get represented. In historical terms a parliament was a circle of equal members representing the electorate to deliberate public affairs in an open and impartial non partisan spirit, subject–in theory–only to their conscience without being subject to direct interference from the electorate, state authorities or private lobbies.

Japan's first modern legislature was the Imperial Diet established by the Meiji Constitution in force from 1889 to 1947 (Baerwald, 1974). The Meiji Constitution was adopted on February 11, 1889. It was given to the people by the emperor, and only he or his advisers could change it. A parliament was elected beginning in 1890, but only the wealthiest 1% of the population could vote in elections. The Diet consisted of a House of Representatives and a House of Peers consisting of nobles and others nominated by the emperor. The House of Representatives was directly elected, if on a limited franchise; universal adult male suffrage was introduced in 1925, for women it was only introduced in 1945. The House of Peers consisted of high ranking nobles. It should be noted that many executive and legislative positions were appointive, rather than elected. Although seats in local, prefecture and the national lower assemblies were elected, the seats in the House of Peers were either appointive or hereditary. The Meiji constitution was largely based on the form of constitutional monarchy found in nineteenth century Prussia and the new Diet was modeled partly on the German *Reichstag* and partly on the British Westminster system.

Unlike Japan's modern constitution, the Meiji constitution granted a real political role to the emperor, although in practice the emperor's powers were largely directed by a group of oligarchs called the *genro* of which the most influential one was Yamagata Aritomo. Yamagata Aritomo (1838-1922), the once poor and low ranking Samurai from rural Choshu (Yamaguchi), who had succeeded to crush not only the Tokugawa shogunate order but was also instrumental in liquidating the morally grounded anti-Meiji rebellion by Saigo Takamori was to become the military and political mastermind and kingmaker of the new Meiji state (Jansen, 2002). As Ravina (2004) mentions Saigo opposed the new Meiji state represented by Yamataga and Okubo because in his eyes it did not embody moral leadership but nothing but centralized bureaucratic rule and regulation for the sake of mere military strength and imperial territorial expansion. The new rulers in Japan had given up Confucian wisdom and replaced it with the 'blood and soil' *Realpolitik* of Bismarck. Yamagata opposed Ito Hirobumi, leader of the civilian party and father of the first Constitution, and exercised influence through his protégé, Katsura Taro to supervise the military.

After the death of Hirobumi in 1909 Yamagata became the most influential politician and remained so until his death in 1922. As president of the privy council from 1909 to 1922, Yamagata remained the power behind the government and dictated the selection of future prime ministers. To strengthen the grip of the state on citizens Yamagata instituted a military circumscription system that relied on militarily trained loyal subjects, expanded its control on local entities by directly or indirectly appointing prefectural governors, city mayors and district heads and by establishing and extending the power of police.

In 1886 he had issued an ordinance prohibiting the petitioning to officials and in 1887 the Peace Preservation ordinance that served as pretext to exclude the political opposition from public participation and involvement. He also strengthened the bonds between the military and the emperor, who–for the first time in history–was put into a military uniform and attended military ceremonies (Jansen, 2002). Although more formal democracy was granted in 1925 by extending the right to vote to all males liberty in terms of freedom of the press, freedom of assembly and freedom of speech was limited at the same time. In the same year the peace preservation law made it a crime to advocate a basic change in the political system or make attempts to abolish private property. Yamagata's legacy was that he had centralized the rule of the state, redefined the role of the emperor in military terms, strengthened the military domination of internal civilian affairs and set the agenda for military expansion abroad.

The legislative process after the war

Before 1947, to become a law or bill, a constitutional amendment had to have the assent of both the Diet and the emperor. This meant that while the emperor could no longer legislate by decree he still had a veto over the Diet. The emperor also had complete freedom in choosing the prime minister and the cabinet, and so, under the Meiji constitution, prime ministers often were not chosen from and did not enjoy the confidence of the Diet. The Imperial Diet was also limited in its control over the budget. While the Diet could veto the annual budget, if no budget was approved the budget of the previous year continued in force.

After the war sovereignty was transferred from the emperor to the parliament. Article 41 of the constitution describes the national Diet as "the highest organ of state power" and "the sole law-making organ of the state". This statement is in forceful contrast to the Meiji constitution, which described the emperor as the one who exercised legislative power with the consent of the Diet. The formal legislative process is today governed by a detailed process. A bill may be submitted in theory to the Diet either by a Diet member or by the cabinet. The cabinet may submit a bill before either house. Submitted bills are referred to an appropriate committee for deliberation. In the case of major legislation, however, the purpose of the bill is explained and subjected to questioning by Diet members in a plenary session before the bill is referred to a committee. Committees play a central role in deliberating over legislation. The purpose of the bill is explained in the committee, the committee member's direct questions at government ministers and other officials involved in drawing up the legislation, experts are called to testify, amendments are proposed, issues are debated, and in the end a vote is taken. Bills that make it through committees are presented to the plenary session as proposed legislation. In the plenary session, the committee chairman presenting the bill summarizes the discussions in committee and reports on the results. Following that, the bill is discussed and deliberated in the plenum before it is put to the vote. As usual also in other parliamentary modern democracies the public plenum de facto only endorses symbolically the decisions agreed in the non-public committee sessions attended by bureaucrats and lawmakers from the government parties and the opposition parties. A bill passed by one house is sent to the other. The bill only becomes law if it wins approval in both houses. Since most bills are proposed initially in the House of Representatives, the House of Councilors is generally the final venue for deciding the outcome of proposed legislation. For decades one single party has succeeded to control both houses and all regular committee chairmanships as well. Due to the crushing dominance of the governing party in both houses all the enacted bills in the after war period have been prepared and drafted by the bureaucracy on behalf of the cabinet or government. The newly revised NPO law of 1998 was entered as a direct floor bill, the first time a bill had not originated in the bureaucracy since 1947.

Before the war the House of Peers was an unelected body that managed to defeat progressive legislation attempts of the Lower House. After the war the new House of Councilors was to be entirely elected and its members were chosen in a different way. The House of Councilors can delay or block the enactment of cabinet laws because its decisions can only be overruled by a two third majority in the House of Representatives–the state budget and international treaties excepted. It has recently gained more political weight and influence since the opposition gained a majority there. Even if it does not succeed to bloc a government initiative the mediatized public debate followed by discussions in the House of Councilors can affect government legislation and public opinion significantly.

Parliamentarism in Asia has a long history of chaotic, immature conflict resolution rituals, pork barrel tactics and obstructionist voting behaviors: the best example might be the physical fist fights quite common and frequent in Taiwan and Korea, attempts to crush locked committee doors with hammers to prevent a vote or discussion and physical obstructionism to delay ballot voting, tactics which amount clearly to anti-political behaviors when benchmarking it against the standards of Hannah Arendt's non coercive and non-violent imperative. Another symbolic detail might be the parliamentary clerks who wear military style uniforms and act as if they want to protect a democratic institution from itself. The military like dress code of clerks in the Japanese Diet compared to the civilian dress code of German parliamentary clerks is more than symbolic. The flaws of public campaigning and the election system have always greatly influenced the outcome of elections in Japan. The preponderance of rural votes over city votes is a well known example. The officially illegal cash bribing of voters is less known but was still practiced at least until the 1990s. The proportional representation system was only introduced in 1994. A party must win 3% of the total number of votes to be represented. Canvassing door-to-door is prohibited by the public office election law. One reason for this is that it could facilitate crimes such as electoral bribery and influence-peddling. But some merits are also pointed out–it causes less sound pollution and annoyance to the general public than street-side campaigning, and it can give voters the chance to gain a deeper understanding of the candidate's political agenda.

The flaws of inherited politics are another significant feature: more than 30% of the lawmakers have inherited their political office function due to their family background and birth privilege. Hereditary handing down of work from parent to child has some unique characteristics. Second and third generation politicians benefit from inheriting the three *bans* from their forebears. These are *jiban* (supporter groups), *kanban* (name recognition) and *kaban* (campaign finance). Heredity candidates run for office with more advantages than entirely fresh candidates. One negative effect of political heredity is that talented potential candidates who do not boast an impressive lawmaker's pedigree are discouraged from running.

Globalization, diversification and borderless world: a comparative perspective

Unlike China or India who have to cope with many pre-industrial issues like manufacturing and ecological impact that Japan has been confronted with in the 50s, 60s, and 70s Japan leads the world in terms of scientific, technological, economic and innovative excellence. The question is if Japan can resist and preserve some it's traditional unique features despite growing pressure from outside and calls from inside to adjust to global standards, open up and deregulates markets further, give up employment safety and internationalize further its education system.

Will the Japanese use the Western model of assimilation to global standards to cope with immigrants and foreigners or will they use their own wisdom and experience to coexist with foreigners? Will the Japanese be able to keep their traditional system of life time employment or will they revert to Western methods of lay off for the sake of shareholder value? Will the Japanese be successful in laying the foundation for multilingual pluralism in local education or will they adopt English as the global dominant culture tool? Will the Japanese continue to imitate the Western global model of material affluence, energy over-consumption and waste production or will they remind themselves of their own ecological past spirit and peaceful coexistence with nature? Will the Japanese remain proud of their cultural folk culture, attitudes and beliefs or will they continue to act as rational animals in a Western sense? Will the Japanese continue to destroy their own important cultural properties for the sake of modernization and affluence or will they preserve their traditional craftsmanship skills? Will they respect the boundaries of natural reserves and wildlife or will they continue to destroy the landscapes, turn the countryside into ghost towns and urbanize the center at any prize? Will they follow the trend towards Western fast food culture or preserve their own traditional food culture?

Japan has experienced significant changes in its social structure since the early 1990s when the neoconservative mainstream government started to liberalize the country and open it up fully to foreign capital. The lasting and sometimes damaging effects of globalization on countries may be observed and studied on case examples such as tiny Luxembourg. Up to the 1970s Luxembourg was a rural, decentralized and very local spot with agriculture and a strong secondary steel industry as its main sources for income. Despite its tiny size Luxembourg has been fully independent and sovereign. The nation-state was delimited by fixed national borders, issued a national currency and had a small standing army. Luxembourg was blessed with nature, clean rivers, convenient public transportation and what matters most public peace and a social consensus. There were few cars or main roads and for shopping one went by foot to the nearby small retail shop. The catholic Church had a strong grip on family life and public values and even workers went to church. Foreign worker immigrants from Portugal and Italy due to sharing the same religious background found it rather easy to become part of Luxembourg and live side by side with Luxembourgers. The public school system although open in principle to everyone was and is still today rather selective and elitarian. Those, who made it to university studies abroad, were few.

However the regional and economic class segregation between farmers, workers and the bourgeoisie in the capital did not cause major distraught or social unrest. Social and public life was very important to Luxembourgers: chatting in public or at coffee shops, shopping at the local vegetables or fish market, joining clubs and social or volunteer mutual aid activities, celebrating various family events, participating in religious and secular, cultural festivals were and–nowadays–still are a central part of public life. There was a mix of self-sufficiency, self-satisfaction, national pride and strong commonsense that unified citizens despite the massive presence of foreign immigrants, despite the social disparity among the bourgeoisie, workers and farmers and despite the dominance of the Church in public life.

Nowadays Luxembourg is fully embedded in Europe and things have changed quite a lot. There are no more that many real workers, small farmers or small retail shops around. Farmland and forests have been reconverted and transformed into industrial zones. Under the umbrella of economic growth and diversification new foreign investors have been massively attracted and new jobs have been created to replace the local industry. Each family household owns four cars in average today, back in the sixties it was only one car. Housing and property prices have risen to outrageous levels due to the presence of many high wage earners. Luxembourgers own properties abroad and go abroad frequently for shopping or spending their holidays. Not only has public life impoverished. The retreat into privacy is another major social change. In the past children used to play in the nearby woods whenever they felt like and socialized spontaneously with nearby neighbors. Festivals were a fixed part of public life and the Church had its influence and moral grip on the community in a good and bad way. These times seem to have gone. Highways have been built, the neighborhood woods have made room for new apartment complexes and commercial buildings, neighborhoods have lost their socializing role and public community life has impoverished as citizens have retreated into their private spheres. The divorce rate has reached unprecedented levels and church services on Sundays are empty. Mental illness, suicide, a deadly road rage among juveniles, prostitution, and drug and alcohol addiction has become issues of serious public concern. The increasing number of foreigners is perceived as threat to the national identity. Educated and skilled office workers from abroad have poured into the country and compete locally for qualified jobs. Luxembourgers shed the pressure of increased competition and prefer rather the job security of civil servants. Citizens who feel overwhelmed, estranged, insecure, threatened by crime, aggressively and intolerance are on the rise. Globalization has brought more foreign capital and wealth to Luxembourg but the social development lacks behind the economic development. Some examples are the disappearance of small retail shops and local community networks, the conversion of farmland into parking lots and industrial sites, the integration problems of immigrants, the prison conditions in overcrowded prisons, an underdeveloped public transport system, raging prostitution, drug and alcohol addiction, lack of decent school infrastructure and debts of private households. By 2015 more foreigners will live in Luxembourg than Luxembourgers. The Luxembourgish language, a symbol of national identity, will probably be replaced by French by then.

Globalization has on the other side created beneficial cultural, economic, touristic, educational opportunities for increased regional cooperation in the formerly war torn Saar-Lorraine-Luxembourg area. More jobs have been created than any time before and the economic and financial boom has created material wealth and affluence. The borderless region stimulates exchanges and mutual understanding among the locals and reflects the socioeconomic changes from a labor intensive agrarian and industrial rooted society to a knowledge and service driven society.

In Japan the change has been similar. Since the burst of the bubble in the 80s a transformation from a traditional producer driven manufacturing economy to globalized, information based and consumer driven high tech and money economy has occurred. The shift from export to direct foreign investment has made it easier for the global economy to step in and take hold of the huge internal market. Japan has exported its local manufacturing capabilities to China and other Asian countries and prevails itself of highly added value technical services and support functions. The embedment of Japan into the global economy has increased material wealth and the statistical competitiveness of the country but at the same time social values of justice and fairness have been neglected. The company model as a social family unit was abandoned, the number of depressed workers increased dramatically as well as the number of reported child abuse case and suicides, the number of regular fulltime employed and insured workers decreased rapidly and the traditional social support network including family and community has declined. The three generation household, a distinctive feature of the traditional society structure has been replaced by anonymous apartment complexes and nursing care homes. The stages of globalization offer similarities in Luxembourg and Japan:

- Traditional manufacturing facilities were hollowed out whereas new jobs were created by attracting investors from all over the world.
- Globalization generated losers and winners. Those who were flexible and competitive found a well paid job, the losers are among those who failed to obtain market compliant job qualifications, school education or language education.
- The public sector created a tax friendly climate and framework for corporate or private investors to boost global competitiveness and attract new industries.
- Public social institutions and civic society have not developed in parallel with the private commercial and financial benefits of globalization. Social disintegration and disparities have worsened.
- The influx of foreigners has created identity diffusion among the native population and immigration policies have failed to tackle the challenge of social integration.
- The older generation has reacted more cautiously to the changes than the younger generation and though the younger generation seems more open it is more vulnerable to the negative implications. Some examples might

be the influx of illegal drugs or the problems caused by fast food and obesity. In Luxembourg as well as in Japan elderly people feel threatened by foreigners, foreign languages or the influx of foreign culture.

Shortcomings of globalization

Subtle racism: foreigners do not legally exist in Japan

The *koseki* family registry, kept by municipal governments throughout Japan, lists a variety of personal details about the family's life, including head of household, address, birthdates, and children. Passports and other documents are issued based on this registration. What the family registry does not list is the name of any foreigner. In cases where one spouse is a foreigner, only the Japanese spouse's name appears on the family registry. This exclusion has its roots in Article 39 of the Basic Resident Registry Law, which stipulates that the names of foreign nationals may not be noted on the official resident certificate. Briefly, the family registration system began with the first national census in 1872 and then became the official system of registration. Following World War II, the family registration system was modified considerably and emerged in its current form. In 1967, Japan made a small step toward addressing the growing number of international marriages by allowing inclusion of foreign spouses who were the head of the household to be listed in the remarks section of the resident certificate. In March 2000, the United Nations Committee on the Elimination of Racial Discrimination (UNCERD) raised questions about Japan's exclusionary policy regarding resident registration during its consideration of Japan's compliance with the International Convention on the Elimination of all Forms of Racial Discrimination. In March 2002, the Minister of Public Management, Home Affairs, Posts and Telecommunications gave permission to include any foreign spouse in the remarks section, provided the foreign spouse requested such listing. Permanent residents risk to be deported if they are on a spouse visa and their spouse divorces them.

Subtle racism: continued violation of the international children convention

The social shortcomings of globalization in Japan become very obvious when looking at the surrounding problems of acquiring of citizenship rights for children issued out of mixed marriages and relationships. The number of international marriages has been steeply rising in the last ten years and so have the unsolved citizenship issues due to lack of consistent immigration policy and adherence to international conventions (Okuda, 2003).

Subtle racism: the pressure to adopt a Japanese name

It has always been a common practice and policy in Japan to pressure and require Koreans and Chinese born and raised in Japan to japanize their name in order to hide their ethnic identity. To get Japanese citizenship and be accepted in Japanese society they need to hide their real identity. This practice is contrary to basic human rights and ethnic diversity. Shigematsu-Murphy (2000) reports from a clinical psychologist perspective on the mental constraints and sufferings related to this policy. Open society asks for ethnic self revelation and open dialogue. Ethnicity as constrained by official language, formal procedures and assimilating norms does not provide for diversity and open dialogue. Japan has its problems when it comes to accepting and promoting diversity instead of ignoring the differences between individuals (Sugimoto, 2003).

Subtle racism: new fingerprinting law as from 2007

A special U.N. rapporteur on racism criticized Japan's new immigration legislation on fingerprinting and photographing all foreign visitors as a process of treating foreigners like criminals. Doudou Diene said at a past press conference the immigration bill that just passed the Diet "illustrates something I have been denouncing in my reports for four years. It is the fact that, especially since Sept 11, there has been a process of criminalization of foreigners" all over the world, he added. The underlying assumption that foreigners may threaten Japanese security is in itself discriminating and a pure act of governmental autocratic thinking especially with regard to permanent residents which means even people who are long-term residents will get fingerprinting reinstated, despite having it seen abolished after decades of protest in 1999.

Press briefing by Mr. Naoto Nikai

On 23 October 2007, Mr. Naoto Nikai, Deputy Director-General of the Immigration Bureau, Ministry of Justice held a press briefing on the New Entry Procedures to be effective as of November, 2007. Excerpts from the briefing arranged by the Foreign Press Center (FPC):

From November 20th 2007, a bio-ID will be required when entering Japan. A machine at the passport control booth will take the prints of your forefingers and your facial photo. But, believe me, this will be the most painless, the least time-consuming, and possibly the most customer friendly system. Plus, we would like to start "automated gate" system where the immigration officers ask no time-consuming question whatsoever. This will even shorten the time you must spend in the queue (line). If you are a re-entry permit holder, the next time you fly overseas, you just show up at the registration counter at Narita airport, fill out the paperwork, have them take your prints and the photo, and you are all set. By the time you have flown back to Narita, the registration is complete and you can quickly walk through the automated gate. However if you are a "stamp collector" I suggest you ask the immigration officers to stamp a seal of permission. We would like to increase the number of automated gates to other airports in future for your convenience. Either way, we have set a benchmark that it will cost you only twenty minutes at the maximum, from joining the queue to the exit. Added to that, we are busy reinvesting into our human capital. The officer at the counter is the "face of Japan". The smile they show you is what you will remember most. If in any way you feel offended, this is your contact point. (…)

Q8. Why do you consider foreigners more dangerous than Japanese nationals and why do you consider "Special Permanent Residents" less dangerous than the status of "Permanent Residents" in Japan? A. "Special Permanent Residents" have the historical background that their parents and grandparents have lost Japanese nationality on the basis of the Treaty of Peace with Japan. So their residence is based on Special Law on the Immigration Control and we have taken into consideration their special status in Japan. Q9. How much has this system cost Japanese taxpayers, and isn't this an overblown reaction in light of the few number of terrorists and the track record of terrorism in Japan? A. It is too late to put a system into place after an act of terrorism takes place. Q10. Will the Ministry of Justice share the bio-information with any other bodies? And has the Japanese government already made any agreement with the government of the United States of America to take part in sharing such information? Has the Japanese been pressured by the United States to introduce this procedure? A. There will be two categories in which information will be shared with foreign governments: ① Information sharing between Immigration authorities, which will only involve sharing information between these authorities under the provision of Article 61-9 of the Immigration Act. ② Official mutual legal assistance requests through diplomatic channels and other forms of information sharing allowed under "the Act on the Protection of Personal Information Held by Administrative Organs." We are not are aware of any such pressure from the U.S. The introduction of this new procedure was decided upon by the Japanese government in December 2004.

Q11. How does the Ministry of Justice define terrorism? A. The Immigration Act doesn't provide a clear definition of "terrorism" or "terrorist." Last year, however, we established the provision on the grounds for deportation of foreign terrorists in Item (3)-2 of Article 24 of the Immigration Act. Item (3)-2 of Article 24 A person who the Minister of Justice determines, having reasonable grounds to believe as much, is likely to commit a criminal act for the purpose of intimidation of the general public and of governments (hereinafter in this item to be referred to as the "criminal act for the purpose of intimidation of the general public and of governments") provided for in Article 1 of the Act for Punishment of the Financing of Criminal Activities for the Purpose of Intimidation of the criminal act for the purpose of intimidation of the general public and of gov-

ernments, or the act of facilitating the criminal act for the purpose of intimidation of the general public and of governments. Q12. Will the Ministry of Justice
take any measures to ensure that the obtained information will not be used for
"racial profiling" under the name of "terrorism"? A. No profiling based on racial
or ethnic origins will be made.

The civil sector as counterbalance to state rule

1995 the year of the disastrous earthquake in Kobe which turned also into a
disaster for government relief operations has been a turning point in history and
led to the creation rush of new NPOs in various areas and social fields. Subsequently a new NPO law has been enacted in 1998 to allow for increased direct
civil political participation. The law for the first time acknowledges and organizes the activities of a not for profit third sector besides the traditional state institutions, parliament and the private profit sector. What is interesting is that the
independence and autonomy of the NPOs has been guaranteed by a law that was
introduced as direct floor bill to parliament, adopted unanimously by all parties
and formulated such as to limit the financial, legal and political regulation and
surveillance of the state to an institutional minimum. The NPO law by guaran-
teeing the freedom to act outside of state control sets the stage for equal political
participation side by side with state agencies or private for profit institutions.
Since 1998 more than 36 000 organizations have been granted NPO status. The
law was revised in 2001 allowing for donations to become tax deductible under
certain conditions and extending the number of activity fields to seventeen. According to the Asahi Shimbun editorial of 3 Januray 2009 only 90 NPOs have
been able so far to obtain the tax favorable treatment allowing them to receive
tax free donations which are vital to support their activities and remain independent from government funds and control.

Besides the NPOs there exist around 25 000 public interest corporations including Japan's largest and most established nonprofits. The concept of public-interest corporations or *koeki hojin*, first developed in the Meiji civil code of
1896 continues to provide the main rubrics for government oversight of civil society groups. Separate laws have been developed for the administration of private school corporations, social welfare corporations, medical corporations, and
religious corporations but all of these groups are subtypes of public interest
corporations. Public interest has been interpreted rather narrowly as for the benefit of society in general or of many and unspecified persons, which excludes
business organizations, sports clubs, alumni associations, and many other groups
which actually function as civil society groups but are registered either as mutual benefit corporations or educational, medical or religious corporations. The
more established public interest corporations include organizations such as Am-
nesty International, the Japan Sumo Association and the Japan Center for International Exchange.

Public-interest corporations have to report regularly to a government ministry, which can investigate a group or revoke its legal status. The corporations, including religious corporations, must submit lists of their annual activities, assets, accounts of changes of membership, financial statements, budget estimates, and other matters. The agency can make on-site inspections and audits. These and similar regulations inhibit the autonomy of these civil society groups. Often there is a de facto agreement by public-interest corporations to employ ex-bureaucrats of the approving ministry, a practice called *amakudari*, which gives those individuals significant influence in how the group develops. This and other widely publicized problems regarding public interest corporations have led to current proposals to make them subject to income taxation. Under a new framework which took effect in December 2008 the status of all public interest corporations will be revoked and they will be obliged to re-register as new legal entities. Under the new system NPOs are no longer required to operate on the basis of an authorization from the agency or ministry with jurisdiction over their field of activities. They simply register with the prime minister's cabinet office or the prefectural government if activities are limited to the prefecture. Upon registration organizations get the status of general incorporated associations (*ippan shaddan hojin*) or general incorporated foundations (*ippan zaidan hojin*). The large corporations must reapply for the new status or they lose their tax benefits and endowment. The reform has no impact on smaller NPOs.

There has been a heightened interest prominently among Western scholars on the civil society boom in Japan such as Chan, 2004 & 2008; Hirata, 2002; Hasegawa, 2004; Kingston, 2004; Schwartz & Pharr, 2003; Pekkanen, 2006 and Haddad, 2007 to name just a few. What differentiates all these approaches is that they look at the civil sector from various angles and perspectives; what unites their approaches is that they agree that an alternative civilian concept relying on democracy, a culturally sensitive, multicultural identity formation and state independent voluntary and proactive citizenship has emerged in Japan. Chan (2004 & 2008) by emphasing agency, advocacy and the narrative construction of reality demonstrates that international norms and standards can positively impact and drive national agendas for improvement and change. Kingston (2004) highlights the changes from an institutional and legal perspective that have enabled citizens to challenge the bureaucracy, access information and reclaim territory. Foreign aid is a key instrument of the soft power of Japanese foreign policy. Hirata (2002) analyzes the growing role and cooptation of civil society actors in Tokyo's aid and development policy and the ambivalent relationship between the controlling state and autonomous civil agents in designing foreign aid policy within the existing institutional frameworks. Hasegawa (2004) looks at NPOs from the perspective of environmental social movements that use their street pressure to influence, correct or initiate state policies. Pekkanen (2006) characterizes NPOs as "dual social capital" without advocacy meaning that they have extensive local-level membership and activities especially in the areas of social welfare and education but that this does not translate into advocacy and policy making on a national level. Schwartz & Pharr (2003) trace the historic emergence of civil society, explore the state's role in shaping civil society and attempt to define the nature of civil society. Haddad's (2007) model of community volunteerism analyzes the emergence of specific types of voluntary local organizations and their role as mediator between the state, local communities and citizens. Japan, with strong ideas of governmental responsibility and weak ideas of individual responsibility, has many embedded organizations–neighborhood associations, volunteer firefighters, and PTAs–that have ties with officialdom. A country like the United States, with strong ideas of individual responsibility and weak ideas of governmental responsibility, has few embedded organizations and instead has comparatively more non-embedded organizations that are distant from the government. In Japan volunteerism has always played a very strong role to supplement the passive role of the state especially in the social welfare and public health sector. Unless Western countries the welfare state in Japan is leaner than in the West and the traditional mission of the welfare state has been covered by the activities of numerous NPOs and volunteer groups. It is interesting to note that traditional Japanese volunteerism is pro bono and viewed as honorable whereas in the West being a volunteer is considered more and more a for -profit- activity that requires professionalism and involves important material and financial resources.

Locally operating NPOs do not get any subsidy or funds from the state. The state welcomes the services of NPOs but not their advocacy and interference in state affairs. The financial lack of support for inbound activities contrasts with the strong financial support given to the four hundred internationally active development NGOs. First emerging in the 1960s, NGOs increased in number and quality in the late 70s and early 80s, mainly through providing assistance to Indochinese refugees. Recent cooperative activities of Japanese NGOs in Irak, Kosovo and Afghanistan are the proof of their steady growth. Another characteristic of Japanese NPOs is their strong international involvement especially since the early 1990s when the state started to encourage them with active financial support to partially complement conventional ODA which used to be sharply criticized as a money channel for public work contracts for Japanese companies abroad (Arase 1995 & 2005). Another reason behind this move was to follow international standards and practices and the search for international esteem to secure a permanent seat at the United Nations Security Council. Initially NGOs referred exclusively to non-governmental and non-profit organizations that work in cooperation with United Nations agencies. The definition has since been broadened to include those non-governmental and non-profit organizations that address such global issues as development, the economy, human rights, humanitarian concerns and the environment.

In the eyes of the state NGOs have become an indispensable part of today's international community. Their mobility and flexibility are vital in providing grassroots-level assistance and emergency humanitarian relief. The Japanese government believes that collaboration with NGOs is crucial in gaining public understanding and support for its Official Development Assistance (ODA) programs. Partnership between NGOs and the government assumes two forms: collaboration and support. Working with them in ODA policymaking and project implementation, the government benefits much from their knowledge and human resources, and in return, provides them with financial and other forms of support. Collaboration and support, of course, are based on a close dialogue. As part of the collaboration, the Ministry of Foreign Affairs (MOFA) launched a joint evaluation program in fiscal 1997. By evaluating and discussing ODA projects and NGO activities, NGOs and MOFA have come to understand each other better and thus are able to work out cooperation schemes. In 2000 a Group of NGOs, the State and Keidanren jointly established a new scheme named the 'Japan Platform (JPF)' to provide emergency humanitarian relief abroad. This system is intended to help the government, the business community, and NGOs cooperate to provide emergency humanitarian relief more effectively and quickly. The NGO Project Subsidy and the Grant Assistance for Grassroots Projects, both introduced in 1989, have been the main pillars of the governmental NGO support schemes. In fiscal 2002, MOFA launched the Grant Assistance for Japanese NGO Projects and the 'JICA' Partnership Program by integrating existing schemes.

In 1991 the Ministry of Posts launched the Postal Savings for international voluntary aid scheme under which holders of ordinary postal savings accounts can donate part of their accrued interest for international cooperation purposes. This quasi governmental scheme was however scrapped after postal privatization in 2007. In late 2008 the Japan International Cooperation Agency (JICA) merged with the Japan Bank for International Cooperation creating one of the world's largest bilateral development agencies with an annual budget of 8.5 billion USD.

Example of a civic grass root movement which has turned political: the Kanagawa Network Movement

The Kanagawa Network Movement or abbreviated as 'NET' is a political party based in Kanagawa Prefecture. It has 3,400 members in 18 municipalities, most of whom are women, and there are 39 local municipal assembly representatives, including four in the prefectural assembly. The organization started as a group of housewives who were initially involved in the consumer cooperative movement. They were working to distribute natural soap to stop the use of synthetic detergents. When petitioning seven municipal assemblies, including those of Yokohama and Kawasaki, to adopt laws to promote the use of natural soap the idea was voted down and this made NET realize that gaining political power was crucial to implementing citizen's policies. One year before NET was formally launched in 1984 the first member of NET succeeded in being elected to the

Kawasaki city assembly. From then on NET increased its membership and number of local representatives gradually.

The fact that the local party consists mainly of elderly housewives and women, who traditionally used to be concealed to more appropriate female volunteering activities such as public health, PTA safety control or traffic security, indicates a paradigm shift at least on the local political level of the basic administrative units in municipalities and prefectures. The public role of contributing to the betterment of society attributed to housewives and mothers has only been tolerated in so far it did not question business as usual and affect the male dominance and male set agenda of what constitutes citizen's needs. NET has been one of the first political movements to trespass the public boundary of male dominated politics and has as such been confronted with a wall of male resistance in local residents associations and industrial groups. Males are often out of touch with what is actually happening in their communities or what local residents want to change. The fight for more political freedom is a fight against traditional male style money politics. One big problem with local autonomy is that power and taxpayers' money are concentrated in the city government which dominates the assembly. In order to make politics more related to citizen's concerns and daily issues NET has an agenda with four clear-cut goals : reforming the way of male dominated politics by seeking for example the abolition of the state pension for assembly members which is dependent on the number of years of assembly membership which induces many to seek reelection for shortsighted selfish financial interests; the strengthening of civil society by providing welfare services based on the needs of citizens such as elderly care services and daycare centers and nurseries for children; changing the assembly by lobbying for direct petitioning by citizens and proposing grass root laws that reflect the wishes of citizens with a focus on environment; finally promoting local and overseas peace activities to reflect the fact that Kanagawa hosts the 2nd largest number of foreign military bases after Okinawa. NET was also opposed to the dispatching of SDF forces to Irak. The four themes may be summed up as public welfare with a focus on disabled, elderly and children, environment and food safety issues, peace, human security and cooperation to give a framework and support local NPOs with appropriate legislation, petitions and funds.

The German way of political equality

The emergence of a nationally representative strong Green party has been unknown in Japan and the United States. The Green party originated as a political movement in the 70s out of concern for peace and the environment. Japan has a similar history of anti-war and anti-US radical student supported movements and terrorist group formation in the 70s but these activities did not result in the formation of a new political party representing radically new values but were rather absorbed by the traditionally established left parties. In Germany however the activities of the civic movements called also 'APO'–meaning literally the extra parliamentary opposition–resulted in a major transformation of the political landscape. Paraphrased as the *Marsch durch die Institutionen*–literally making one's way right through the institutions–the Greens contributed to a renewed and different political culture in Germany and inspired many citizens to challenge the traditional way of doing politics. The parliamentarian representation of the the Green party was founded in 1980, in 1993 the Green Party merged with the civil rights movement 'Alliance 90' of the former German Democratic Republic. Since 1983, there has been a continuous representation of either the Greens or Alliance 90 in the German parliament. For nearly 25 years the Greens have been working in the parliament for environmental protection and sustainable development, democracy and human rights, social justice, peace and multilateral international policies. From 1998 to 2005–that is for two electoral terms–the party formed the federal government together with the Social Democratic Party (SPD). During this time the Greens played a substantial role in establishing Germany as a reliable and trusted partner for sustainable and peaceful development, both at the national and international level. Since 2005, Germany has been governed by a conservative-social democratic coalition. The Greens are one of three parties in opposition, each with a similar number of seats.

The parliamentary group is made up of 51 members - the largest representation of ecological/social policies in any parliament around the world. Members of the German Green Party also make up a significant share of the Green parliamentary group in the European Parliament. 13 of the 42 members of the Green European parliamentary group belong to 'Alliance 90/The Greens'. The Greens have impacted political culture in areas like non-violent resistance against state rule, a critical foreign policy keeping respectful distance to the U.S., introduction of elements of direct democracy supplementing representative democracy, introduction of a fixed quota to obtain equal statistical representation for women in offices, job rotation from party functions to parliamentary representation and vice versa to prevent lawmakers from becoming too much entrenched in professional politics, restriction of the number of electable terms, incompatibility of being at the same time a minister and member of parliament, separation of party and parliament functions and radical environmental policies like the abolition of nuclear power.

The Green policies rely on four basic principles: ecology, social justice, direct democracy and non-violence. Ecology encapsulates the diverse teachings and philosophies represented in numerous environmental movements. Central tenets include a recognized need to reduce the negative impact of human civilization on the natural environment, the biosphere, and the planet, and to find new, alternate ways to cohabitate harmoniously with earth's other life forms. Social justice reflects the general rejection of discrimination based on distinctions between class, gender, ethnicity, or culture. Green parties are almost universally egalitarian in their outlook, seeing that great disparities in wealth or influence are caused by the perversion of or total lack of social institutions that prevent social imbalance. Grassroots democracy or participatory democracy is embraced by Greens as the only reliable governance model for achieving social change. Many Green parties have rejected or constrained the traditional role of leaders as party boss, in favor of having figurehead leaders or spokespeople. Green party manifests are configured to prevent the party bureaucracy from accumulating too much power in the organization, in favor of more decentralized or member driven processes.

Non-violence reflects the Green movement's policy of rejecting violence as a means to resolve conflicts with the state. Green philosophy draws heavily on Gandhi and other traditions, which advocate measures by which the escalation of violence can be avoided, while not cooperating with those who commit violence or threaten citizens with violence.

The deep shift of political culture that happened in Germany may be best understood when looking at the law to compensate former foreign slave laborers initiated by the Greens (Hein P., 2000). The law regulates the access to a state pension for all foreign slave laborers regardless of their current residence. The Greens were the first ones in Germany to initiate the debate on compensation for unjust treatment during the war and the law that was finally enacted by the German parliament was a major step forward of coming to terms with history, whereas in the Japanese case the international community has continuously raised concerns on unsettled war issues such as the comfort women issue, the textbook controversy issue or the Yasukuni shrine issue. The Hiroshima debate on whether Japanese were victims or perpetrators is unnecessary. The debate on Hiroshima is futile as it is well known that from a military viewpoint Johnson's decision did not add any value. On the other side taking the victim role is not helpful if it serves as an excuse for war responsibilities. There are museums glorifying the *kamikaze* as national heroes despite knowing that they were sent against their will into their death, a museum on the warship *Yamato* opened some time ago to glorify the military past and the government has recently supported the opening of a center for the study of Anne Frank and the German holocaust but why is it impossible to have a museum of the Japanese aggression war against Asia in Japan? A museum is the most important tool to preserve the past memories. Forceful suppression of unpleasant memories increases the risks for history to repeat itself.

There are many other examples which prove that Japan has not freed itself from its inglorious past: the misappropriation of Indian Justice Pal to justify that the world war Tokyo trials were unfair and unjust is politically outrageous as is the denial or distortion of the Nanking massacre. The latest move to amend the peace article 9 of the Japanese constitution under the pretext of allowing Japan to engage in collective defense of its allies or combat international terrorism is yet another attempt to give up established peace principles. Germany has opted to keep distance to the U.S. foreign policy, to make the world a civilian place and only engage in UN mandated humanitarian dispatch activities. Japan has gone a step further by initiating a debate on non UN mandated military overseas operations. The dispatch of troops to the Irak is one recent example of the policy shift. Regarding self defense Japan has enough military capability to defend itself and is in no need for building up offensive systems.

Why did a similar shift of political culture never occur? Japan is an island nation; the oppositional social movements never managed to consolidate as an institutionalized political force or party and consequently attempt to establish a non-violent, grass root, ecological platform failed. Japan has never been integrated in a regional cooperative network compared to Germany which has learned from the lessons of the past by showing real remorse for the sufferings it incurred to its European neighbors and this has by the way been very much appreciated by the Europeans. In Germany the youth have rebelled against their parents and the authorities representing the past whereas in Japan the youth rebellion never materialized in a national institutionalized opposition to the mainstream thinking. Germany and France finance joint cultural institutes in each country and Germany maintains a central agency for political citizen education called *Bundeszentrale fuer politische Bildung*. The German Bundestag agreed to compensate slave laborers, apologized to the victims of aggression and built a national war memorial. Germany has made real efforts of reconciliation with its neighbors by sponsoring visits of students to concentration camps and promoting the exchange of cross border school visits. The crimes of the German army against civilians were documented and exhibited nationwide in local museums. The Japanese school and education system has never made any attempts to teach the historic facts and educate the young about the crimes committed by their grandfathers or try to overcome mutual animosity by initiating reconciliation projects by bringing together people instead of separating them. Germany has intensely promoted the influx of foreign students to enable them to learn about the new Germany and initiated forward-looking immigration policies. Japan has never symbolically broken with the wrongdoings of the past and this failure constitutes psychologically a major barrier to renewal and rebirth (Orr et al, 2001). The only two after war politicians who stand out are former socialist Prime Minister Tomiichi Murayama who apologized honestly and sincerely for past crimes in public and Yohei Kono, the speaker of Parliament's powerful lower house who proposed to build a neutral public national memorial to honor all the victims of war.

The stereotype antagonism between Eastern shame cultures versus Western guilt culture needs to be reevaluated in a comparative context if one wants to understand why Japan went a different path when facing its aggressor war legacy compared to Germany. The assumption has been made that Japanese cannot apologize because, as members of a shame society, have no sense of guilt. Ruth

Benedict (1989) argued that the West operated as a guilt culture concerned with strict morality and personal responsibility whereas Japan reflected a Confucian shame culture, in which the individual was, concerned with external public shame exposure rather than with internal guilt feelings. Benedict's concept has been adopted at face value by some scholars (Buruma, 1994) who claim that Germany is more guilt culture and Japan more shame culture even though the culturally simplistic 'they versus us' dichotomy of guilt versus shame cannot be maintained from both a psychological and philosophical modern viewpoint.

Regarding shame which is closely connected to the concepts of honor and loyalty, Nitobe (2007) wrote that is must be located inside rather than being viewed as an outside phenomenon. Ikegami (2003) in her analysis of Yoshida Shoin's motivations to disregard an edict of the Tokugawa rulers demonstrated that loyalty to his individual conscience was more important to him than being exposed to external shame pressure. She called this attitude ethical individualism. Shame in a positive sense protects something intimate from the public eye and in a negative sense emphasizes what is wrong with oneself. It has a much more inward focus, and as such, leads shameful parties to feel poorly about themselves, rather than simply the actions they have taken. The result is often an inward-turning behavior avoiding others, hiding the face, removing oneself from social situations.

The psychiatrist and neurologist Dr. Viktor Frankl insists that every human being has a right to become guilty and be punished. Without accepting guilt there can be no room for dignity for Frankl. If one takes away the right to become guilty one takes away the human dignity itself he claims. The human being has not only the right or freedom to become guilty but also the responsibility to overcome its guilt. As a result, guilt is an important tool in maintaining standards of right and wrong in individuals and society as a whole. Frankl's argument clearly demonstrates that guilt is not limited to internal feelings but submitted to the judgment of the outside world as well.

Both shame and guilt can have extensive implications for one's self perception and one's behavior towards other people, particularly in situations of conflict. The difference in attitude between both countries is not only the fact that Germany has come to terms with its past whereas Japan has not but. The underlying question is rather how it could be that ordinary civilian people who, dressed in uniforms, committed abominable and horrendous crimes against other civilians could keep on living with a clean conscience after the war without being driven to insanity or madness? How could it be that the many ordinary war criminals that followed orders instead of following their conscience had not been brought to justice by civilian criminal courts after the war? How could it come that the conspiracy of silence and the secrecy surrounding war crimes against civilians had never been fundamentally questioned in Japan after the war? Why do the schools still teach children that the war against Asia was just and that it was just to sacrifice oneself for the emperor? How can there be spiritual renewal if there is no sense of wrongdoing and any willingness to mourn and grief?

The German psychoanalyst Alexander Mitscherlich wrote in 1967 an influential book titled 'The inability to mourn' to highlight the belief that Germany did not want to be reminded of its wrongdoings of the past on purpose to keep its conscience clean. The book gave inspiration to the subsequent youth revolt against perceived authoritarian thinking in German society at the time. Despite some inaccuracies such as the claim that the Holocaust had been intentionally negated in the after war in Germany the book offers very important insight for the theory that mourn and grief are psychologically crucial to come to inner terms with a crisis or loss. The four stages of grieving are generally believed to be shock, anguish and pain, depression and recovery or rebirth. Recovery takes time, but time alone is not enough to heal the wounds of loss and bereavement. Finding out how to grief and mourn is what helps the healing process. Talking about and remembering the victims and other symbolic activities facilitate the process. Little by little this leads to recovery and rebirth. Recovery means accepting what has happened in the past to the victims as painful reality. If there is no mourning on the side of the aggressors how could the victims ever forgive? German politicians have always shown great willingness to honor the memory of the dead victims of German aggression whenever there has been an opportunity during a state visit abroad.

The reasons for silence and secrecy in Japan have less to do with lack of shame or guilt then with arrogance, lack of conscience, suppression of negative memories, blaming of the victims and refusal to show remorse for past wrongdoings. Contrary to Germany the Japanese did not give moral or financial compensation to victims such as comfort women or slave laborers; they did not document the sufferings of the victims like the Germans did by establishing a national archive and documentation center to track the biographies of war victims and keep their memories thereby alive.

The lingering stigma faced by *hibakusha* atomic bomb victims is another example of how shame and guilt have interacted in a pathological way. By blaming its own faults or problems on the *hibakusha*, Japan as a nation avoided guilt and shame and at the same time it refused to compensate *hibakusha* or acknowledge their human rights because by stressing its victim role it could not express or feel any responsibility for the bombings. Radiation came to be perceived as a polluting, defiling substance, and thus became integrated in a larger system of beliefs about purity and pollution, which are highly developed and systematized in Japanese society and rooted in Shinto and Buddhist conceptions. Contamination fears are an integral theme in community reactions to *hibakusha*, which are suspected of transmitting the impurity of death through genetic transmission or through contagion via bodily contact; this motivates discrimination in marriage and the workplace.

In her study Catherine Lu (2008) recognizes the importance of both shame and culture for successful reconciliation work but cautions that unfulfilled and insincere experiences of shame and guilt can have counterproductive implications if they are not undermined by a mature political culture. She uses the victim role self-image of the Japanese after the war as a striking example of unfinished shame, guilt repentance and grief work. Lu asserts that

> "In threatening old identities, values and beliefs, experiences of shame and guilt may provoke defensive, reactionary and violent political responses, and thus may precipitate hideous rather than salutary transformations" (Lu, 2008, p.367).

The Japanese never built a publicly financed, national memorial to the victims of war and apart from former Prime Minister Murayama never apologized–from the bottom of their heart–in public to the victims of war. In Japan it is politically correct for a member of the Diet to pay his visit to a nationalist shrine in an official or private function and pray for the souls of condemned war criminals whereas in Germany it would be unthinkable that lawmakers, either in private or officially, visit for example the graveyard of Rudolf Hess to pray for his soul or honor him. In Japan the after-war conservatives stuck to blind loyalty and obedience towards the U.S. as they had done before the war not out of love for the U.S. but because it was the only way for them to politically survive whereas the left aimed in its nationalist naiveté at becoming independent from the U.S. Civil society researcher Iokibe concluded that "neither of these ideological positions was successful in fostering respect for human dignity or providing a firm rationale for the importance of private (PH, civil sector) initiatives" (Iokibe, 1999).

The idea that Japan and the emperor were victims of the military class, that the military rulers pursued no ideology and could thus never have been able to commit a Holocaust in the sense of systematically and deliberately exterminating a targeted population like the Germans had done and that Japan has been victimized as a nation by the atomic bomb droppings has been an influential one. Some foreign and Japanese scholars have asserted that the Germans were more prone in their ideology to mass kill humans and commit a Holocaust and that the Holocaust constitutes a bigger evil than the Japanese aggression of Asia.

In an interview (Delanty, 2004, p. 400) Eisenstadt mentioned an unnamed Japanese scholar who had claimed that in the case of Japan there had been no ideology behind the killings of people and tried thereby to trivialize Japanese evil against the German evil. In her book 'The banality of evil' Arendt defined the radical evil as a symptom of thoughtlessness, dumbness and lack of depth. Both German fascism and Japanese ultra nationalism have produced a similar intensity of evil. The question if the German Holocaust is a worse evil than the

Japanese genocidal crimes in Asia is meaningless, lacks insight and does not add any value as Chalmers Johnson notes:

"It may be pointless to try to establish which World War Two Axis aggressor, Germany or Japan, was the more brutal to the peoples it victimized. The Germans killed six million Jews and 20 million Russians; the Japanese slaughtered as many as 30 million Filipinos, Malays, Vietnamese, Cambodians, Indonesians and Burmese, at least 23 million of them ethnic Chinese. Both nations looted the countries they conquered on a monumental scale, though Japan plundered more, over a longer period, than the Nazis. Both conquerors enslaved millions and exploited them as forced laborers – and, in the case of the Japanese, as prostitutes for front-line troops. (...) The German government has long recognized that, in order to re-establish relations of mutual respect with the countries it pillaged, serious gestures towards restitution are necessary. It has so far paid more than $45 billion in compensation and reparations. Japan, on the other hand, has given its victims a mere $3 billion, while giving its own nationals around $400 billion in compensation for war losses. One reason for these differences is that victims of the Nazis have been politically influential in the US and Britain, forcing their governments to put pressure on Germany, whereas Japan's victims live in countries that for most of the postwar period were torn by revolution, anti colonial movements and civil wars. This has begun to change with the rise of Sino-American activists. The success of Iris Chang's The Rape of Nanking (1997), a book the Japanese establishment did everything in its power to impugn, heralded the emergence of this group. More significant, however, are differences in US government policies towards the two countries. From the moment of Germany's defeat, the United States was active in apprehending war criminals, denazifying German society, and collecting and protecting archives of the Nazi regime, all of which have by now been declassified. By contrast, from the moment of Japan's defeat, the US government sought to exonerate the Emperor and his relatives from any responsibility for the war. By 1948, it was seeking to restore the wartime ruling class to positions of power (...). The US keeps many of its archives concerned with postwar Japan highly classified, in violation of its own laws" (Johnson, 2003).

What matters is not to compare the amount of sufferings inflicted, because from a victim's perspective every suffering and loss of life is equally worse, but what lessons - if any- were drawn from past wrongdoings and there the gap becomes obvious (Saaler et al, 2008; Hein, L. 2000; Hashimoto, 1999; Orr et al., 2001; Seraphim 2006). Some examples of Japan's failed attempts to reconcile with its history, conscience and neighbors speak for themselves. In 2008 one of the highest ranking commanders of the army and as such one of the highest serving civil servants claimed in a paper reproduced nationwide that Japan had been the victim of the second world war and that the war against Asia had been justified. Instead of publicly criticizing the contents of the paper and having the commander revoke his outrageous comments in public the minister of defense found it enough to send him into retirement and pay him on top his retirement allowance. The commander did not show any feeling of guilt or shame and the chance that he will be continuing to preach his hatred theories as a private person is great. No wonder that the irresponsibility at the top is reproduced at all levels of society. Until today Japanese school children are not aware that the war against Asia was unjust and a violation against international law and humanity and believe that it was morally right to sacrifice oneself for the glory of the emperor. The distortion of history in school textbooks continues up to the present and the protest of the democrats against it too. In Okinawa more than one hundred thousand people demonstrated in 2007 against the state censorship of historical facts in the history textbooks and crimes committed by Japanese imperial troops against civilian Okinawans during the final assault of U.S. troops. Unlike Germany who has settled border conflicts peacefully and reconciled successfully with its former victims such as France, Poland, Benelux Japan has failed to work on reconciliation and worse upholds territorial conflicts with Russia, China and Korea over disputed islands or rocks and its courts continue to reject claims for compensation for slave laborers and comfort women. The issue of the comfort women, an euphemism to describe the systematically planned and approved rape and prostitution of thousands of Asian women forced against their will to sexually serve Japanese soldiers in war brothels has been well documented (Tanaka, 2001; Hein, 2001) and widely supported by Japanese anti-war and women rights NGOs. Unfortunately the government authorities joined the ultra right movements in blaming the victims for having been abused and refused to compensate them financially and morally. It is sad to see how poor the diplomatic relations are with its Asian neighbors and how few respect Japan gets compared to Germany. Germany is seen as a reliable and trustworthy partner in the world whereas Japan follows blindly U.S. foreign policy, struggles to come to terms with its past, and needs to convince its neighbors desperately that it is not anymore a threat to them. ODA and the UN World Food Program are tools the Japanese government has used to pay for getting friendship and recognition abroad but as the German example shows the only way to be treated as a respected partner on a global level is to demonstrate a mature political and civic culture of non-violence and peaceful policies, true environmental concern, neutrality and respectful distance to the U.S., true remorse and reconciliation with victimized neighbors and respectful coexistence with and treatment of foreigners.

The purpose of the civilian reconstruction work the Germans are doing in Afghanistan is radically different from the Irak mission of the Self Defense Forces (SDF) or the refueling mission in the Indian Ocean. The Japanese government supported both subsequent U.S.–and not UN led–Irak wars with massive financial and staffing resources knowing that both wars were aimed at toppling a legal government that for a long time had served the national interest of the U.S. as reflected in the quotation of a U.S. representative who once said that "Sadam Hussein is a dictator but he is our dictator" but had become a persona non grata even though the claim that Irak had threatening mass destruction weapons could never be proven. Irak became the biggest individual recipient of bilateral development assistance aid of Japan who supported and followed the offensive US aggressor agenda and intervened when Japanese NPOs tried to circumvent the state mission and activities. Afghanistan shattered by a civil war has become the battlefield for anti-Taliban military operations who threaten the legally elected government. Germany has declared that the purpose of its military intervention under the framework of an UN mandate–The United Nations Assistance Mission in Afghanistan (UNAMA)–is defensive in nature by being limited to safeguarding physical security and by preparing the ground for later civil reconstruction. The German focus has not been blind support for the U.S.

toppling of a legal government as happened in Irak but stabilization of a legally governed country that has been threatened by civil war disruption. It may also be noteworthy that the German parliament almost unanimously supports the Afghan mission whereas the Diet has been deeply split on the Irak issue. The Germans work hand in hand with their NPOs whereas Japan has been suspicious of parallel NPO activities in the Irak (Georgeou, 2006).

The latest move in Japan to revise the peace constitution constitutes a worrying development for several reasons, the most important being perhaps the least obvious and least threatening from a factual perspective knowing that any revision requires a two third majority of both houses in the Diet. Since 1999 a Japanese NPO has tried to organize public awareness and protest against revision plans. In 2008 a large international symposium gathered in Tokyo to voice opposition against the conservative government plans.

Social disparity and new poverty

Non regular workers, including part-timers, made up a record 35.5% of the workforce in Japan in 2007, a government survey has shown recently. Since the end of the asset-inflated bubble economy in the early 1990s, many employers have moved to hire non regular workers while reducing regular payroll jobs to cut employment costs. Even during the period of economic expansion in 2007, many companies boosted the number of non regular jobs, hiring more part-time baby boomers and housewives. Of all male workers, 19.9% were part-timers or contract workers, while the figure for females was 55.2%, both record highs, according to a report by the Ministry of Internal Affairs and Communications. In 1987, the figure for men was 9.1% and for women 37.1%.

The OECD asserts that social inequality will not be reduced by increased social spending efforts. "Instead, the priority should be to increase the returns from work by reducing labor market dualism and by better targeting existing social programs on the most vulnerable groups. The priority is single parents, who have a poverty rate of over 50%. This would also help to reduce the rate of child poverty from its currently high level. With 98% of child poverty in working families, measures to increase employment are unlikely to reduce child poverty significantly. Instead, it is necessary to improve family benefits for employed persons, while limiting the creation of work disincentives and poverty traps. In the absence of such targeted policies, there is likely to be increased pressure to reduce poverty through steps to create a more generous overall welfare state. However, this would require substantial increases in public spending and revenue, with possible adverse economic implications at a time when coping with population ageing and raising potential growth from its low level is a priority in Japan (...). In addition to better target social expenditures, the reform of the tax system should aim at reducing the relative share of the tax burden that is borne by low-income households" (OECD, 2007, p.26). The OECD takes a typical neoliberal stance when asking for a deregulation of the labor law so that it will become easier for employers to lay off and fire established employees.

Educated housewives and labor shortage

There are currently millions of well educated housewives who are bored at home doing nothing while at the same time Japan experiences a very serious labor shortage due to the aging of society (Japan Labor Review, 2009). The reasons for failing to have integrated housewives as fully established and equally paid employees into the active workforce are manifold:

- Long commuting hours. The separation between workplace and home is one of the biggest challenges for family live. Especially in urban areas one-way commuting times of one hour or more makes it impossible for citizens to have a better work life balance.
- Unequal family responsibilities. Traditionally women bear the full responsibility for rearing and educating children whereas males are reluctant to do housework or take responsibility for childcare. The root cause for the current aging of society, high divorce rate, high percentage of singles. childlessness and low fertility rate and the confinement of women at home is the male earner who is more concerned about his own status, career, physical health, pleasures, leisure and hobbies then about his wife, family, children or local community.
- Unfavorable tax system that gives no financial incentives for women to independently earn enough money to make an independent living. If the annual income does not exceed 1030 000 yen, which is a little less than 10 000 U.S. dollars, they do not have to pay any tax; women can be covered by their husband's health insurance and can receive their old-age basic pension without contributing to the system. When their husband dies, they will receive two-thirds of their husband's old-age pension as their survivor's benefit, which often is higher than the old-age pension for working women because of the income difference between men and women.
- Few maternity and child care benefits for mothers. Compared to European countries Japan offers few incentives apart from a symbolic lump sum payment to become pregnant and give birth to children. There is financial compensation up to 66% of base salary for income loss during the 14 weeks of maternity leave, the financial support for child care leave in one of the most expensive countries is around 40%, the income limitations to receive child allowance do not offer incentive for wanting more children. The chronic shortage of public nurseries is beyond imagination. One of the most affluent countries in the world is not able to supply enough nursery places for the 0~3 year olds.
- No flexible work times for established full time employees. Japan is one of the few advanced countries in the world that offers no part-time working hours for full time employees. Whereas in the Netherlands parents can

choose to work half days to spare time for child care and education Japan factually excludes parents and especially mothers from the workforce by requiring employers to offer either fulltime positions or under qualified and undervalued part-time positions. The reason for this focus on male earner fulltime employment is culturally rooted: Japanese are paid for the time they spend at the office and not for the productivity and results they produce.

A child care leave that does not relieve parents

The legal framework for child care and parental leave has been adjusted step by step to make it easier for parents to raise their children despite work pressure and gender inequality. The child and nursery care leave law was designed to give working women and men more support and time off for raising children. The law stipulates that parents may take a leave until the child becomes 1 year old and this may be extended by another 6 months if no nursery place can be found. Some advanced companies offer an unpaid child care leave up 3 years fully protecting employment for the parents. Employers and employees are exempted from pension and health insurance premiums during childcare leave and up to 3 years renewable for every newborn. The child care leave allowance is paid through the local unemployment insurance office called Hello Work and comprises 40% of the base salary but only up to 1 year. 30% are paid upfront and 10% will be paid after returning to work. The employer is exempt from paying wages during child care leave. That means if a parent wants to take up to 3 years child care leave them will only get financial support (40% of salary) for the initial first year i.e. for a total of 18 months if special extension has been granted. Even though this amount has been increased to 50% from October 2007 the measure factually excludes males from taking child care leave considering the fact that most males account for the biggest part of household income. Any reduction of the male income would lead to serious income insecurity and deterioration of existing living conditions. The child care leave law has suffered from various side effects such as the de facto reduction of the number of established fulltime employees who fall under its provisions and the increase of non-regular employment types. In reality the child care leave law excludes the following categories or non-regular workers: part-time/contract workers and day laborers and employees employed for less than 1 year. Other questionable restrictions have been applied to limit the scope of eligible applicants for leave such as "workers who spouse is able to care for the child in a normal way" or "a spouse who's mental or physical condition is appropriate for bringing up the child". These practices postulate that males are main earners and must be prevented from taking leave. Employers may allow single parents to take leave if the spouse no longer lives together with the child concerned due to dissolution of marriage or separation. On April 2005 certain contract employers also became eligible for child care leave as a result of revisions made to reflect the reality that many of those who were contract employees actually worked for the same employer for a number of years with renewed contracts. There has been a recent trend to deregulate labor market and increase the number of non-regular employment types to reduce overhead and personnel cost for employers. Apart from the legal improvements that help working women to keep their jobs after childbirth, childcare is still considered a woman's job and statistics speak for themselves: mostly women apply for child care leave although the ratio of males who have taken leave has risen from 0.02% in 1992 to 0.56% in 2004. Kanno concludes in her study that society is not yet ready to accept that males have to share a bigger burden in child care and rising. She asserts that women

> "...are racing against the clock between their workplace, a childcare facility and home. That is the main role of a working mother. It is doubtful the birthrate will increase under such conditions. It is only natural for working mothers to want a quick end to such hard work (child care) and for the prospect of such hard work to deter them from having children in the first place" (Kanno, 2007, p. 50).

Fortunately there have been some grass root efforts on a small scale to challenge that child care is a woman's job and act for social change but the obstacles that need to be removed are big: flexible and shorter working hours for working parents, sufficient daycare centers in near neighborhood, income gap between male and female employees and last not least the outdated belief and notion that child care is a woman's job and responsibility and males are not able and willing to do housework. A sound and healthy work-life balance depends largely on changing the mentality and attitudes of males and reducing their power and domination in society. Even considering that a working parent decides to take the common 1 year child leave it will be extremely challenging to find a day care center or kindergarten after expiration of the legally granted minimum 1 year child year leave (up to 3 years can be taken). One reason why many refrain from taking the leave is because they are not sure if they can get a place in an approved day care center after the 1 year leave expires. It has been highlighted previously that it is extremely difficult to find appropriate and reasonably priced approved public or private day care centers for children under the age of 3 in Japan. Though preschool education is not compulsory in Japan, over 95% of children at age 5 attend one of two distinct educational / childcare institutions: kindergarten (*youchien*) for 3- to 5-year olds, many operating only for half a day, under the auspices of the Ministry of Education, Culture, Sports, Science and Technology and based on the school education law, or daycare centers (hoikuen) for 0- to 5-year olds, for more than 8 hours a day, under the supervision of the Ministry of Health, Labor and Welfare and based on the child welfare law. The separation of jurisdiction among Ministry of Education and Ministry of Health may be surprising but makes sense when looking at the philosophy that lies behind. The daycare centers with their flexible opening times cater to the needs of working mothers whereas the kindergartens with their high degree of inflexibility and very short opening times of average 4 hours a day cater to the needs of the fulltime housewives. It is often a difficult choice to decide whether to put a child under the auspices of the Ministry of Health or Ministry of Education. More than 26 000 children have been waiting for a place as of 2004 in day care centers despite plummeting birthrates. The discrepancy between supply and needs may be ultimately related to the growing number of women who opt to work after childbirth and in fact the number of female part-timers has rocketed over the last years. In 2001 the government eased the public monopoly for day care centers. Until then they had been managed by semi-public social welfare foundations which have been heavily subsidized by taxpayers' money and under strong political influence. They run 6300 day care centers across the country. Their political arm is the Japan Day Care Center Promotion federation and its political support groups. To get a child in a public day care center is like gambling: everybody tries to get in but few win and nobody knows what the criteria are to get shortlisted for one of the few available slots. The Japanese day care year runs on the same schedule as the school year that is from April 1 through March 31. As a rule applications are accepted from about January and decisions are made by early or mid-March. There are circumstances in which applications are accepted mid-year. Public daycare systems are administered by local governments so the services differ from community to community. The process of selection is in transparent and civil servants are not accountable to anyone. Applicants are chosen according to their needs and general preferences: civil servants/teachers, single working mothers, low income parents, placing of siblings and those with no backup support systems have priority. As a matter of fact it is easier for self-employed to get their children into the nursery because the husband can easily issue a certificate that the wife is employed by him. The formal process of applying is bureaucratic. If there is not enough room in a particular nursery school, the child may be placed on a waiting list. This list will be evaluated once a month. Not to say that public day care centers are of bad quality or socially unfair. The opposite is true: contributions are decided on a sliding scale considering income: high income has to pay highest fees ranging from 5000 Yen to 65 000 Yen per month. The quality of day care centers is very high.

Approximate # of Daycare Centers: 32,000		
Approved: 22,355 as of April 1, 03	Unapproved: 9,645 as of March 31, 02	
Public 12,255 (1,075, 404)	Private 10,100 (914,891)	e.g. -Facilities for employees: 3,534 (51,904) -Baby hotels: 1,184 (26,442) -Others, such as small-scale daycare centers/rooms: 4,927 (142,679)

Table 1-1: Number of daycare centers and their legal status. ( ) indicates the number of children enrolled. Source: http://www.childresearch.net/ RESEARCH/ MJ/MJ0002.HTM

In principle, there are two types of daycare centers: daycare centers approved by the government (about 70% in 2002) which can be public or private, and daycare centers not approved by the government (*muninka hoikuen*). In many instances, these unapproved ones can serve to compensate for the disparity between supply and demand created in the regulated childcare market, and admit the children who could not get into the (approved) daycare centers otherwise. However, in certain regions, even these unapproved centers are also operating beyond capacity.

Discussion on teacher-child ratio

	Japan	USA (California)	England	Germany (Berlin)	Sweden
Age 0	1:3	1:4	1:3	1:6	2:5
Age 1-2	1:6	1:4-12	1:3-4		
Age 3	1:20	1:10-12	1:8	1:10	1:5
Age 4 and 5	1:30				

Table 1-2: Comparison for the Teacher-Child ratio at Daycare Centers in different nations. Source: http://www.childresearch.net/ RESEARCH /MJ/ MJ0004. HTM

As reasons for the high teacher-child ratio in Japan, some cite different expectations of teachers and education for children upon reaching the age of three: teachers are considered to be mother-like figures for children under 3 who lack maternal care and more as educators for children over 3 to foster their independence and a sense of membership in a group. Others justify it with the expertise of teachers and their low turnover rate, though this argument is limited to public approved daycare centers. Concurrently, there are some Japanese who prefer a smaller size daycare center and lower teacher-child ratio should there be a choice.

Housewives were part of the system created to pursue economic growth after World War II. Japanese women have failed to win full equality with men because women were divided between housewives and those working outside the home. Japanese women face a big challenge in harnessing the two forces to realize full gender quality. It is not fair to criticize housewives as indulgent and think that only working women are participating as full members of society. When a vigorous economy demanded more workers, Japan took a very different strategy from the labor policies adopted by Scandinavian countries, where women were encouraged to join the workforce. In Japan, a system was created to force men to do twice the work, by paying them a salary for two people. And to encourage women to serve as housewives, the government introduced various benefits, such as tax reductions and dependent allowances, but all those benefits went to the husbands. Sometimes, housewives are used as a valve to adjust the workforce. It is not true that housewives do not work, as many of them work part-time for low pay and under precarious working conditions. And unpaid work, such as child rearing and efforts to secure safe food and water, cannot be measured financially. It is not reflected in the gross national product or gross domestic product under the prevailing value system. But that value system should be changed because unpaid work is absolutely necessary for securing one's lives. It should be properly recognized and shared by men and women. Without changes in the value system and the sharing of unpaid work, there will be no gender equality. Many middle-aged women work as part-time workers. The Bureau of Statistics, Management and Coordination Agency, defines part-time workers as those who work no more than 35 hours a week regardless of their status or their term of employment. The number of female part-time employees was 1.3 million in 1970, 2.6 million in 1980, and 5 million in 1990. Of female part-time workers, one-third were aged between 35 and 44, one-third were between 45 and 54; 15% were over 55. So most of the part-time workers are over 35.Middle-aged married women prefer to work part-time because they wish to work without cutting back their household duties, and they want to be home before the children come back from school.

The average income difference between men and women is one-half, which is worse than that of the U.S. Moreover, husbands can qualify for a special tax deduction for full-time housewives and can also receive a spouse allowance from their employers. Many working women are trying to abolish this type of system, not only because they feel it to be unfair, but because if these married women pay their premium, it would solve the financial difficulties of the social security system, or at least postpone the arrival of higher premiums and lower benefits. Many Japanese housewives are enjoying this privilege as full-time housewives but at the same time the current system prevents them from becoming mature and equal citizens and keeps them trapped and financially and emotionally dependent on their husbands.

The government sponsored abuse of Asian trainees

Japan has 101 independent administrative agencies that cost the taxpayer a lot of money but do not produce any results. These entities have come under criticism because they have been involved in unnecessary projects and because they merely exist to provide jobs to former bureaucrats. The Diet has been considering a bill to reform and overhaul the system but the government continues to place high priority on protecting its own organizations. Since 1993 the 'Japan International Training Organization' (JITCO) a semi-governmental foundation has set up a training framework to match the needs of private companies with the supply of unskilled trainees from Asian countries, the majority being from mainland China. Foreign trainees spend three years in Japan, undergoing job training in the first year and hands-on training in technical skills in the remaining two years. Specialized Japanese recruiting companies maintain offices in China to offer introduction services for Chinese trainees wanting to work in Japan. The Japanese embassy in China supports JITCO by issuing trainee visas. What was intended as development cooperation derailed into an exploitation program for cheap labor force. Due to their ambiguous legal status trainees are not considered to be regular workers and do not fall under the jurisdiction of the labor law. Due to the legal loopholes in treating trainees there has been an abuse in overwork and underpayment. A Japanese NGO representative used the term slave labor to describe the status of the right less trainees.

Education without ethical principles

The greatest educators in the Meiji era have been people such as Inazo Nitobe, Yukichi Fukuzawa and even Saigo Takamori, all of them of Samurai descent. What unites them is that they were global minded, action oriented and ethically strongly principled in their approaches. The strong influence of Samurai principles on pre-modern education in Japan has been almost forgotten after the war. From a perspective of strong individual principled ethical beliefs Nitobe states in 'Bushido' (2007) that the ultimate goal of education must be to form the character and the personality of the individual. In Nitobe's view knowledge and education should be aimed at fostering a spirit of wisdom, conscientiousness, righteousness and compassion for others. Education should serve to achieve the goal of refinement of the character, well groomed behavior, self control and modesty. Wisdom is superior to mere knowledge, intelligence or logical thinking. There must be a strong connection between conscience, knowledge and practical doing and he maintains that it is not enough to know and to do but "to be- to exist as you, yourself" (Minato, 2003, p. 46). Education is foremost aimed at cultivating one's personality, gaining experience and engaging in responsible public action. There can be no personality without responsibility as he used to say. The personality of a person is best assessed by looking at his handwriting and Nitobe stresses that calligraphy is indicative of a person's character. As a visionary educator Nitobe promoted equal access to education for women and equal opportunities to children from a less privileged social background. Unlike many others who talk about education without ever having worked in the field Nitobe did what he preached by founding the first women's university in Japan, by establishing and heading a night school for socially disadvantaged children in Sapporo and becoming headmaster of a higher school preparing young men for their future role as leaders of Japan. Nitobe's humanist concept of education went much further than just acquiring knowledge, studying, attending classroom activities or getting a professional degree. It resembles the Greek educational concept of *paideia* in many ways. As Mumford (1957) puts it *paideia* is the lifelong formation and socialization of one's personality. "It is not merely learning but making and shaping; and man himself is the work of art that paideia seeks to form" (Mumford, 1957, p. 187). *Paideia* transcends mere education because it never stops and because it is grounded in experience and doing rather than knowing or studying.

The Samurai rejected intellectualism, logical rationalism, perfectionism, specialist technical skills or expertise and selfish financial gain as contrary to their educational goals. A teacher occupied the highest status and authority in society despite the low financial reward.Yukichi Fukuzawa the influential Meiji educator played an important role in introducing people rights ideas. In his work 'An encouragement of learning' he insists that learning will give power, help to keep a minimum level of social stability as education will prevent unjust government, maintain mutual respect among people regardless of their strength and wealth and make oneself aware on one's relative capacity compared to other people. As history has shown Japan failed to respect other nations when it attacked and occupied its neighbors and one of the big shortcomings of Fukuzawa has been that he adopted Western thinking only on a formal and superficial basis. His anti-Chinese stance for example helped to prepare the ground for later imperialism.

The intentionally anti-Western imperial edict on education of 1879 marked the first step towards a backward change in education reforms. Subsequently the public good was defined as national state interest and education was completely subjected to state control to support nationalism and the war economy. Gender bias, radical social selection and extreme elitism and competitiveness characterized the education system before 1945. Unlike after the war weaker or mediocre pupils who failed had to repeat the class and the obsession with passing exams was the primary reason for the U.S. to propose changes to the pre-war school system. The U.S. occupation forces brought institutional changes to the school system without removing or exchanging those who had designed the pre-war education system. In early 1946 the Ministry of Education had commissioned an expert committee that came up with a pre-war very segregating two way career track school system which would have reduced the chances of the majority for academic advancement. Against this proposal the mission had the current single-track high school system implemented to give to everybody the opportunity to access higher education. Under the authority of the U.S. occupation force the education aim was democratized under the heading of "love of truth and peace" and "esteem for individual dignity"–at least on paper. The individualized democratic American guidance model replaced the pre-war militaristic moral training.

The Fundamental Law of Education was compiled as the basis for postwar education in Japan, and was enacted in 1947. The law stipulated the basic principles of education, providing ability congruent equal opportunities and compulsory education to be provided for a period of nine years. Equal opportunity in education led to a Japanized egalitarian interpretation meaning that all children were formally viewed as having the same homogenous disposition, ability, potential and it meant for teachers to treat them all the same way. In the name of economic development objective and scientific knowledge acquisition became the cornerstone of education and the goal was to get a formal diploma or technical degree to secure a job in one of the leading industrial conglomerates or the booming manufacturing sector. The companies would take care of teaching social skills such as business manners. All the efforts of education were geared towards passing a prestigious university entrance exam that served as an entry ticket to a leading company and secure a lifetime job. The brand value of a company or university or school was and is still defined by ranking preference.

Equal opportunity and ability have been Japanized to a large extent by learning through imitation and effort. The purpose of learning is not to improve results but to improve through applying and repeating processes in a rigorous way: whether the Kumon method or the Suzuki method these methods all rely on a specific learning method or process that can be learned by anybody willing to put effort into practicing on a daily base. To master the processes daily repetition and ritualized drills are necessary. Effort overrides ability and ability is defined in formal or objective terms rather than based on individual uniqueness and subjective distinction. Ability has been narrowed down to nurturing the ability to memorize words and numbers, reproduce letters, read, sing, jump or calculate but not as the ability to be individually distinct, unique, thoughtful, wise, ethical, critical, respectful of all living beings, independent, creative, caring or empathize with others. Furthermore the removal of qualitative differences and distinctions has led to the myth that every child has the same basic features and what differentiates them is their level of effort. Children being perceived as less able were believed not to put enough effort. Similar in companies less performing employees were believed not be arduous enough in their hardship and efforts. Within the existing school structure the vertical ranks have been preserved. Conduit (1996) who reflects back on her boys' experience with a Japanese primary school laments that it "seems a pity that the objective of a primary school can already be his or her ultimate position in adult society" (Conduit, 1996, p.203).

Lower ranked children are not anymore excluded from the group as in the pre war era, cannot fail and must not repeat classes. They are rather ignored or left aside. Similar later on in companies less performing employees are usually not fired but ignored and put aside into a corner. The extremely high number of pupils per class in Japan makes individual guidance and attention practically impossible as well. The rigid vertical ranking school system has been questioned by some educators. According to Tachikawa (2007) the school reformator Saito tried to overcome the rigid vertical ranking thinking by nurturing equal abilities among all the pupils and refused to acknowledge that some pupils were superior or more able then others and that this approach made learning more enjoyable. Saito seems however to have focused his efforts on nurturing formal abilities whereas the current paradigm has shifted to more individualized life skills, responsible behavior in society and ethical concern for the community.

There has been much confusion among teachers, ministry officials and the media in what ways the Japanese concept of personhood, personality or individuation–in Japanese *kosei*–impacts learning. The question is not if the Japanese are culturally apt or able or not to be individual but who or what hinders them from developing a sound ethical personality. A simple example might demonstrate how *kosei* is prevented from being nurtured from the perspective of a school child. More than the ability to think the willingness to conform to what is regarded as right response is valued. The child adapts his answer to the norms represented by the teacher without reflecting. It is thoughtless learning which can be potentially dangerous. For example in a Japanese school setting a child is supposed to answer the question: do you think Hitler was good or bad with 'bad' without knowing why 'bad' is supposed to be the correct one whereas in a Western school setting it might happen that a teacher asks the child "what do you think was good or bad about Hitler" to instill reflection and have them justify their argument. Since Meiji children have been systematically prevented from being individual and under such circumstances Nitobe's educational dictum "be yourself" cannot work. Success is the result of conformity to the majority not the ability to think or reflect. Ravina (2004, p.31) mentions that traditional education before Meiji placed great emphasis on the individualized ability for moral reasoning.

The pursuit of absolute equality in Japanese schools negates individuality and the right to being different, is more quantitative in terms of factual learning then qualitative in terms of character formation and is undemocratic because it ranks children in superior and inferior according to criteria of either difference in ability or difference in effort. In order to make the system look equal, the curriculum has been the same in all schools, multiple choice examinations have been given preference over essays and rote memorization of facts, data and information has been given preference over critical thinking and individual competency.

As a result of high government spending on education, the commitment of private employers to recruit and educate new employees on the job and parents that place high emphasis on formal scholastic achievement, the education level of Japanese soared to top levels among OECD countries after the war. The image of the Japanese as being detail and fact oriented, diligent, intelligent, rational, and hardworking and perfectionist has been forged at that time.

The myth of absolute equality negating individual uniqueness and diversity worked well as long as the economy grew and the industrial output could be raised. In the postwar period several educational reforms brought about major changes and raised the general standard. One of the major trends has been the sharp rise in the ratio of students going on to high school from 42.5% in the 1950s to 97.7% in 2007 and to university from 10.1% in 1955 to 53.7% in 2007. The other major trend is the advancement of women to academic studies from 5% participation in 1950 to 52.5% in 2007.

In the 1980s a new neo-liberal reform agenda was launched after politicians became aware that Japan had been overly egalitarian in terms of treating everyone the same way and that it should shift its emphasis to realizing a school system that helps children develop their individuality and gives them diverse choices—shifting from excessive emphasis on egalitarianism and uniformity to a diverse, flexible educational system that encourages individualism in a Western sense. Education risked becoming again a privilege for the few. The neoliberal shift in education was briefly interrupted by an unusual schooling experiment that was badly received. In 2002 a regular five-day school week was introduced in public schools to create a *yutori* or literally pressure free relaxed learning environment including the reduction of the curriculum by 30%. In order to eliminate the harmful effects of overheated entrance examination competition and so-called rote-learning education, the current guidelines advocated pressure-free education to break away from the overemphasis on knowledge and formulated curriculums. It aimed at letting the children spend more time free from pressure at home and in the communities, and engage in social contribution activities and nature-oriented experiences to nurture the zest for living in their daily lives including the abilities to learn and think by themselves, and the existence of a rich humanity, and healthy development and physical strength to lead vigorous lives. This system was to be realized with mutual cooperation among schools, families and communities.

The relaxed education policy practiced in public schools did not lead to a positive reception. The experience with *yutori* has been badly received with employers as well. It seems that employers refuse to hire graduates who got their school education at public schools during the *yutori* years. Parents reacted negatively to the perceived lowering of teaching quality. Affluent middle class parents took their children out of the public system and enrolled them in private high schools and private universities and this is a remarkable change compared to the past. The growing social status of private schools is correlated to higher income background of the parents, class and birth privileges. In terms of academic competiveness private high schools have displaced public high schools over the past 40 years. The majority of those schools are six year schools combining middle and high school. There has also been a perception that the unified six year curriculum in private schools keeps away problematic students. Schools look more and more at formal criteria of physical looks, family background, well groomed behavior, overall conformity when they admit students.

As a reaction to unified six year curriculums in the private school sector the Central Council for Education has made proposals ranging from introducing public unified six year secondary education by combining middle schools and high schools as an option for public schools to modifications of the entrance exam system, including permitting superior students to enter university directly from the eleventh grade, skipping the final year of high school. The trend towards unifying the secondary school track has major implications for those who want to enroll into upper high school. It is not uncommon for example that a child placed in the private kindergarten will graduate from the same private university. Six year track schools will select the students by admission exam at an earlier stage and this will prevent outsiders from joining in between. Tachikawa suspects that Monbusho's goal is to impose an elitist model on public schools similar to the one practiced in the private sector regressing back to the pre-war status of a two-track secondary system.

Subsequent conservative governments have made efforts to overhaul and reform the education system towards individualism, deregulation, decentralization and competition to bring it in line with business demands and national economic interests. The national postwar consensus of treating everybody the same way has been substituted by the new neoliberal dogma of personal choice and self-responsibility which means that class background, social status and birth define the chances of getting the most suitable output driven education leading to a higher probability of high income and high social prestige. The fact that most high schools regardless if private or public are geared to prepare for university entrance has worsened the social gap and disparity especially on the backdrop of changed hiring practices among private employers making it difficult for inexperienced university graduates to secure a job, reduced hiring's in public sector and public spending cuts on education, oversupply of schools, low pays and unsafe short-term working contracts for teachers and a the absolute statistical decrease of children. Unemployment among general course high school graduates or *mugyo-sha* who leave high school or refuse to pursue higher education is very high. Another result of deregulation is that universities will be almost run like private for profit companies in the future. Currently private schools are operated by educational foundations that are prohibited by the private school law from seeking to turn a profit. They also must meet the standards stipulated by the Education Law in such areas as curricula, facilities and equipment, teachers' qualifications and financial stability. Regulations have been eased, however, in deregulation zones established for education projects, to allow for more flexible and diverse programs, and stock companies and nonprofit organizations are allowed to open schools. Securing a sufficient number of enrolled students has become crucial factor for financial survival. Universities compete and struggle to make sure they can enroll enough students.

Reflecting on the purpose of after-war education may help to elucidate why things have gone so awkward after the 1980s, why a minimum consensus on the basic purpose of education has not been achieved till today and what this implies for teachers, parents and students. The private human concern for welfare cannot be separated from the public concern for public goods such as human rights, democracy, justice, freedom, peace or coexistence with nature. From a global private / public perspective it is assumed that the crisis of education Japan faces today is not so much a crisis of not having the means, infrastructure or talent but rather a crisis of the education concept itself threatened by private for profit interests and a neoliberal public discourse centering around increasing the eco-

nomic results and material output of education. It is not a conflict of choice between public or private schools but a conflict of goals and aims of what education should stand for. Amid growing concern over the lowering of educational
levels, the Central Council of Education, an advisory body, proposed in 2008 an
increase of 10% in classroom hours for major subjects. Under the new curriculum to become effective from 2011 students will take more hours of science,
mathematics and English, while English lessons will become mandatory in elementary schools. At the same time the number of parents who feel that the academic level of public schools is insufficient has dramatically increased and the
number of students who attend cram schools after normal school hours as well.
The dual system of official education and in official afterhour's additional education is unique in the world. The number of elementary and junior high school
students receiving after school instruction in private rather expensive cram
schools in on the rise. To prepare for junior high school and university entrance
examinations after school education has become indispensable. Apart from the
psychological and sociological implications of having children attend school at
night or on weekends the financial implications reflect the growing correlation
between high income and high education levels and a move from the *gakureki
shakai* (educational achievement society) to success rooted in economic privileges. Many parents spend time to think about what they should do so that their
children can attend a specific school or enter a specific company upon graduation. There is no room for letting children imagine experience or decide on their
own what is best for their future. Job decisions are gender specific as well and
even emancipated women still consider a good match making with an educated
male as being crucial to their future. Career counseling in high schools, intern-
ships at companies during summer school break and experimental first hand experience is virtually unknown in Japan.

The Japanese constitution guarantees every student the "right to receive an
equal education correspondent to their ability". The fundamental law of education specifies that "the people shall all be given equal opportunities of receiving
education according to their ability". In short all people regardless of their so-
cio-economic origin have equal value despite their individual differences. Both
conservative and progressive political parties have violated this principle, conservatives ignoring the "equal" part and progressives the "ability" part. Conservative members have sought to improve the performance of top level students.
By contrast, the Japan Teachers Union (JTU or Nikkyoso) and the Socialist and
Communist parties have concentrated on reducing the gap in performance level.
The new neo-liberal dogma classifies students into superior and inferior categories in terms of presumed ability level, giving better and faster education opportunities to the presumably more able, which happen to come from wealthy families. Both conservative and progressive approaches fail to recognize that the respect for individual difference and diversity is crucial to safeguarding both relative equality and relative ability.

In Japan education in terms of knowledge acquisition, formal curricula, so-cio-economic status and work are overvalued whereas a balanced, fulfilled, ab-undant, meaningful life is undervalued. That is precisely the reason why many children have no dreams or refuse to learn and drop out of school. For Conduit (1996) the extreme focus on factual learning and academic achievement has been responsible for depriving Japanese children of their childhood and she maintains that one of the main reasons why adults behave in childish ways is because they never learned to be naturally enjoying freedom, playing and expe-riencing friendship by themselves when they were children. Perfection as educa-tion goal is simply not attainable or even desirable.

Even though the state has allowed letting every school form its own ethos this does not necessarily guarantee a principled education philosophy. The pop-ular free education or *jiyu kyoiku* in Japanese–literally a free anything goes modern education syndrome–ignores not only the differences between the pupils, but also, which is worse, the differences between teacher and pupil. The teachers in Japan spend considerable time on writing administrative reports and attending training courses or undergoing continuous learning. Teachers trying their best to be viewed by pupils as peers and friends rather than as authority figures or role models become depressed, go on permanent sick leave and the parents who blame teachers for their own shortcomings of failing to have taught basic man-ners at home are regarded by teachers as monster parents. Housewives who as-sociate their self worth with the educational success of their children put pres-sure on teachers. Paradoxically the introduction of more relaxed education in public schools and a five day school week can be traced back to the demands and concerns of parents. It was the same parents who asked for relaxation who were the first to criticize relaxed education and start to transfer their children to private schools.

In a lecture to the Foreign Press Center in 2006 noted psychiatrist Hideki Wada maintained that it is today possible to enter a high school or college with-out studying hard and that the image of diligent Japanese belongs to the past. Children are de-motivated. According to him time spend in the classroom has become the lowest among OECD members and public spending on education as well. He also maintains that social problems at schools have increased in parallel with the trend for children not to study hard anymore. As a way out of the crisis he proposes to reduce the size of classes and introduce graduation exams. The enhancing of emotional wellness and cultivating pupils as emotionally well-rounded human beings and countering the growing decay of school educa-tion as witnessed by bullying, violence, nonattendance, and the breakdown of classroom order has been high on the agenda. In 2001 finally after having faced a serious increase of social problems at schools such as disruptive behavior, vi-olence, bullying, school dropping out and school absence the government em-barked on a new project of financing part-time school counselors. *Seito shido* or pupil guidance aims at the full development of personality and consists of personal social development, development of a healthy lifestyle and helping children solve personal and interpersonal problems. The current Japanese school counseling model is based on a clinical approach and targets the individual separated from family or peer issues. Nakano Y.(2003) proposes a paradigm change to make school counseling more effective. Educational objectives for the future include the establishment of reliable school education, promotion of university reforms, restoration of the ability of the home to educate children, and fostering a sense of civic responsibility, respect for tradition and culture, and a sense of love and respect of the country, home and internationalism. In 2006 the government under the pressure of conservatives amended the educational aim to "loving our country and homeland". The corresponding Japanese text passage of the law reads as follows:

伝統と文化を尊重し、それらをはぐくんできた我が国と郷土を愛するとともに、他国を尊重し、国際社会の平和と発展に寄与する態度を養うこと。

The newly enacted law calls for developing an attitude which respects tradition and culture and loves the nation and homeland that have fostered them as a goal of education. Instilling patriotism among students will be one of the objectives of elementary school and junior high school education. The hissing of the flag and singing of the anthem from elementary school onwards are part of the same move. Mishima in his book on 'Hagakure' maintains that the love for an abstract intangible thing such as a country is a meaningless concept. Neither does it help to prepare children for the challenges posed by adulthood neither does it show concern for their immediate educational needs.

Other proposals have been made to implement community volunteer activities, compulsory martial arts training or introduce a new system to renew the teacher's licenses every ten years by taking a 30-hour training course. Those who are judged incompetent by a prefectural board of education must take an additional training course for up to one year. Those who are still judged incompetent after the course can be deprived of their license. The four principles of moral education proclaimed by the Ministry of Education are to learn self-control; to learn to live and communicate with others; to learn to respect the environment, nature and beauty: to understand the importance of life; and to learn to respect the rules by which people live and society is organized: justice, equality; enjoyment of one's work. In private schools, part or all of the time for moral education may be replaced by religious education. It strives to promote moral education by developing and distributing *kokoro* memos and allocating *kokoro* teachers. Principles of moral education are also emphasized in the learning of all other subjects in Japanese elementary and secondary education, and in various daily activities called special activities or homeroom activities which children are expected to carry out in school. Students in each class are usually divided into groups of five to six children, with each group being responsible for specific duties, such as cleaning the classroom; serving school lunch; preparing the class newspaper; looking after the class animals. The groups take turns in taking such responsibilities every week or month. This kind of group arrangement is also made use of in the teaching of individual subjects such as science and maths, where children cooperate with each other working within the group and gifted ones help slow achievers spontaneously. The members of the groups are not fixed, but change around regularly. Through such arrangements, children learn automatically how to cooperate and help each other; to contribute to the interests of other members and the group itself; to discuss to reach an agreement; to guess and consider the implicit opinions and feelings of other members.

In his assessment of Confucius Jaspers states that Neo Confucianism contributed to a degeneration of the original ideas of Confucius. With regard to education he notes

"knowledge that was inner action degenerates into rote learning. There arose the class of scribes who distinguished themselves not by personality but by formal learning and maintained their prestige by a system of examinations. (...) instead of making antiquity his own, the student learned to imitate it. School learning produced an orthodoxy which lost its bond with life as a whole" (Jaspers, 1962, p.62).

Learning from the wisdom of Japan : *kateika* education

Home economics is an integrated science, a practical science centering on family life. Research is conducted to determine the interaction between human beings and the environment surrounding them, while natural, sociological and anthropological studies are made on the material as well as the human aspects of life. The results thus obtained are used as the basis for improving the living conditions as well as promoting the welfare. Home economics is not limited to the study of life skills at home. It also deals with lifestyles in general as well as their cultural significance. The following areas are covered by home economics: man's life and its development as well as health issues, the family as basic unit of human life, family relationships as well as family management and administration, human life is studied mainly from the cultural viewpoint centering on design and aesthetic factors, from a welfare standpoint, family and its members are studied in its relation to society. How information is input to and output from families is studied. Sorting and use of information are also studied. Attempts are made to clarify various aspects and varied levels of environments that affect lifestyle. How to create and maintain good environments is also an important item taken up in this area. A variety of household items and the dependence on them are studied from a scientific and sociological viewpoint. The industrial systems of production and distribution are studied with a view to clarifying how households are involved in terms of production and consumption.

Japan has continued to grow economically, and the high level of economic stability has contributed a great deal to improving living conditions and raising health standards. On the other hand, a number of social problems have appeared.

The divorce rate has gone up; the birth rate has continued to decline; juvenile delinquency has been on an increase; death from overwork has been taken up by mass media; and the aging society with its problems just to name a few. In the shadows of consumer-oriented affluence are emerging a variety of environmental problems. Family life is directly or indirectly connected with the performance of local community, national and international economy, and regional environmental problems. All of the strains and contradictions produced by society closely affect family life. For example, many of the world-scale environmental problems often stem from the quality and quantity of garbage produced by households. Therefore, these problems should be viewed and studied from the family and individual viewpoint. Home economics which was traditionally studied only by girls has been made compulsory for boys as well. The purpose of this change is to ensure that both boys and girls are equipped with the skills that they will need to survive in an era of 80-year life expectancy and to enable them to acquire the knowledge and techniques needed to create a fulfilling family lifestyle. In the area of vocational education, information-related subjects have been enhanced and increased to ensure that students can cope with a changing industrial society. Other improvements to subject areas and subjects include the introduction of project studies as a means of developing problem-solving skills and creativity. In addition, composite courses, such as agricultural economics and electronic engineering, are being offered as standard courses.

One of the controversial issues on the substance of education was a gender differentiated curriculum, the home making/economics offered only for female students. Campaigns to make both girls and boys study this program were extensively organized by teachers through the 1980s and 1990s. Since 1994, the same home economics program is offered to both girls and boys. Reviewing the content of textbooks and writing textbooks to raise student's awareness on gender equality have been carried out by different groups of women. Translation of books and materials that are used for the promotion of education on gender equality in other countries is a more recent activity carried out by NGOs. Since the Education Board of the local government in some regions has the authority over the selection of textbooks for adoption, side-reading materials are important tools for gender-sensitive individual teachers to rely on. Some public women's centers have produced guiding manuals and brochures for education on gender equality in collaboration with experts and NGOs.

Case study on Brazilian government schools

The Yomiuri shimbun reported that the government decided the creation of a fund in 2007 to support the education of Brazilian children in Japan. When President Lula da Silva of Brazil visited Japan in June 2005, it was decided to establish the Japan-Brazil Council for the 21st Century. Since then, the Council has been involved in the consultations on the Japan-Brazil Exchange Year in 2008 and bilateral exchanges thereafter. In addition to bilateral exchanges in the fields of politics, economics and science, the proposals also focus on cooperation for the improvement of living conditions of Japanese descents in Brazil and Brazilians in Japan. One of the proposals concerning the latter is to improve their children's learning environment, including through assistance to Brazilian schools in Japan by both governments. In addition, it is proposed to establish a fund for scholarships, distance learning of Portuguese language, development of Portuguese teaching materials, distribution of textbooks and other purposes, with a view to supporting the education of Brazilian children in Japan.

There are currently more than 300 000 Brazilians residing in Japan. According to the survey concerning the admission status of foreign pupils and students who are in need of instructions on Japanese language, conducted by the Ministry of Education in the academic year 2005, children whose mother tongue is Portuguese represent the largest proportion (36.5%) of such students. The issue of non-enrollment, including dropout during or at the end of the compulsory education period, has emerged among them partly due to language difficulties. The issue of their education was also highlighted at the Symposium on Issues Concerning Brazilians in Japan, organized by the Ministry of Foreign Affairs in 2004. According to the Brazilian Embassy in Tokyo, 50 of the approximately 100 Brazilian schools in Japan have been accredited by the Brazilian government. But none of them has been given official school status in Japan, and only two Brazilian schools–one in Aichi Prefecture and another in Gifu Prefecture–are granted "miscellaneous school" status, which is given to international schools that satisfy a number of conditions. Miscellaneous schools receive tax deductions and their students are entitled to student discounts, but their graduates are not considered to have completed Japanese compulsory education. Most American and European international schools in Japan fall under the miscellaneous school category. Among them, those approved by the Western Association of Schools and Colleges, the European Council of International Schools or the Association of Christian Schools International enjoy special status, which enables their graduates to take public school entrance exams.

Abduction and kidnapping of citizens

The North Korean kidnapping of Japanese citizens has been in the news for some time and one cannot but wonder about the attention the international community has given to this case. Producing knowledge to support the reality it wants is one of the key characteristics of politics in Japan. The knowledge about the abductions has long been suppressed and kept away from the public. The fact that people had been kidnapped and the reasons behind the kidnappings had never been investigated by media or police at the time they happened. People who dared filing a missing report were regarded as hysteric at the time when the kidnappings happened. When looking at the sheer amount of citizens kidnapped–up to several hundred victims might have been involved–Chang (2006) notes that it seemed very strange that the government did not take action earlier. The inconvenient truth is that the Japanese state, its representatives and the media have been actively supporting the sovereign and legal state of North Korea for the last 40 years or so despite the kidnappings in the 70s and despite all the wrongdoings and international violations of the regime in the past. The official state policy at that time was to please North Korea as much as possible and give them as much development assistance as possible. Japan was one of the major sponsors of the nuclear revitalization KEDO project and has contributed massively with rice food deliveries via the UN World Food Program to the political survival of the regime.

It can be regarded as the biggest merit of the Yokotas to have pushed their own government for action and bringing up the issue. The real opponent of the Yokotas is not North Korea but the Japanese government itself and the Yokotas have made it clear in their statements that they have not been happy with the delayed, concept less and undetermined actions of their government. It has been supporting its North Koreans counterparts for decades with support and thus helped in prolonging the survival of the regime and prevented democratic peaceful change. Dealing with a ruthless state that relies on a privileged clique to legitimate its power base is probably one of the most difficult issues in foreign affairs as there is not much room for negotiation or influencing. The Japanese government has been very naïve in believing that it can promote change by trying to influence and please the top leaders. As the German reunification example shows what brought about change was peaceful protest from within by social movements. A regime can only change if it loses its legitimacy in the eyes of its own people. In that sense the decision to broadcast NHK messages into North Korea may be welcomed as it seems primordial to allow North Koreans to access different sources of information.

The tactical mistake the Yokotas made in promoting their just and right cause was to rely primarily on traditional diplomatic bilateral intervention and foreign policy tools to solve the problem and delegate the problem solving to incompetent and careless politicians and bureaucrats. During a stay in Korea with their counterparts they had to face another inconvenient truth: it was the Japanese state who had previously abducted many Korean citizens as comfort woman and slave laborers and the Korean NGOs were hoping very much for the Yokotas to acknowledge these facts and overcome their rather private and limited views on the subject: only a broader borderless social movement against abduction of citizens by any state could make their cause more efficient and credible in the eyes of the Asian community. The message must be that every abduction for any reason is unjust, constitutes a human rights violation and must be condemned.

Abduction of citizens by a state is not the only issue at stake. In Japan private child abduction by spouses seeking divorce or having divorced is another source of concern and again the government, courts and the media instead of protecting human rights and the principle of fair and equal treatment tolerate the private abductions. It is very easy to file for divorce and even with a forged signature a Japanese spouse can get easily divorced from his foreign partner and get legal recognition, child custody and the right to monthly aliments. Abduction of children is a growing concern and the government, courts do nothing to instill a public debate on the issue, redress illegitimate acts or live up to the spirit of international agreements by protecting the wellbeing of the foreign spouse and abducted children.

Killing in secret

Johnson (2002; 2005; 2006) has offered compelling evidence for the lack of public debate on capital punishment and the secretive killing of citizens by the state. As Johnson puts it legal killings and starting a war are the strongest prerogatives a state can have and therefore a public debate is needed on the criteria, reasons and rationale for killing people deliberately in the name of law and order. The problem is not limited to the death penalty itself but includes the absence of public discussion on the subject which shows that Japan is not a mature democracy that allows for an open, balanced and fair discussion and as a result state killings are arbitrary, random, in transparent and even illegitimate if innocents die. Nobody knows why some people are punished to death and others not, why they have to wait many years on the death row without knowing if and when they will die, who sets the criteria and selects those to be executed whilst others including Shoko Asahara, the notorious convicted leader of the Aum sect, are allowed to keep on living for years despite having been sentenced to death for a terrible terrorist crime involving 12 dead and 5000 injured. All those questions remain unanswered and this puts doubt on those who are responsible for preparing and implementing the killing process. According to Johnson (2006) during the Meiji era the average annual number of state killings was around 800 whereas after the introduction of Western criminal law and punishment the number fell to about 18 by 1930 despite unchanged homicide rates. Johnson describes the state's policy of secrecy and explains how it emerged as the product of an historical imperative–the Meiji rulers needed to appear civilized to Western powers–and the self-interested actions of powerful elites in the occupation and in the Ministry of Justice. Since the 1960s the homicide rate has continuously fallen and Japan is considered to be a relatively low crime society in international comparison terms. Despite the lowered nominal homicide rate compared to the U.S., the probability for a murderer to be put on the death row is statistically as high in Japan as it is in the U.S. That means in other words that the certainty for a murderer to be sentenced to death is very high in Japan. The low tolerance for murder may be explained by cultural factors. Taking away the life of somebody is considered an extremely serious and unforgivable act. That also explains why medical doctors are for example very keen to preserve the biological life of a seriously ill or ailing patient at any price. It must be understood that death convicts are not considered to be part of society anymore and therefore their treatment is de-humanizing in many ways. Showing no remorse and regret and offering no sincere apology to the victim are additional criteria for deciding upon the severity and harshness of a punishment. The door to rehabilitation and reintegration remains often closed for death inmates.

From 1995 to 2004, 99 persons were sentenced to death. In 2007, 46 people were sentenced to death, a 20-year high. According to the Japan Death Penalty Information Center 110 people were on the death row as of December 2007. The increase in death sentences goes hand in hand with a murder rate that has been declining at least since 2003, reaching a postwar low of 1,199 in 2007. Murder, robbery, rape, and indecent assault reported to police all fell, continuing a downward trend since 2004. The success of the low serious crime rate policy compared to most other industrial nations may be partially explained by the deterrence effect reflected in both the certainty and the severity of punishment in case of murder. Another reason may be the propensity not to direct violence against others but against oneself as Johnson (2005) argues when he compares the elevated lethal rate–as combined rate of homicides and suicides–of Japan to other countries.

The government has defended its secrecy as means to protecting the family from shame. Shame and apology are two key concepts to understand the cultural framework. Shaming punishments rely on, and ultimately reinforce, the notion that the offender is a valued member of the community. It seems that the offender feels shame precisely because he values his position in the community. Thus judges hand down lighter punishments only when they think the offender values his position and will want to restore it to its earlier status. In that sense, then, shaming punishments are not about dehumanization, but about hope and reintegration into the community: the punishment is based on and recognizes the hope that the offender will feel a strong enough connection to the community that he will feel ashamed, and that the community will value that person's connection to the community enough to react to the offender. It must be noted that–despite high recidivism rates–the judicial system puts much effort in reintegrating criminals into society by making use of a nationwide system of volunteer probation officers called *hogoshi* who are often selected among Buddhist monks.

Under the current system, a convict can obtain a pardon or leniency if the Cabinet approves the application following a screening process at the national offenders rehabilitation commission, a justice ministry panel. But, in reality, since World War II it has been extremely rare for inmates on death row to obtain a reduced sentence or a pardon. If a convict is to obtain leniency, the prisoner must confess and express remorse because it is usually understood by justice authorities that a leniency petition is accepted only if the convict admits to the crime and expresses remorse.

Some victims of crime prefer the death penalty because life imprisonment in Japan permits the release of criminals. Life imprisonment provides conditions for parole after completing a decade in prison, which is why it is rejected by traumatized victims, making the death penalty the only option. The state support for crime victims is almost inexistent in Japan. The Japan Federation of Bar Associations has regretted that not enough actions have been taken to assist crime victims who are not receiving enough support for financial compensation and medical/mental care. The Federation has strongly requested to immediately establish a law concerning compensation for crime victims and introduce a system to provide court appointed attorneys for crime victims.

Juveniles are exempted from the death penalty even though the age at which somebody can be executed is 18. In 1997 the public outcry about the cruel murder of a child by another child (Smith, 2008) led to the lowering of the age limit for criminal accountability. Another recent high profile case has been the mediatized support for a 30-year-old man known only as Hiroshi, who has lobbied relentlessly for the death penalty for the defendant who received life imprisonment for raping and killing Hiroshi's wife and the 11 month-old daughter. The Hiroshima High Court had to review its March 2002 life sentence handed down to the killer who was 18-years old at the time of the crime. In April 2008 the same Court converted its life sentence to the death sentence and set thereby a precedent for the future treatment of young serious offenders.

In rare cases the convicted himself has requested to be put to death. If the personal decision was taken based on rational grounds or in a state of mentally impairment remains controversial. The concept of mental incapacity remains in this regard unclear and its application for defense purposes seems restricted: in the case of a Chinese married, distressed woman who had killed two neighbor children she had driven to a kindergarten the prosecution asked for the death penalty and rejected the plea for mental incompetence. A new lay judge system has commenced in 2009. This system allows crime victims and their bereaved families of cases to be examined by lay judges or those cases involving professional negligence leading to injury or death to attend trials, question witnesses about circumstances, question defendants, and make statements including demands for punishment after examination of evidence, if they so wish to. This system is such that those members of the general public, who have been selected by lot, will participate in trials for the most serious of criminal cases. They will determine the sentences, including whether or not the defendant is guilty or not guilty, together with professional judges. The flaws of the newly introduced system that does not even encourage a public debate on the death penalty taboo are obvious: appointed civilians or lay people will have to bear shared responsibility for sentencing convicts to death.

Does the death penalty really reflect the wish of the people as is often stated through surveys sponsored by the Justice Ministry or is the fact that most people do not like to engage in a public debate reflecting a high level of disinterest and indifference and an immature political culture? Johnson (2006) argues that the secrecy maintained around the death penalty is unworthy of a civilized and democratic nation because by doing so it sacrifices democratic values such as accountability, transparency and public debate. He also claims (2005) that the alleged increased insecurity, terrorism risk and subsequent calls for vigilance against crime are artificial constructs to produce a reality that serves the electoral interest of politicians. The European Union has deeply regretted that the death penalty is still being applied in Japan, a country with which it shares common values and principles such as freedom, democracy and the rule of law. It has called on Japan to renew its commitment to promoting respect for human rights by joining it in abolishing capital punishment in line with the international community view.

Protecting the spirit of the peace constitution

In 2007 the government took an important step towards revising the pacifist constitution by having a bill approved in both houses to hold a referendum on the issue as early as 2010. Amendments to the constitution have to be endorsed by a two third majority of all the members of both houses and need to be approved by a majority of cast votes in a national referendum. Some fear that the latter may lead to a victory to fervent supporters to change and criticized the government for not establishing a minimum turnout in the referendum. Article 9 of the constitution renounces war as a means of settling international disputes and prohibits the maintenance of armed forces and other war potential. It is not just a provision of the Japanese law; it also acts as an international peace mechanism towards reductions in military spending, promotion of nuclear weapon free zones, ending violence against women, supporting conflict prevention, and mitigating the negative environmental impact of the military (Akira, 2007).

With its Preamble and Article 9, the Japanese constitution proclaims pacifism as one of the nation's fundamental principles. Article 9 not only renounces war and the threat or use of force as a sovereign right for itself; it also demands that all wars be made illegal. Japan's constitution provides the right to live in peace – a basic human right not only for the Japanese people, but also for the people of the whole world. The preamble reads as follows:

> "We, the Japanese people, desire peace for all time and are deeply conscious of the high ideals controlling human relationship striving for the preservation of peace, and the banishment of tyranny and slavery, oppression and intolerance for all time from the earth. We recognize that all peoples of the world have the right to live in peace, free from fear and want."

Article 9 has acted as a restraint on the militarization of Japan, which has maintained what it calls an "exclusively defense-oriented policy" and limited Japan's Self-Defense Forces (SDF) capability to the "minimum necessary level." In addition, Article 9 prohibits dispatching SDF to foreign territories to engage or participate in military combat overseas. Japan has also interpreted Article 9 as prohibiting the country from exporting arms, thus preventing the resurgence of Japan's pre-war military industry complex. Furthermore, Article 9 prevents development of an arms race and nuclear proliferation in East Asia.

Article 9 was born out of the direct experience of the Hiroshima and Nagasaki bombings. The devastation and immense suffering that followed these attacks led Japan to commit to the three non-nuclear principles which prohibit the country from possessing, producing, or permitting the introduction of nuclear weapons into its territory. The spirit of Article 9 rejects dependence on nuclear weapons in security policies and promotes Nuclear-Weapon-Free Zones world-wide–an idea long advocated by the victims of the atomic bombings. It also demands that nuclear weapons be outlawed. Article 9 prohibits the threat or use of force as a way of settling international disputes. As such, Japan cannot pose a threat to the security of other countries. This principle has played an important role in establishing trust relationships between Japan and the Asia-Pacific region, and has contributed to keeping the peace for more than 60 years. Article 9 is of paramount importance for the prevention of conflict. In July 2005, the Global Partnership for the Prevention of Armed Conflict's Action Agenda declared that Article 9 of the Japanese Constitution has been the foundation for collective security for the entire Asia Pacific region.

The move towards revision of Article 9 partly comes from the U.S. demand for Japan's full-fledged military support and participation in its war on international terror. Washington has consistently used the Asian-Pacific region as a hub for launching attacks against Afghanistan and Iraq. Indeed, the U.S. needs logistical support from its bases in the region to dispatch and sustain any deployment in the Middle East. The United Nations has been calling for a decrease in military spending, and reallocation of limited resources to solve global problems such as poverty, hunger, epidemics, disasters, and to protect human rights. Japan's Article 9 supplements the UN Charter Article 26's call for regulating armaments and minimizing the world's resources used on military expenses, and promotes disarmament for development. From air, water and land pollution produced by wars to the environmental and social stresses caused by the presence of military bases, the negative effects of military activities on wildlife and the environment have long been recognized. Growing awareness of climate change has led the debate to focus on what could be achieved with the colossal resources currently being spent on the military, if instead governments invested such sums in protecting our planet from the extreme impacts of climate change. Article 9 distances itself from the state-centered, militaristic approach to national defense, and brings a human dimension to security, which must be based on sustainable human development and the fulfillment of basic needs by non-violent means. First developed in 1994, the notion of human security was consecrated by the 2005 World Summit outcome document of the United Nations.

Direct democracy to supplement the representative system

Currently referendums have no legally binding character but are consultative by nature. Public-drafted legislation has been proposed that would require local governments to hold a plebiscite if at least 10% of local voters petition for one, and make the results binding if they reflect the will of over a third of the registered voters. The legislation sought by the Forum for Plebiscite Legislation, a group made up of lawyers, scholars, municipal assembly members and other members of the public, also requires municipalities to abide by the results of such plebiscites if the results are supported by at least one-third of eligible voters. Currently, plebiscites are nonbinding and local assemblies can decide if such voting can be held. The group's members said such legislation is necessary to have the public voice properly reflected in local administration.

The group has continued since 2000 to call on Diet members from both the ruling and opposition camps to propose such legislation in the Diet. The citizens' group wants to influence similar moves by the ruling bloc as well as the Democratic Party of Japan by announcing their own version. Unlike in most U.S. states and many European countries, holding a plebiscite in Japan requires the enactment of a local ordinance. While a petition for a plebiscite must bear the signatures of 2% or more of a local electorate, a vote can take place only after the petition is approved by the local assembly regardless of how many voters demand one. The current system is causing increasing frustration for citizens' groups nationwide as one plebiscite proposal after another gets rejected by municipal assemblies despite support from a substantial portion of the voting public. In addition, even if a plebiscite actually takes place, the local government is not legally bound by its result. Plebiscite proposals filed by citizens on such issues as building nuclear power plants, military facilities, waste disposal facilities and airports have been rejected on 34 occasions since January 1998, and only 10 plebiscites, including the vote in Tokushima over the contentious Yoshino River dam project, have taken place so far. While an eligible voter is defined by the election law as a Japanese citizen at least 20 years old, the citizens' group wants local governments to expand the range of eligible voters to include both Japanese and foreign residents age 18 or older. Even if binding the results of a local referendum may not affect the national government or national policies. The dilemma is exemplified by the nuclear powered warships calling in Japanese ports. Even if a referendum to prohibit warships from entering local ports might be locally binding this would not affect international agreements ratified by the government to uphold its security commitments towards the U.S. or other Allies.

A critical review of Fujiwara's bestseller 'The dignity of the nation'

In his bestseller book 'The dignity of the nation' Masahiko Fujiwara (2007), the new star among the neoconservative rightwing establishment, has criticized the emphasis on Western logic in Japanese society and called for a return to what is described as ancient Japanese virtues according to literary critic Andrew Rankin. Fujiwara stands against globalism and claims that it is a method employed by the United States to attain world domination in our post-Cold War setting. Other disputes are directed against the market economy, which Fujiwara claims is widening the economic gap between the wealthy and impoverished in Japan and that this economic system has been slowly eroding the supposed egalitarianism in postwar Japan. The first half of this book constitutes a critique of Western ideals: democracy, freedom, logic, equality, and globalization. Fujiwara is fed up with all of them. Now that slavery has been abolished, freedom has lost its meaning, and is merely the promotion of selfishness. The industrial revolution enabled the West to dominate the world, he writes, but globalization is nothing more than worldwide homogenization. Communism and imperialism were products of magnificent logic, hence their spectacular failure. Meritocracy has created societies where the individual is surrounded by enemies. Fujiwara wants lifetime employment and promotion through seniority in the aim of achieving social stability, which he sees as the fundamental strength of any nation. Companies should not belong to shareholders, who offer no special loyalty, but to the employees who sustain them. He is good at exposing the hypocrisies of Western morality. Freedom and equality, he rightly points out, is contradictory, and cannot coexist; that is why 35 million Americans are too poor to afford medical care. His attacks on media-based populism and the dangers of free-market economics–such as the use of derivatives for speculative purposes–are spot on, though these are easy targets. The disintegration of family values he diagnoses as the failure of Western logic and the rational spirit. Fujiwara is right to mention that people have become indifferent to crimes and are overflowed by information. The success of the book is due to the fact that Fujiwara seems to have reflected the feelings of many of his readers that something has gone wrong in Japanese society. The book attracts readers because it appears to offer stable values in unstable, insecure times. Such a value or principle might be dignity. Fujiwara offers this polemic slogan to his readers. The former Prime Minister Abe liked to use the term dignity, but he took the least dignified way of resigning. However when he offers his solution in guise of the samurai spirit Fujiwara starts to losing ground and slips into muddy ground. Money-based social structures must be replaced with ethics based on *bushido*, the way of the warrior. Unsurprisingly his definition of Samurai spirit lacks detail and seems to denote anything he finds noble in Japanese tradition such as empathy for the weak, filial piety, awareness of the fragility of the human condition–which are not Japanese at all, but originate in the teachings of Buddhism and Confucianism. One might add that even the Greek polis embodies those in way global principles. Fujiwara falls short of grasping the true sense of *bushido* namely the quest for peace, freedom and political equality. His shortcomings open the door for scary misinterpretations and dangerous nationalist and militarist talk.

It needs to be strongly reiterated that the root cause for today's social problems and social instability is not the alleged U.S. led globalization of the world but Japan's own self imposed nationalist ideology, male gender superiority, ethnic arrogance, disrespect for its own traditions and culture, an education system without principles, material selfishness and a general mental and emotional state of complete indifference and lack of compassion for others.

Chapter Two.

The invisible impact of globalization on psychopathology and mental health

The chapter sheds light on the mental health damage caused by forced economic globalization. The chapter gives an overview on psychiatry from 1900 to 1950 when repression and seclusion from society was the mot d'ordre to deal with mentally ill and thereafter when laws were adjusted to reflect modern developments. The chapter will analyze the changing patterns of psychopathology since the Meiji restoration, try to explain the success of the Western client centered therapy represented by Carl Rogers in Japan besides traditional psychotherapy, discusses recent trends in anti-social behavior, puts a comparative focus on the fatherless society discussion and deals with the rising mental health issues in the context of multiculturalism and ethnic diversity.

Introduction

Few English studies have highlighted the crucial role of mental health in the making of modern Japan and its interactions with globalization (Weng-Shing et al, 2005; Tsuchiya et al, 2004; Ito, 1999). Curiously, the role of NPOs acting independently in the area of mental health reform has not been given particular attention in the recent debate on the civil sector revival maybe because those NPOs operate mainly on a national or local community level. On the other hand leading psychiatrists and clinical psychologists such as Masatake Morita (1998) from a Buddhist perspective, Takeo Doi (1992 & 2004) from a Neo-Freudian perspective and Haruo Kawai (1995) from a Jungian perspective have tried to explain what are the constitutive inner elements of Japanese psyche such as *amae* or the maternal or motherhood principle. Those internationally acknowledged contributions in the field of psychology have however contrasted with the rather ineffective and inappropriate domestic state of mental health services as expressed in the excessive number of in-patient hospitalization. The voluntarist separation between the public and private sphere has been nowhere so pervasive than in the prevention, diagnosis and treatment of mental illness and disabilities. Whereas the state as embodiment of the public sphere has restricted its legal, financial and supportive involvement to a minimum–or to say it more bluntly–has refused to take proactive responsibility for mental health care such as reforming state hospitals or taking effective measures towards suicide prevention, the private market sector represented by private hospitals and psychiatrists has largely profited from the treatment of patients. The shame associated with the public stigma of mental illness has been responsible for the indiscriminate private seclusion of patients within hospitals or the private family home setting.

Through intense lobbying, voluntary advocacy activities and public pressure NPOs succeeded in helping to change and improve the negative public perception of mental illness and facilitated the reintegration of patients into local communities. Their activities started already locally in the 1960s long before psychiatric reforms on a state level were initiated. More recently psychiatric domestic reform has been speeded up by global trends, norms and standards of best practices such as deinstitutionalization and normalization that helped to redefine the roadmap for psychiatry and treatment in Japan. The changes in treatment for schizophrenia serve as positive example for public NPO involvement. With regard to the common but controversial treatment of mild depression with antidepressants the conflict of interest between private gains and public health wellbeing has been triggered by the globalizing influence of the pharmaceutical lobby. NPOs such as the suicide prevention NPO Lifelink, the Japanese branch of the international mood disorder association, the international mental health providers association (IMHP), the English telephone counseling NPO TELL and the 24 hour Japanese language nationwide represented telephone counseling association *Inochi no Denwa*–literally life phone line–have been incremental in promoting alternative self enhancing Western style talk treatment therapies to counterbalance the overreliance on the Western medical model on one side and traditional self negating Japanese style counseling therapies such as Morita or Naikan on the other side. Their example shows that it is possible to counterbalance the neoliberal medical globalization model with an alternative globalized Western counseling model.

There are roughly two distinctive periods in the treatment of mentally ill: from 1900 to 1950 repression and seclusion from society was the mot d'ordre to deal with mentally ill. In a second wave Japan adjusted its laws to reflect modern developments in psychiatry and treatment of mental illness. Since the 1980s Japan has undergone a number of mental health law reforms aimed at reducing hospitalization and institutional seclusion of psychiatric patients. In 1995 the mental health law was reformed and for the first time legally defined mental illness as a–less threatening–disability and established strict criteria for involuntary hospitalization. The law promotes the concept of normalization viewing mental illness as a disability and encouraging the integration of psychiatric inpatients back into the community. The November 2005 revision of the mental health and welfare law had three main aims:

• Change the public's attitude toward mental illness

• Reorganize and reinforce psychiatric medical services

• Reorganize and reinforce community support systems

Crimes by mentally impaired offenders

Following the implementation of the 2003 forensic law known as Medical
Treatment and Supervision Act various problems have been pointed out about
the treatments of mentally disordered offenders in Japan. The Medical Treatment and Supervision Act–hereafter called the Act–came into effect in 2005.

The Act is to provide proper medical care and supervision for mentally disordered offenders who caused serious harm due to insanity or quasi-insanity and
to achieve rehabilitation without re-offending through relapse prevention. Mentally disordered offenders are psychiatrically examined from two perspectives:
whether they are criminally responsible for their crimes; and whether they require medical care under the Act. These two types of psychiatric examination
need to be standardized. Under the Act, medical care is provided through collaboration of multiple agencies and groups, such as designated medical facilities,
probation offices and mental health welfare agencies. The Act study group re-
views actual cases with judges, prosecutors and rehabilitation coordinators. Under the new citizen-judge lay system that will go into effect in 2009 court decisions are made by a collegiate court comprising 3 judges and 6 citizens.

Cultural perceptions and regulation of the profession

Mental illness used to be defined in terms of mental and spiritual weakness.
The Japanese have been taught to suppress feelings and personal opinions from
childhood. Outward displays of negative emotions are discouraged as signs of an
immature and weak character. Sharing intimate private information with others
outside the family is taboo which makes it difficult for people to seek counseling.
A depressed person is supposed to save his face in public and pretend to function normally. Family matters use to be dealt with by the family and not external
agents. This approach conflicts with the process of openly talking about oneself
that is inherent to most Western style psychotherapy. Whereas in the West
counselors would encourage patients to exercise and connect to people and raise
self-esteem, strengthen independence or self assert their ego strength and independence Japanese psychologists, suspicious of Western style therapies, refer to
the custom of relating and positioning the individual to the group, especially the
family, rather than trying to achieve his self-fulfillment. There is also a partial
aversion among clients against taking drugs because of significant side effects.

Psychiatrists are certified, licensed and accredited through the Ministry of
Health whereas clinical psychologists or *rinsho shinrishi* in Japanese are licensed and certified via a private association supervised by the Ministry of
Education. The counselor profession itself is unregulated. Whereas in the U.S.
only licensed counselors are allowed to offer their services in Japan anybody can
call himself a counselor and open a private cabinet. State licensure requirements
in the U.S. typically include possession of a master or doctoral degree in professional counseling from an accredited higher education institution, a minimum of

3000 hours of post master's supervised clinical field experience in a hospital or community setting, passage of a national state recognized counselor examination and strict adherence to a national Code of Ethical Standards and Behavior. Counselors are monitored by the state's counselor licensure board in the U.S.

Japan has a rather elevated ratio of 9.4 psychiatrists per 100 000 individuals and 7 clinical psychologists per 100 000 individuals. Japan has been well-known for having the highest number of psychiatric beds per capita in the world (28 beds for 10 000 people) with a 95% occupancy rate, long inpatient custodial hospital treatment (almost 380 days) but recently a shift towards more community integration and integration is observable. Only physicians are allowed to prescribe medication or treat patients. Due to the financial burden involved of becoming a psychiatrist and maintaining income through medication prescription psychiatrists see patients in average only 3 minutes per session. Counseling as an additional therapeutic instrument is not state licensed and not reimbursable through national health insurance. Japan has been criticized for relying heavily on long in-patient hospitalization stays, institution based care instead of community based care and insufficient emergency services.

The most frequent disorders psychiatry has to deal with are schizophrenia, mental disorders, substance abuse, suicide, child abuse, domestic violence, depression and more recently anti-social behaviors, social avoidance and reclusion also called *hikikomori*, eating disorders and sexual gender identity issues. One of the shortcomings of psychiatry is the lack of qualified specialists in forensic psychiatry, child psychiatry or psychiatrists trained in suicide prevention or specialized in the treatment of cultural alienation among the ever-growing number of Japanese returnees who lived for a long time abroad and experience cultural reintegration difficulties upon return. In a recent report completed after a field trip to Japan in 2008 the Australian psychiatrist Professor Chee Ng concludes that "there are significant challenges facing the mental health system in Japan" (Ng, 2008, p.3).

Prefectural mental health: 25 years 'Kanagawa Women center'

The public prefectural Kanagawa Women's Center is promoting empowerment of women and equal participation of both women and men in all aspects of the society. The center envisions a gender-equal society where every person can express and exercise one's individuality and ability regardless of one's gender. For the realization of this gender-equal society, the center carries out a variety of activities. The Center is committed to protect and promote the human rights of women through working on the issues such as violence against women and sexual harassment and providing services to assist self-sustainability of women. Since 2002, it has been designated as a Spousal Violence Counseling and Support Center in the Law for the Prevention of Spousal Violence and the Protection of Victims. The counseling services are provided free of charge by women counselors only and temporary shelter services is offered as well.

Overview of structural and cultural aspects of psychopathology since Meiji restoration

The ways one looks at a problem also defines he solution to solving it. An overview of psychological disorders since Meiji restoration shows in what way they are linked to societal developments and what treatments have been applied (Weng-Shing et al, 2005). In Samurai society inner motivation and moral principles, subjectivity, individual ethics, a strong self awareness and self worth prevailed over seeking of harmony, self-interest or conformist behavior. With the Meiji transformation more attention was given to the objective world, rationalization, harmony and conformity to the group.

The context of psychopathology: family patterns and motherhood expectations

Psychopathology may be best understood in the private social context of family and motherhood. Japan is–or better used to be–a familial society where marriage, child bearing and childrearing provide a woman her place in the society. The family as basic social micro unit of society reflects strong vertical interpersonal relationships and induced changes in the family structure allow for assessing changes in psychopathology. Mumford (1957) argues that the social nucleus of archaic life is the village centered large family that offers respect for the past and to the elders. In Meiji times the three, four or even five generation family was the norm as was the absolute and sometimes violent authority of the father, whose role model as master of the patriarchal household was never put into doubt. However within the changing social context of modernization, commercialization and rationalization a conflict between paternal authority, established traditions, strict values inside home and the pressure to conform to outside norms of harmony and self negation for the sake of either military strength or economic affluence took precedence. Nishizono (2005) describes this conflict between Western forms and Japanese spirit, between the self who tries to assert his rights in the wake of Westernization and a family consciousness that remains loyal to the established order.

What triggers psychopathological reactions? Psychopathological reactions occur when the self image does not match with the perceived reality or does not match social norms in place and consequently a conflict or crisis breaks out. Maladaptive behavior happens through dysfunctional observational learning from parents. The inability to cope with a situation in a healthy way is either due to a perception of inefficacy, excessive standards or a dysfunctional expectancy or self-evaluation. When tensions arise incongruence may appear and the defensive processes like denial or distortion may occur. The trigger for an incongruent self is a gap between perceived self and experience. During a crisis the client becomes aware of the inner tensions, confusion and this causes emotional stress, anxiety and depression.

The Morita psychotherapy was developed by Japanese psychiatrist Masatake Morita in the early part of the twentieth century (Morita, 1998). He was influenced by the psychological principles of Zen Buddhism. His method was initially developed as a treatment for a type of anxiety neurosis called *shinkeishitsu* (hypersensitivity). In the latter part of this century the applications of the Morita therapy have broadened, both in Japan and in the West. The standard Japanese treatment is nowadays applied to the *taijin kyofusho* (fear of others) disorder as well. This traditional form of psychotherapy has close links with Buddhism and the cure involves patient isolation, enforced bed rest, diary writing, manual labor, and lectures on the importance of self-acceptance and positive endeavor. The self is defined in relationship with mother nature and the ultimate goal is the acceptance of things as they are as well as integration of the self and the world by rectifying distorted cognitions of reality. Problems arise when the self looses touch with the natural flow of wholeness. Focus is on the development of a self that incorporates nature. Since the 1930s, the treatment has been modified to include out-patient and group treatments; this modified version is known as neo-Morita therapy.

Taijin kyofusho

The founder of the Morita therapy defined *taijin kyofusho* as anxious concern of how others–especially near friends or family members–might think about one or might react. In the West, *taijin kyofusho* is usually described as a form of social anxiety or social phobia, with the sufferer avoiding social contact. However, instead of a fear of embarrassing themselves or being harshly judged by others because of their social ineptness, sufferers of *taijin kyofusho* in Japan report a fear of offending or harming other people. The focus is thus on avoiding harm to others rather than to oneself. In the authoritative statistical manual of diagnostic criteria DSM-IV casebook (American Psychiatric Association, 2000) reference is made to a typical clinical case of a woman afraid of thinking aloud. The patient in question is a single or unmarried woman in her late 40s living with her mother and sister and brother together. She reports that she is thinking aloud and thereby hurting the feelings of other people around her and believes that her habit of thinking aloud is offensive to everybody in the neighborhood. As a result she avoids social contact. She describes herself as being conscientious, prudent and tender and she has always been receptive to the feelings of others and always been seeking the acceptance of others. The fear of others, insecurity and shyness are symptoms of shunning the public, avoiding social contact and being occupied with oneself. The pathological concern with other's opinions and how one will be regarded and received by other persons is regarded from a psychiatric perspective as social phobia disorder. In this case the psychiatrist diagnosed the patient in question as having a delusional disorder.

Nishizono (2005, p.45) and most other Japanese clinical psychologists explain this culture bound disorder with the concept of externalized shame culture developed by Ruth Benedict but it remains unclear how the mechanism of shame relates to extroverted fear and overreaction to social interaction. What others might think about oneself becomes the source of alleged shame feelings. Jugon in his study of social phobias in Japan concludes that already in early childhood socialization

> "the Japanese mother preferentially uses the lever of self-sacrifice as she wants her baby to be a good child. It means she puts herself more or less unconsciously (and more or less easily) in the position of a victim for soliciting her child to react as she wants" (Jugon, 1998).

The child learns to see his mother as a victim to keep her love. This basic relation is transposed later on the framework of interpersonal relations in society. A person may have distorted feelings of empathy towards the other which allow him to get in his status of victim.

The myth of the selfless ideal mother

For male clinical psychologists the idealized picture of the self sacrificing mother who gives eternal equal love to all her children is an unquestioned dogma and principle. Motherhood in Japan is much more idealized than in the West: the ultimate role of the mother is to raise children, contribute to the community and be a loving and faithful wife to her husband. The Ajase complex is part of the alleged guilt conscience derived from debt of gratitude and relationship of son to mother claimed to be unique to Japan and completely separate from the Oedipus complex in that the Ajase complex is "pre-Oedipal and does not involve the father figure or sexual matters" (Weng-Shing et al, 2005, p12). For Freud the Oedipal stage was central to the development of the super-ego, with its capacity for generating guilt, which creates a social conscience. It seems useful to elaborate on this important concept developed first by Kosawa and expanded by Okonogi focusing on the themes of matricide and prenatal rancor in contrast to the Oedipus complex emphasizing incestuous desire, patricide.

The Ajase complex

Bimbisara was a powerful king in India. One of his sons Ajase was a close friend of a Buddhist monk who convinced him to kill his father and become himself the King. The plot was discovered and the father upon knowing the murder intentions of Ajase decided to abdicate in favor of his son and retire. But Ajase put him in prison with the intention to let starve him to death. Queen Idaike was the only allowed to visit the father and brought him secretly food. Ajase took revenge on his father by torturing him finally to death. So far for the facts. The legend that evolved from there found its way with Buddhism to Japan and was readapted to suit the established imagined motherhood ideal. Queen Idaike worried about the King's lack of love for her wanted to bear a child so she could retain her status. Impatient about becoming pregnant she killed the hermit thought to be reborn as the king's son who cursed her by saying that he will reincarnate as her son but will kill his father. Instantly the Queen became pregnant and the child that she bore was named Ajase. The queen, fearful of what she had done, tried to abort and kill the baby, but she failed and Ajase survived. When he grew up and learned the secret surrounding his birth, he became angry with the queen and attempted to slay her, but was dissuaded from this act by a minister. At that moment, he was attacked by a severe guilt feeling and became afflicted with a dreadful skin disease.

Only his mother stood by and lovingly nursed him. Eventually, the Prince was cured to become a widely respected ruler. The deformations and additions to the Japanese legend by Okonogi have been questioned and it has been asserted by Nagera (2005), who compared the historical facts with later adaptations, that the Ajase complex is not only not separate from the Oedipus complex but rather part of it. As an example Nagera mentions that the fact that Queen Idaike secretly brings food to to the King shows that she is devoted in love to her husband and that the irrational reaction of Ajase to this is part of the oedipal conflict in him. Another example is Ajase's willingness to kill his mother and Nagera wonders if it "should (it) not be considered Oedipal to want to kill the mother because she loves more the father than the child" (Nagera, 2005, p.7). Kamipebbu (2005) argues that the Japanese version of the legend was readapted to fulfill a male oriented motherhood ideology and adds that Okonogi idealized the mother figure Queen Idaike "and added a sweet conclusion to the Kosawa's Ajase Story that focuses on the conflicts associated with human living as much deeper problems (then Oedipus complex) and highlights it as the story originated in Idaike's egoism as a woman" (Kamibeppu, 2005, p.17). The expectation imposed on mothers to love their children and sacrifice themselves for others eventually collapsed.

After the war and with new freedom given by the U.S. occupation the previous tight gender relations became looser, the nuclear family began to become stronger but also the social pressure to compete for entering university and getting a safe lifetime job in a big company. The father became a symbolic figure, as male earner but absent from home whereas the female stayed at home, raised the children and worked part-time to make ends. In this time anxiety disorders and hysteria among women bearing all the responsibility for child rearing, household and cooking began to spread. Kamibeppu (2005) reports a clinical case of a daughter, in the typical after war family setting of four with the father being the earner and the mother the housewife, who never had experienced any motherly love in her life. The myth of motherly love is contradicted by the reality of motherly abuse of the elder daughter who happens to become the victim and suffers from not being able to initially fulfill her own postgraduate study career dreams. The emotional confusion of the daughter caught in between the broken relationship between mother and father became such that she was "wondering whether she is a victim or victimizer" (Kamibeppu, 2005, p.26). As mentioned previously the Japanese mother is socialized into the role of self-negation and victim and she passes this role on to her daughters. The distressed elder daughter for example looked down on her mother because she accused her of not supporting her father fully. Through her arrogance the elder daughter perceives herself as victimizer more than victim. Kamibeppu who treated the patient successfully concludes that from a therapeutic viewpoint only the "symbolic death" of the mother and not the "symbolic killing" suggested by male psychologists can lead to the full mental and emotional recovery of abused patients. She also strongly invites Japanese society as a whole to stop pressuring mothers into the ideal selfless ever-loving mother image and relieve the burden put on mothers by involving more fathers in child rearing and other social agents that help to prevent isolation of the mother. The family therapist Tamura also strongly suggests to include fathers into family therapy but cautions that under current social circumstances it would be rather difficult to just empower mothers or force them to become more emancipated and comments that for "the housewife who stays home all the time, the children are the only objects she can exercise her power" (Tamura, 2001).

The latest collapse of the nuclear family characterized by one person household, singles, childless society, high divorce rates in the aftermath of the bubbly economy has caused new social frictions leading to an increase of mental health related disorders more common to the West such as gender identity disorders, anti-social behavior, social withdrawal or eating disorders. Globalization and commercialization of society have led to the social construction of new disorders such as depression once regarded as a natural state of feelings whereas nowadays it is regarded as a disease requiring treatment with medication.

The reinvention of depression as a disease

It is difficult to find an exact reason for developing depression in each individual person. It can be triggered by psychological trauma, stress, illnesses, unemployment, and many other problems. The decline of the private sphere, disrupted family structures, experience of conflicting needs for dependence and autonomy, stress at the workplace and in school have led to a steep rise of mental disorders–more than 3 million people seek either inpatient or outpatient treatment for depression according to the latest statistics available from the Health and Welfare Ministry. Depression is a condition characterized by loss of energy, fatigue, a sense of worthlessness, guilt feelings, bad mood, difficulty concentrating, and even thoughts of suicide are just some of the many symptoms. Freud viewed depression as representing the symbolic loss of a love object accompanied by the turning inward of anger toward the parents. Depression is exacerbated by a lack of social contacts, peers and friends. Biological approaches view depression as resulting from an insufficient level of serotonin, a neurotransmitter. Treatment by so-called SSRI's or selective serotonin reuptake inhibitor seems to be effective for some depression prone disorders (Kobayashi et al, 2003) even though they can have serious side effects. Pharmacotherapy is indicated particularly for endogenous depression with an alleged physiological basis. Medication is thought to act more quickly on symptoms than psychotherapy but the effects of medication are not as enduring unless continued. Depression is quite common and the World Health Organization lists depression as one of the most serious conditions. One of the major barriers in treating depressed people is getting sufferers to admit that they need help in the first place. With proper and professional treatment depression is treatable and curable. Economic globalization has contributed to a commercialization trend leading to a cultural remodeling of private sadness feelings into a public disease called depression to be treated with medication. It has been overlooked that antidepressants actually treat what is a common symptom of depression, rather than the condition itself. A public debate on the appropriate diagnosis and treatment for symptoms of mild depression has been hindered by a rigid system that relies on conventional medical treatment administered exclusively by medical doctors often more concerned about financial gain then about the mental wellbeing of their patient and by aggressive marketing of pharmaceutical companies aimed at pushing through their selfish marketing plans. The success of Western style talk therapy counseling techniques in Japan has shown that a global minded approach to depression rooted in neutrality, empathy and active listening can overcome some of the limitations of the medical model. In her critical article 'Did antidepressants depress Japan?' the journalist Kathryn Schulz (2004) retraces the cultural history of depression in Japan and by recapturing the socially constructed remolding of depression from a generally accepted Buddhist feeling of existential sadness, melancholia, sensitivity and fragility to a medically defined mass disease that needs to be treated with modern anti-depressant medication. The question is however if *kokoro no kaze*–as a mild depression is called in Japan–is a medical condition that needs to be cured by medication or if talk therapy is largely sufficient. How one looks at things often defines the solution one is looking for: the relabeling of a cultural phenomenon as a medical disease involves a huge financial stake as health insurance covers the treatment (Schulz, 2004). Psychiatrists and the health care or pharmaceutical industry profit most from the boom in anti-depressant usage. In the late 1980s market research revealed that there was no need for selling anti-depressants but in 1999 a Japanese company began selling SSRI's via medical representatives to the medical community. Since then globalization has stabilized the market demand for anti-depressants in Japan. Doctors often unfamiliar with Western pharmacotherapy have adopted a purely pharmacological approach to treating mental illness. A mid-1990s study conducted by the World Health Organization found that Japanese doctors misdiagnosed mental illness very frequently. At the same time the mental health system is preventing people from getting non-medical professional care. Well trained and qualified clinical psychologists are not allowed to examine patients independently of medical doctors.

Schizophrenia

The latest edition of the diagnostic and statistical manual of mental disorders DSM-IV (American Psychiatric Association, 2000) lists six major psychotic disorders–among them schizophrenia–and describes three subtypes of schizophrenia. The most common type in the U.S. is paranoia. The exact root causes for schizophrenia remain unknown but it is believed that biological and social factors contribute to the onset of the disorder. Experts agree that schizophrenia develops as a result of interplay between biological predisposition - for example, inheriting certain genes- and the kind of social environment a person is exposed to. There is currently no physical or laboratory test that can absolutely diagnose schizophrenia for sure–a psychiatrist usually comes to the diagnosis based on defined descriptive clinical symptoms. What makes the diagnosis accuracy difficult is that the six DSM-IV listed psychotic disorders all present similar symptoms such as hallucinations, delusions, distortion or impairment of memory, reduced or lacking reality awareness and reality loss, suicidal ideation and a wrong diagnosis can therefore not be excluded. Schizophrenia tends to run over generations in families and women tend to have less severe forms than men. Treatment for the disorder foresees medication as well as psychotherapy and family support. During or after psychotic episodes hospital treatment may be required but in general it is limited to a two week stay at most. The prognosis for full recovery of the disorder is not good and the relapse risk high. Continued lifelong treatment and aftercare is required even after the alleviation of symptoms has been obtained.

Japan has a proportionally exceptionally high number of diagnosed schizophrenic patients. Tsuchiya et al (2004) report that two thirds of all in-patients in have been diagnosed with schizophrenia in 2000 with this percentage dropping to 53% by 2002. In absolute nominal terms the number of in-patient individuals has dropped from 216 600 in 1996 (Ito et al, 1999) to 202 012 in 2002 (Sato, 2006) and this trend will probably continue. Schizophrenia treatment until recently used to rely on the principles of secrecy, conspiracy of silence and private seclusion and confinement within hospitals or family setting until psychiatry reforms for deinstitutionalization, normalization and community care took effect. Until then psychiatrists as well as the public opinion contributed to maintain a culturally negative perception by regarding schizophrenia to be an untreatable disease (Sato, 2006) or a personal character weakness (Griffiths et al, 2006). For example, the formerly used official medical term for schizophrenia–seishin bunretsu byo–implies that schizophrenics have split minds and corrupted souls. Various reasons have been advanced to justify the practice of not informing the diagnosis to the patient to keep away shame from the family or to protect patients from committing harm against them by preventing the patient from committing suicide if faced with his diagnosis. Sato (2006) reports that as a result of conventional practices many in-patients were not aware of their diagnosis on average for more than one year considering that the average length of stay is believed to be 8.5 years (Oshima et al, 2007). With the adoption of the more neutral term of *togo shitchosho*–literally dysfunction of integration or integration disorder–in 1992 the reporting frequency of the diagnosis to the patient increased dramatically (Sato, 2006). Based on a survey Oshima et al (2007) estimate that 40% of all current schizophrenia patients with one of more year of hospital stay could actually be discharged and treated on an out-patient basis in their local communities if sufficient community resources were made available.

As Ito and Sederer (1999) mentioned earlier the state has never been the primary agent responsible for fighting public stigmas, supporting voluntary public health associations with subsidies or protecting the human rights mentally ill in Japan. For a long time it has been the strategy to keep the mentally ill out of the public discourse by confining them to seclusion at home or in hospitals. As early as in 1970 civilian voluntary grass root efforts have been undertaken to take schizophrenic patients out of their social isolation, integrate them in local communities and offer them meaningful lives. The major driving force acting publicly against the negative social stigma associated with schizophrenia and inactivity of the state bodies has been a civil sector advocacy group called *Zenkaren*, a national association of families of mentally ill patients. *Zen* means all, *Ka* means family and *Ren* means unite –in short all families unite for mental illness. It was established in 1965 in response to a proposed amendment to Japan's Mental Health Act. At that time an incident involving a young man with schizophrenia who had stabbed the U.S. ambassador had served as a pretext to the national government to subject people with mental illness to strict supervision by the police. The government stance triggered a public outcry and some 500 participants from across the country had called for the mentally ill issue to be a local government–not a police–responsibility. Since then, *Zenkaren* has grown into one of the largest and most influential mental health non-profit groups in Japan. It has over 1600 affiliated local groups with 120 000 members from all 47 prefectures. Its activities have developed to address deficiencies in Japan's mental health system and it has pressed for the establishment and improvement of social welfare polices and rehabilitation programs by governments at both the national and local level self-help. *Zenkaren* provides counseling, guidance and information services for people suffering from mental illness and their families, organizes workshops that serve as job-training and social centers for the mentally ill, conducts public awareness campaigns to correct misconceptions about, and promote better understanding of, mental illness, educates its members and the public and keeps them up to date and conducts research to improve the mental health system, social welfare policies, rehabilitation programs and the skills of community mental health workers.

Eating disorders

Family relations have played an important role in the development of eating disorders in Japan. For the family therapist Tamura (2001) the rise in the number of dysfunctional family patterns is due to the symbolic and physical absence of the father paired with the dominant role of the mother. According to him the overdependence on the mother has caused enmeshment. An enmeshed family pattern is a pattern in which members are over involved with each other's affairs and over concerned about each other's welfare: "As a result, mothers took on the major responsibility in child rearing, and maintained very closed (often enmeshed) relationships with children, not only in childhood years, but also in adolescents and young adults up to their twenties" (Tamura, 2001). Especially in the later phase when the child seeks to become independent it may be induced through family enmeshment to develop an eating disorder. According to another theory ineffective parenthood may cause eating disorders as well. Ineffective parents feed their children with food when they ask for love. Parents of teenagers with eating disorders tend to always know what their children need and people with eating disorders worry much about how others view them or seek to conform to others who tell them that thinness and diet are valued as being cute by society or the peer group. Pike and Borovoy (2004) describe in their voluminous detailed clinical study on eating disorders in Japan what they call "Motherhood as the only route to maturity" (Pike and Borovoy, 2004, p.502) covered up by a "conspiracy of silence" (Pike and Borovoy, 2004, p.507) that compels women to accept social norms of marriage, motherhood and gender role expectations imposed on them. Pike and Borovoy show evidence for the fact that the image of women in Japan is still seen from a traditional viewpoint despite Westernization and modernization. They argue that there is no economic incentive for women to live independent lives and those women are encouraged to stay at home as fulltime housewives fulfilling at the same time a public role of support to community life. Marriage as a social institution serves to cement the motherhood ideology even at the expense of spousal love. Westerners often complain that the mother focuses exclusively on children after birth. Pike and Borovoy mention that love is secondary to a spousal relationship and that "women need not fear divorce and poverty should their husbands fall out of love with them" (Pike and Borovoy, 2004, p.505). In Japan it is the custom that after a divorce has been legally validated husband and wife cut all ties. The saying *kateinai rikon*, de facto but not legalized divorce, and *fufu tanin*, separate spouses, reflect the social reality of mutual spousal estrangement. Pike and Borovoy highlight that a divorced mother has better chances to get public support than a divorced woman.They also reflect the fact that in Japan there is no in between stage from girl to motherhood and the female teenager image creates tension and confusion because they do not belong to either the girl category or mother category.

Several clinical case studies illustrate the dilemma of the Japanese woman caught between the desire to become independent and the pressure to conform to social norms of good housewife and wise mother. The social phenomenon of "parasite single" (Pike and Borovoy, 2004, p.509) concerns women who delay their marriage, continue to live with their parents and spend their money on shopping sprees and travel exemplifies the challenge. Losing weight is seen as a silent protest means to symbolically regress back to the nostalgic times of pre-marriage, youth and carefree life. For Pike and Borovoy disordered eating behaviors are the only means to give way to one's protest against over-indulgence and over-dependency on others.

Amae or fostering dependence on others

The Ajase legend is closely related to the strong mother-child relationship which is the basis for dependant-indulging love called *amae* (Doi, 1992 & 2004), in Freudian terms defined as passive object love. Japanese culture does not regard dependence as problematic or undesirable but as a human quality. In the statistical and diagnostic manual of mental disorders DSM- IV–the authoritative source on Western impregnated psychiatry norms–dependence is clearly viewed as a negative attitude and labeled as dependence personality disorder with a high incidence of diagnosis for women. Somebody who matches criteria and symptoms of being overprotected or maintaining too strong family bonds risks falling under this category. In Japan children do not want to separate from their parents as in the West and enjoy the socially accepted mutual sometimes lifelong dependence. Independence, high self regard and self esteem is not valued that much. Relying on the family and group comes first. Japanese do not like to openly disagree with others and feel only well in the group. They like others to take care of them and assume responsibility and make collective decisions for them. They like to be told what to do by others and do not like to take initiative. Japanese would probably rename this disorder to independence personality disorder to fit their cultural values, customs and beliefs. A pity that the DSM-IV classification (American Psychiatric Association, 2000) does not take sufficient account of values, beliefs, attitudes and customs that differ from the Western standard.

The child who *amaes* wants to merge and become one with his mother. The English word mollycoddle helps to understand the meaning of *amae*. Someone who wants to be mollycoddled does not articulate his desire but hopes by his person or his actions to elicit indulgence from someone else without verbalizing. The psychoanalyst Takeo Doi argues that *amae* is the desire to merge with the other, as if still not an independent entity, and puts forward a theory of individuality that says that being an individual is to linguistically articulate oneself and one's desires. For Doi the ideal social relationship occurs when social expectations match the individual self-development. He claims that no Western equivalent term to *amae* exists and describes it therefore as unique Japanese emotional experience even though this natural symbiotic mother child bonding exists definitely also in Western societies. What is different is that in the West children are taught to develop their own personality, become independent and make decisions for themselves when they come out of age, whereas in Japan enmeshed family relationships, continued over-dependence on others, a father-less society syndrome and gender cleavage lead to continued dependence on the mother even after adolescence. Everything the mothers do is for the child and everything the child does reflects on the mother. According to Watanabe "the mother needs her child to be good in the eyes of the public, to save her face and prove her competence" (Watanabe, 1992, p.28). Too much *amae* and overde-pendence negate the child's own wishes and desires whereas lack of *amae* leads to emotional abandonment of children. In a negative pathological sense *amae* is the unwillingness to go or be allowed to go down the path to linguistic and mental individuation and self-hood. Sacrificing mothers who have lost their nat-ural sense of intuitive *amae* tend to have children with emotional problems.

The oppressed mother who either lives out her suffering without ever verba-lizing it or who becomes abusive to her child; the either spoiled or abused child; the either socially withdrawn or anti-social juvenile and the either emotionally absent or abusing husband are examples of either excessive or inhibited *amae*. The rise of eating disorders, child abuse and social withdrawal is the result of motherly restrained or inhibited *amae* as Watanabe (1992) puts it. In 2006 the Japan Times reported a national child abuse crisis in one of its editorials. News-paper ads of a crying child draw for the first time attention to an ugly reality no parent would ever have wanted to admit. How could it be that in a country va-lued for social harmony and goodwill dependence on others private, hidden sexual and physical violence against babies or even worse the failure to provide basic survival care such as food and daily meals to one's biological children made headlines in the news? After the 2004 revision of the child abuse preven-tion law the number of reported child abuse cases had increased from 12 000 cases (2004) to more than 40 000 reported cases in fiscal 2007. The increase in reported numbers and more proactive child protection policies reflect a heigh-tened sense of civic involvement and public concern (Goodman, 2001). The re-vision made it easier for anybody to notify police in case of suspected child abuse even if there was no concrete evidence. The increase in reported number is also due to a broader definition of what constitutes abuse. For example child-ren who are forced to witness their parents suffering intra-family or domestic vi-olence may also be considered to be indirect victims of witnessed psychological abuse and violence. Furthermore a revision to the operation policy for child consultation centers apparently led to a rise in reported cases because the revi-sion encouraged child consultation centers to not only take care of abused child-ren but also of their siblings by taking them into temporary custody. A lack of resources is partly responsible for enforcement flaws in the legal system: at present there are only about 2100 child welfare commissioners in the nation. Another alarming trend is the rise of abuse among very young parents who mar-ried out of convention after having conceived a child. *Dekichatta-kon*, a shotgun marriage induced by an unplanned, unexpected pregnancy, has become fairly common in Japan. Marrying out of social convention just because the woman has become pregnant can cause distress and frictions especially if social support systems such as a neighborhood or community network or family is lacking. Social isolation especially in urban centers where most abuse cases occur can increase the risks for abuse.

Hikikomori

Takeo Doi explains the prevalence of *hikikomori* as originating in the pathology of *amae* in terms of over-indulgence on the mother and atrophying paternal influence in nuclear family child pedagogy. *Hikikomori* are mostly young male people who keep staying indefinitely at home and lock themselves up in rooms. Their fathers are usually weak or absent from home. Those people do not know how to step out to society or school. They take power at home and intimidate their helpless mothers. Though acute social withdrawal in Japan appears to affect both genders equally, due to differing social expectations for maturing boys and girls, the most widely reported cases of *hikikomori* are from middle and upper middle class families whose sons, typically their eldest, refuse to leave the home, often after experiencing one or more traumatic episodes of social or academic failure. The problem is viewed as largely a family and social issue, caused in part by the interdependence of Japanese parents and children and the pressure on boys, eldest sons in particular, to excel in academics and in the corporate world (Zeilenziger, 2006).

The success of client centered therapy in Japan

In the early 70s Japanese psychologists got acquainted with Carl Rogers client centered therapy and since then this counseling approach has been the most popular approach in Japan besides traditional Freudian psychiatry and local therapies (Hayashi, 1998). The success of Carl Rogers's talk therapy has demonstrated that there is a strong individual desire and need for sharing one's innermost private issues with trained and competent mental health professionals. In fact every counseling process starts with an initial kick off voluntary decision to enter into contact with a helper at a given moment or time chosen by the client. Voicing feelings and thoughts through verbal or non-verbal communication to a counselor in a deep crisis represents the first step towards individuation, ego strength and freedom. The phenomenological theory offers both a holistic, tolerant and non-dogmatic approach to the understanding of human personality. Rogers has a humanistic and positive belief in personal human growth potential and assumes the purposeful meaningfulness of life. There will always be a tension or discrepancy between the existence, the now and future oriented meaning or aspiration between the current self and the ideal self. Existence does not exist for its own sake but is transcended by future oriented meaning, values, beliefs and goals. Becoming a mature and responsible, free person is the ultimate goal of personality development and in that sense it is non-conformist (Rogers, 1995).

The client centered theory builds on the five pillars of personality theory: structure, process, growth, psychopathology and change. From an overall perspective less attention is however given to structure and psychopathology for good reasons explained below in more detail.

Structural aspects

Personality and the universe have a common basic structure called organismic experiencing which encloses our biological, cognitive, emotional and behavioral aspects on one side and the self on the other side. The self is only the smaller conscious part of this bigger organism. The self-concept is as well a structure as a process. As a structure it very much shaped and molded by interactions with the environment. The theory lays the ground for a natural, actualizing tendency of the organism towards a higher interconnected and complex order, integration, autonomy and independence away from control by external forces. Mind and body are not separated in the thinking of Rogers.

Process

Rogers is more interested in the processes our self is going through than in the fixed structural aspects of the self. The main process describing human functioning is called self-actualization through which we are maintaining and enhancing our self-concept and our self-awareness. The need to preserve a congruent self-concept in relation to the environment and certain values, goals, ideals associated with self is crucial. Our self-concept is not static but open to change through experience. The need for positive regard influences the way we perceive ourselves and how we act. People try to behave in accordance with the self-concept they have of themselves. The theory is undermined by a belief that people are constantly in a process of becoming what they are already or have always been.

Growth and Development

Rogers acknowledges the significance of childhood experiences in shaping the personality and our self-regard. Society, culture and parents impose powerful conditions of worth on us which again influences our positive self-regard and self-esteem. Children who grow up in a fostering, non-invasive home develop better social skills and more self-esteem. As part of development towards adulthood it is important to value our own experiences independently of the valuation of others. Intrinsic motivation lays the path to growth. From a developmental perspective the phenomenological theory helps to identify minimum environmental parental and educational requirements needed for nurturing of high self-esteem, high self-consistency and positive self-regard in children.

Psychopathology

The phenomenological theory does not treat mentally ill people differently from healthy people. Rogers finds it a rewarding experience to learn from psychotic people. He is never giving up hope on them because even under the most adverse circumstances people are striving to become. There is no etiology for mental disorders in Roger's theory. Incongruence is a mismatch between actual experience and self-concept. The low self-concept and self-inconsistency becomes a barrier to recover from distress. Usually defense mechanisms like distortion and denial help to keep experiences out of awareness and avoid anxiety or other unpleasant feelings. In case of a psychosis the defense mechanisms have been overwhelmed and the person will have altered perceptions of reality, experience odd thinking, delusional beliefs or have inappropriate emotions or behavior. Rogers does not judge or label those people and in that sense his approach is truly accepting and understanding the client in his contradictory and ambivalent wholeness.

Change

Here again the process is more important than the structure. Change happens if the social, cultural and interpersonal context is warm, genuine, empathic, supportive and accepting. Understanding people permits them to change according to Rogers. This theory allows people to own their feelings, be different, contradictory or non-conform. Rogers's message is that not every other person must think, feel and behave the same way as one does. Diversity, pluralism and tolerance set the context for change and in that sense Rogers questions also the mainstream understanding of mental health care and political correctness.

The public reaction to suicide

Despite being one of the world's richest and most advanced countries and enjoying the highest life expectancy suicides surpassed 30 000 for the tenth straight year after a steep increase since 1998. Reacting to public pressure the government enacted for the first time a law on the prevention of suicide in 2006. Civil society groups such as Lifelink perceived the law as too weak and ineffective and took action on their own to address the problem in public and seek more effective prevention measures. Approximately 70% of the suicide victims have been elderly, unemployed males in the age range from 40 to 60. Many suicidal depressed Japanese men, afraid of being exposed as weak, either act without ever thinking of asking for help or just refrain from revealing their despair or troubled feelings to others. The media solely blame the economic pressure and globalization for the suicides but the fact that the suicide rate in times of postwar poverty was very low and did not fall despite a recent economic recovery turns the attention to other significant factors which play a part in a person's decision to choose death over life. Japan's high suicide rates are socially rooted in a denial complex preventing sufferers from asking for help, a cultural belief that regards suicide as a self chosen act of freedom, an inefficient mental health care system, poor community based prevention programs or mutual self help networks and the unavailability of proper medical treatment, rather than in the recent economic crisis. It is supposed that the higher the education and IQ levels of a person are, the bigger the risk becomes to commit suicide. An overeducated, over rational person is believed to lack self love.

The nonprofit organization Lifelink found that the top motive for suicide among people who left suicide notes when they took their lives was financial or living problems. The next two reasons were suffering from illness and family problems. The report shows that suicide is triggered by an average of four linked factors: depression, anxiety, family rifts and debt. By job status, the highest number of suicides occurred among the unemployed, followed by employed people, and then the self-employed. It was found that victims were exposed to multiple risk factors; only 4% were found to have committed suicide due to one single risk factor. The most common risk factor was depression, followed by family discord, debt, physical ailments, hardships of life, and relationships at work, changes in working environment, loss of job, poor business, and overwork. These 10 factors covered about 70% of all suicides. The risk factors were often tied together. A company employee's job transfer, for example, could lead to overwork and trouble in relationships with others at work, which in turn could lead to depression. In the case of business executives, poor business would lead to lifestyle hardships, which would lead to multiple debts and then depression. There were also other linked factors where the causal relationship remained unclear, such as bullying and loss of job, and the death of family members and alcohol problems.

The myth of honorability attached and social tolerance given to suicide needs further examination as it confuses more than it helps to explain the motives behind committing suicide. In his thoughts on 'Hagakure' Mishima argues that "suicide is the ultimate expression of free will in order to protect one's honor" (Mishima, 1978, p.46) but recognizes at the same time that "fate over which one has no control plays a part" (Mishima, 1978, p.103). The Samurai were not death prone as suggested by Mishima and suicide was only accepted in order to die for a great cause such as an ultimate protest against a big injustice of the Lord-master or as a protest act against fundamental immorality. The quasi suicidal *kamikaze* style death of Saigo Takamori in his fight against Meiji immorality might serve as ideal example. His death was not really an act of free will but he was coerced into this situation by reacting to the irresponsible action of others. In so far his suicide might be considered as involuntary death. Furthermore presuming that a true and real Samurai knew when it was right to die, his death had a social purpose and meaning as well. Nitobe notes that "to die for something which is not right is foolishness, not courage" (Nitobe, 2007, p.15). Seen from this perspective suicide cannot be seen as an isolated individual act but an act embedded in a social context. Mishima categorically negates the teleological approach of self-sacrifice for a higher cause:"we tend to suffer from the illusion that we are capable of dying for a theory or belief" (Mishima, 1978, p. 105). Ironically the author of 'Hagakure', Yamamoto who instilled the death drive in Mishima was convinced or prevented from committing suicide after the death of his master and died peacefully of natural causes. Even at that time when Samurai were prohibited by the Tokugawa rulers from changing their master dying without a deep reason or meaningful purpose was not accepted. The tragic failure of Mishima ending in his ritual suicide can be interpreted as an ultimately meaningless and even irresponsible act of desperate escape and extreme social isolation. His death cannot be conceived as a reactive protest and even less as an act of selflessness rooted in freedom. It was an act of pure self-destruction.

Mishima was right to criticize the modern society by accusing its moral decadence when he claims that "at the end of freedom is the fatigue and boredom of a welfare state" (Mishima, 1978, p. 25) but the conclusion he draws was utterly wrong and self deceptive when he says that the suppressed death impulse must eventually explode or that what matters is the "purity of action" (Mishima, 1978, p.104) of "how" one dies not "what for" one dies.

The suicide of a 62 year old Minister of Agriculture, Forestry and Fisheries who hanged himself in May 2007 hours before he was to face questioning in the Diet over a series of scandals underscores the fact that modern suicide is often neither honorable nor excusable but simply a socially coerced escape from accepting public responsibility. Nitobe calls this act foolish as it does not serve anybody or any cause. From an individual perspective this kind of suicide makes no sense and conveys no meaning. From a socially embedded perspective suicide is tragic because it is the irrational reaction of others that conditions one's own behavior in Japan. Bullying victims commit suicide because they feel abandoned. Suicide prevention is possible if society accepts individual failure or becomes more tolerant of individuals facing problems instead of putting a social stigma on them and offers a network of support to those who are exposed to risk factors. Motohashi et al (2004) who compared Western suicide prevention programs of the 80s conclude that

"The contents of these suicide prevention programs resemble one another since the causes of suicide are to be considered multi-factorial, including individual predisposition, mental disorders, socioeconomic factors, and family problems and social isolation. As a result, prevention programs targeting a single cause are not as effective" (Motohashi et al, 2004, p.4).

Ethnic identity confusion

In today's era of globalization the movement of people across borders is growing rapidly. In order to ensure equality, human rights and freedom for all there is a need to understand indigenous cultures and languages and to reexamine the concept of nation-states from a multicultural and diversity perspective with the goal of ensuring respect for all identities within the nation-state by establishing a balance among diverse cultural traditions and ethnic customs. On an intrapersonal, micro-level identity is to be seen as a social and cultural concept of belongingness and personhood. Adjusting to global phenomena without compromising on one's perceived core identity is a precondition for mental health. It is believed today that identity is not a fixed entity but an ever evolving situational category. Also how the process of identity formation is handled is seen as having important implications for later personality development. Identity problems encompass a variety of doubts about self-image and involve such issues as values, friendships, family, group loyalties and goals.

As Murphy-Shigematsu (2000) notes, the self-concept in Japan is highly responsive to group demands and being different or deviating from perceived group standards leads to social exclusion. Where demands for social conformity are high or a sense of self esteem is manipulated by external means the experienced antagonism between individual self and social self can lead to identity confusion–not knowing where one comes from, who one is or where one belongs to. Identity confusion is frequent among children, adolescents and adults of mixed origin who may feel pressured to accept wholesale a set of group values that may be unacceptable to them or disagree with a socially perceived standard of right and wrong.

Subtle disguised or unintentional racism conditioned by cultural stereotypes may worsen identity confusion. In a social setting of ethnic concealing of one's identity and unspoken agreement on cultural assumptions unintentional racism must be challenged either to become intentional or to work towards modifying attitudes and behaviors. A relativist cultural stance allows for a more balanced approach to solving or finding relief for an identity crisis. Multicultural counseling is aware of the influence of the dominant culture on minority individuals and accepts that depending on the cultural perspective from which a problem is considered, there can be several appropriate solutions. Furthermore a multicultural approach seeing and understanding the world from the subjective perspective of the other helps to understand that cultural differences and identities are positive attributes that offer new perspectives, add richness to relationships and society as a whole.

A monoculture focused construction of national identity formation relying on what separates people and nations works with static concepts: sometimes it is called blood purity, racial or genetic differences, sometimes national character, sometimes physical looks, language or simply *kokoro* what allegedly differentiates or separates the pure Japanese from the non-Japanese. Those concepts ignore that identity formation is an ever evolving process and that reality is not only given and conditioned by social norms but can also be reconstructed through active agency. The Japanese ethnic uniqueness claim has been described as myth and it is true that from a genetically, racial and ethnic viewpoint the Japanese uniqueness has never existed and the debate has been funneled to boost nationalist feelings and the spirit of togetherness and solidarity among the Japanese against alleged impure elements. In Japan ethnicity, education and identity have since long been narrowly connected. The official assumption has been that regardless of their ethnic background people from Okinawa, Ainu people, mixed Japanese, Japanese of Korean and Chinese descent and descendants of Japanese immigrants, so called *Nikeijin* share all the same identity and roots as the other

Japanese although for example for *Nikeijin* the state does not confer citizenship on them without going through the naturalization process whereas for example Ainu who are de-facto Japanese citizens consistently have claimed ethnic group and minority status. Only after public pressure did the government engage in a symbolic act of public relations and took action ahead of the G8 Hokkaido Summit in 2008 to recognize the ethnic indigenous status of the Ainu officially. Despite the symbolic gesture towards the Ainu the Japanese authorities are still sticking to a monocultural, assimilating approach when addressing minority issues instead of switching to a multicultural, integrative approach by accepting factual multiculturalism and co-existing identities (Lie, 2001).

A barbarian, as foreigners used to be called during the Tokugawa seclusion, is basically not belonging to the human race. When the author first came to Japan in 1989 he was told that Japanese would not regard foreigners as humans as long as they do not speak the Japanese language. The language barrier was a cultural barrier that kept people apart. Fortunately enough the author became proficient in Japanese and it allowed him to establish a real relationship with his parents in law and share his subjective world view with their subjective worldview. Language as a tool is no guarantee for mutual understanding but at least it creates opportunities for direct and authentic verbal communication.

For clinical psychologist Murphy-Shigematsu (2000) the secrecy surrounding non-Japanese who are assimilated and socially expected to conceal their ethnic identity is a "source of constant psychological stress" (2000, p.381) and prevents problems from being addressed in a suitable way. His clinical case example of a young female Korean-Japanese juvenile, with a Japanese mother and Korean father, who came for counseling because she was suffering from an identity crisis illustrates not only that social pressure to adjust to the dominant national culture exists but also confirms that identity formation is a ongoing never-ending process of influencing and being influenced. In this case the Korean-Japanese client suffers at first from having to conceal her real ethnic Korean identity in public but after having undergone therapy and having spent some time abroad she regains confidence in her and accepts herself as she is as a human being. She finds that under the new circumstances there is simply no need to reveal her second Korean name and concludes "Now that I am more strongly Korean (...) I don't need to use a Korean name (...) Nationality does not matter. What matters is how an individual thinks and acts in life" (Murphy-Shigematsu, 2000, p.380). Murphy-Shigematsu calls this process a successful narrative reconstruction of a new self despite the dysfunctional family setting and amidst a social environment rooted in a conspiracy of exclusion, silence and secrecy. He concludes that "minority individuals in Japan are likely to challenge the limitations of the social system by asserting their ethnic background" (Murphy-Shigematsu, 2000, p. 382). This challenge should by no means be viewed as something threatening or negative. What is interesting in this case is that the client through gaining inner strength, self-esteem and changing her self perceptions also redefines what it means to be Japanese in a globalized world. The implicit acceptance of her Korean part and statement that nationality does not matter reflects a truly global mindedness and sets in fact new borderless transcending norms. By openly exploring and reinforcing her individual ego strength and by becoming resistant to group conformity and manipulation attempts she has established and achieved a new sense of identity and psychological stability.

Violent anti-social behavior among juveniles and early adults

A personality disorder is an enduring pattern of personal experience and behavior that deviates noticeably from the expectations of the individual's culture, is pervasive and inflexible, has an onset in adolescence or early adulthood, is stable over time, and leads to personal distress or impairment. An anti-social personality disorder is characterized by a pattern of disregard for and violation of the rights of others. To qualify for such a diagnosis the symptoms by definition must begin before the age of 15.

The severity of symptoms of anti-social personality disorder can vary. People with this illness are likely to be irritable, egocentric and aggressive as well as irresponsible. They justify their behavior and project blame for their difficulties on others. They may have numerous somatic complaints and perhaps attempt suicide. Due to their manipulative tendencies, it is difficult to separate what they say about themselves that is true from what is not. People with this disorder lack secure and stable parenting and grew up in dysfunctional families with overburdened mothers and father who were unavailable. Therefore as children they failed to develop positive attachments with others. In Japan the terms *kireyasui* and *mukatsuku* are used to describe the instant and sudden bouts of rage and irritability towards others without a particular reason among mostly males (Tsuchiya et al, 2004).

In Japan there have been some spectacular cases of juveniles or young adults killing people–either family members, former schoolmates or just anyone–out of impulse and for no apparent reason. The most mediatized and shocking case is probably the murder of a boy in Kobe by another juvenile in the early 1990s (Smith, 2008). Although the number of violent crimes and murders committed by juveniles aged 14 to 19 has been on the decrease according to the statistics of the National Police Agency, the Diet enacted a package of new juvenile crime laws in 2007 that lowers the minimum age at which a child can be sent to a reformatory to "about 12". Social scientists have been trying to identify the patterns of deviancy such as family background, cultural patterns, mental health related issues or school problems to try to explain juvenile delinquency (Foltjanty-Jost, 2003). The lack of empirical criminological data might be due to the traditional cultural pattern of saving the face and not addressing embarrassing issues openly. It is worrying that the offending perpetrator gets more publicity, care, help and attention then the victim or the victim's family. The data lack might also be related to legal issues of informed consent and privacy protection. Furthermore it is not clear what causes actually violent or criminal anti-social behavior.

The following case study although not from Japan shows that anti-social behavior does not happen out of the blue or overnight but is the culmination of a long process of diverse influences and factors such as past child abuse, physical health condition, genetical dispositions, family background and socialization, socioeconomic status, cultural environment, previous medical evaluations and follow up treatments that lead to the development of a severe mental disorder or escalate eventually to an outburst of violent behavior. Generally speaking it seems that the absence of a local juvenile professional crime prevention and intervention network of social workers, child care centers, family and marriage therapists, school counselors and police will increase the risks of a sudden, unpredictable outbreak of indiscriminate violence. There is a need for more empirical case studies on juvenile crime behavior.

The Cho case

The clinical case study on Seung Hui Cho who suffered from a pervasive selective mutism disorder that led him to commit on April, 16 2007 the U.S. Virginia Tech killings of fellow students permits to elucidate some of the motives behind sudden outbursts of violent anti-social behavior among young males. Even though the crime did not happen in Japan the cultural, educational and social family background of the offender, the circumstances that surround the crime and the failures of the public care system to address the problems timely and in an efficient manner may be applied to the Japanese context as well.

Cho, a male, was born as second child in Korea on January 18, 1984 and migrated in 1992 with his family–father, mother and elder sister–to the U.S. for economic reasons. Cho was reported to be medically frail since early childhood due to a diagnosed defective heart condition. Selective Mutism as primary diagnosis which is a rare childhood disorder of shying public speech and in addition a major depression, single episode had been diagnosed for Cho in 1999. It is a separate, standalone and independent child disorder according to the DSM classification (American Psychiatric Association, 2000). Associations with other conditions like social phobia may however be possible and the question if selective mutism is related or not to other anxiety disorders is currently debated. If not properly treated at onset at early age the disorder may become pervasive and worsen. The rare disorder is also known in Japan (Suzuki, 2005). It is characterized by the following criteria: the failure to speak in public social situations is consistent whereas at home this does not apply for systematically. The disturbance does interfere severely with the developmental growth path to becoming a mature adult in later life and ability to develop social skills and competence patterns. The observed duration of the disorder must be longer than one month to rule out expected short-term shyness problems due to change of an environment. The failure to speak must not be induced by formal language comprehension difficulties or speech pathology or stuttering. The disorder is not better accounted for by a communicative disorder or a pervasive development disorder, schizophrenia or another psychotic disorder. The onset for selective mutism disorder is before the age of five years but in the case of Cho the diagnosis had been given only when he was already aged 15. The cure prognosis for this disorder is uncertain to very good at early detection and treatment. Most children do not simply grow out of the disorder. Excellent treatment results have been reported by administering psycho pharmaceutics, involving the parents proactively into the therapy process, by using play therapy, desensitization and stimulus fade techniques and by treating simultaneously existing marital issues or parental depression. If not detected or treated it can develop into the more serious violent prone anti-social personality disorder such as in the case of Cho.

Typical symptoms of selective mutism

Associated features and symptoms include pathological shyness, persistent anxiety, social isolation, depressed pessimism and goallessness in life. Cho had been taken for the first time to a psychiatric evaluation in June 1999 because he consistently had not spoken in public to others- peers, teachers, therapist- and even at home had restricted his verbal communication channel mainly to his sister. Specific presenting symptoms and their duration that justified a diagnosis and treatment were identified as follows: Cho did not express his feelings to anybody verbally; he avoided eye-contact; was extremely shy; did not speak to others in public and remained all times quiet; he was withdrawn and did not socialize with peers or go out; he had no friends; he did not join associations or clubs; he played and studied alone at home; he did not have real conversations with his parents; he did not socialize with friends or date women; he had never worked to earn money and he assumed no responsibilities at home; he appeared as being goal-less in his life when he changed his major suddenly and without reason from mathematics to English or engaged suddenly in poetry. Other symptoms that gradually intensified in the case of Cho were sadness, anger, disruptive behavior, stalking women, controlling and manipulative behavior patterns as well as manifest suicidal as well as homicidal thoughts. Cho had no previous recorded history of mental illness.

Social relations

There is no information available on any early reported childhood trauma or abuse except for the poor medical condition, the extreme reported shyness and the refusal or inability of talking/speaking to others. Due to his loner and socially withdrawn nature nobody of his classmates seems to have remembered Cho in Korea as if he had never existed. A class graduation picture of him was not available. In the US the Cho's lived an isolated social life and changed location several times to resettle. They were not fully integrated as others in the local Korean community. Cho did not develop any meaningful or long-lasting friendships within his community or with his various school classmates. A meaningful social life was inexistent. A note on bullying as possible root cause stressor after immigration to the US: Sometimes bullies pick on people who are disadvantaged by being new immigrants or are from a cultural minority group. Victims tend to be timid and, in the case of boys, tend to be physically weaker and less skilled than bullies. In Cho's case no evidence has been available to support that he had been systematically bullied even so he might have been teased occasionally.

Family history

Cho's early childhood in Korea seems not to have been untroubled and the family history reveals that his mother, a woman from a well educated family of landowners from the North who was ten years younger than her husband had been more or less forced into an arranged marriage with the father, a construction worker from a poor family in the South. After marriage and to make ends meet the father had been absent for a long period on work assignments overseas and the mother had often been alone at home. Arranged marriages - as opposed to western style love marriages - are the norm in many Asian countries and this reflects the influence of patriarchal thinking and traditional values. They offer seldom mutual individual satisfaction and are meant to fulfill the needs of both families. The mother seems to have been the primary care giver and bonding person to Cho in his early years. Cho did not talk much to her though and this had worried her and the family. It was learned later that the father had been reported as having always been negative towards Cho and never had been praising him. Cho's parents had always worked very hard day and night and this could have restricted their time for parenting and focusing more on the emotional needs of their children and especially Cho. A formal family history of mental illness could not be established and no records are available. As traditional Asians Cho's parents had put every effort and all their money into education and academic achievement of their two children. Cho's IQ had been reported as being over average and his academic grades had always been fair or good in Korea as well as in the US school system. Cho had always excelled in natural sciences and mathematics until the day he suddenly and without specific reason had changed his college graduation subject radically from math to English and thereby had put his graduation overall at risk. English skills were definitely not his strength. It was later learned that Cho had taken this move because he had been afraid of graduating and having to face the challenges of life and finding a job. In Asia more weight is put on natural science education as compared to humanities especially with regard to boys who have a higher social status than girls and are expected to work for the economic success of their family and nation. Cho's parents had not appreciated that Cho's sister had succeeded to graduate from

Princeton instead of Cho himself. Cho did not follow the path his parents had wished him to follow. A boy who does not succeed academically in Asia is a disappointment and shame for the whole family. Psychosocial and environmental problems and stressors that might have exacerbated Cho's mental health conditions are a family history of unstable marital parental relations and other stressors that had been reinforcing his existential anxiety and refusal to speak such as immigration stress, a possible unknown early childhood trauma or the cultural pressure to excel in academics and science education.

The failures of the system

In December 2005, two years before the killings, Cho had been assessed independently by two different professional mental health care providers: by one psychiatrist he had been assessed as being no danger to self or others and in no need of treatment, but before that another mental health professional had diagnosed Cho as being a serious danger to himself and to others needing urgent hospitalization and medical treatment. The inconsistency in diagnosis and assessment of two equally qualified and experienced professionals is surprising and the clear misevaluation by one of the two psychiatrists, who failed to protect Cho from himself and from the public, has contributed to the fatal outcome as shown later on. One of the failures of the public care system lies in the fact that the patient information, records and files relating to Cho's disorder had not been shared by the treating psychiatrists for reasons of legal patient privacy protection and professional negligence.

The fatherless society syndrome

In 1963 the German neo-Freudian psychiatrist Alexander Mitscherlich published a ground breaking study titled 'On the way towards the fatherless society' where he described the German after-war society where the father had lost his authority as a role model to his family and children. A role is described as an ideal to which people try to adhere in the making of the self and the positive identification with the father is a prerequisite for role modeling. Mitscherlich described after-war Germany as an authoritarian system preoccupied with negating the past war memories and maintaining law and order. The norms and values of the fundamentally pre-war authoritarian society had not really changed after the war and that was the reason why the youth rebellion took place in the 1960s. Some of the anti-order revolutionary attempts ended in violent acts of terrorism whereas the peaceful anti-establishment protest culminated in the birth of a new political party called the Green Party.

The after-war generation of fathers had not changed from the pre-war generation because their fathers had failed to symbolically acknowledge guilt, shame and grief for their victims and had such failed to be ideal role models to their sons. They were more "other-directed" than "inner-directed" (Riesman, 1950) in their norms and values and this prevented real democracy to emerge. Mitscherlich describes a free and open society as a society that allows for non-conformity, asking questions and being disobedient to negative authority. He paved the way for social protest and represented the spiritual values of the social movements that emerged later and may therefore be called the father of a new democratic and freedom oriented political culture in Germany that broke up with the past authoritarian, submissive and intolerant traits of Hitler's generation. At a time when Germans were still viewed as former enemies not to be trusted and the opposition against anything German was somehow strong a personal visit to the Mauthausen concentration camp in Austria and to the Hartheim castle where mentally ill had been mass murdered during the war triggered ambivalent feelings against Germans. Could the Germans of today be trusted? Could this horror happen again? Could history repeat itself under the same given circumstances? The author had decided to take up the challenge of confronting his views on Germany by studying social sciences in Germany, a country he had criticized but also admired in many ways. The university years in Germany proofed to become a fruitful and enriching personal life experience. Being directly exposed to a culture perceived as frightening, strange and distant helped overcoming prejudices and feelings of animosity. The author experienced a new generation of sensitive and global minded Germans who had grown out from a culture of authoritarian thinking into a culture of positive regard and concern for world peace, the environment, foreign cultures and democracy.

The Germans and Japanese have accepted individual guilt and shame for their wrongdoings to different degrees. What differentiates Germany from Japan is that the painful reconciliation with the past and the after war fatherless society crisis prompted a new political culture paradigm symbolized by the four famous value pillars of the Green Party: ecology, social justice, direct democracy and non-violence. This paradigm change has not occurred to the same degree in Japan for reasons stated previously and Japan is still struggling with fully coming to terms with itself and liberating itself from negative past memories in a positive and forward-looking way.

Mitscherlich, a trained psychiatrist, highlights in his study the often difficult and painful relationship between father and son in the modern mass society where the father is alienated from his family, his home, his community, religion and work. The oedipal conflict characterizes the fundamental conflict between son and father in the Western Christian patriarchal model. From a developmental human growth perspective an ambivalent process of differentiation and identification of the child is necessary on his way to later independence and adulthood. In Japan the father has been the pillar of patriarchal society until pre-war. He had unspoken authority over the household and he used his authority for the sake of preserving the family unity. The mother had to fulfill strict responsibilities inside the home and submit to the authority of the father. The children feared the physical presence of the father more than they loved or respected him. He embodied more authoritarian features than positive authority.

In the after-war period the father became physically absent from home and gradually lost his former place and status at home. His role as authority figure and identification symbol blurred and faded away. The biological and emotional bonds to the children severed. In a recent nostalgic advertisement of the Japan Ad Council the loss of the father-son bond is deplored under the heading 'Returning to the way we were':

> "The popular comic strip *Sanchome-no Yuhi* depicted life in Japan in the 1950s. It captured a time when we learned from our fathers, who were our role models. The people around us-our older brothers, even the elderly woman next door- taught us lessons about life. We may have been poor, but we felt a strong connection to one another. Today, it seems we are losing the valuable relationships we felt back then (...)"

After the war the socio economic changes caused a profound change in the family structure and women's social status. The father was physically and emotionally alienated from his family and sacrificed his life for his company instead. The company family system had replaced the traditional household structure as basic social unit. The *tanshin funin* system that consisted in dispatching salaried workers to different work locations kept fathers on purpose separate from their biological families to channel all their energies to the company and economic reconstruction of the country. The mother had to feed, educate, raise the children and play the symbolic father role. Many of them suffered nervous breakdowns, became hysteric or in the worst case became violent against their own children. The toll taken on the family in terms of mental health has been considerable in the 50s, 60s and 70s. As Tamura (2001) concludes the father could neither be an authority role model nor a friend to his children. He simply did not exist in their eyes.

In modern society there has been a shift from a vertical authority directed behavior towards vertical other-directed more conformist behavior styles (Riesman, 1950). Clinical psychologists have noted the rise of a peer-based self in Japan whose identity is shattered and emotionally distressed because it does neither attach to familial and filial value systems nor inner directed convictions or principles. Peer directed education coerces children to orient their behavior towards others and adjust to their standards. Whereas in Germany the teenagers revolted symbolically against their fathers which according to the developmental stages described by psychoanalyst Erik Eriksson can be viewed as a necessary step towards independence and maturity, the revolt took not place in Japan as the fathers were physically and emotionally absent. Adolescence is not a marked transition as in other industrialized countries and despite gender equality the women did not seek more equality and rights but rather preferred to stay dependent economically and emotionally on the male earners. Unless in the West where the son tries to detach himself from the mother, the strong unique and lasting mother son relationship in Japan has prevented men from making the necessary step to a mature male adulthood and some studies suggest that failed relationships between mother and their sons may explain why sons suddenly turn violent against the person they are most attached too. Is there any correlation between excessive mother attachment and male juvenile crime propensity? Tamura maintains that dysfunctionalities in family and society may be responsible for these violent outbreaks:

> "The identified adolescent has a symbiotic relationship with his/her mother. Most fathers of these cases have been absent because of, for example, work commitment, marital conflict or difficult in-law relationships. They could not function as the third person and intervene with the mother-child relationship. This also created difficulties for the child to form personal relationships with people outside the family. It is very interesting that they may not have problems before puberty, but as they get into the adolescent age, their relationships with friends suddenly become difficult. They become self-conscious, and the ambivalence of the sense of being accepted and the fear of rejection become an important issue. Those adolescents who have close relationship with their mothers and distant relationship with their fathers cannot regulate the distance with other people. Often they have this omnipotent illusion that their close friend can fulfill all their needs like their mothers" (Tamura, 2001).

The father-son role identification model Freud described for early childhood development might still be of use today. A positive symbolic identification with a father ideal is a prerequisite for healthy mental development and non-violent behavior. Supportive fathers and mothers are those who set boundaries, exercise respectful authority, challenge others, care for others, accept disagreement without punishing, respect autonomy and show open affection to others.

The absence of paternal authority does not stop in family settings. In fact many other social agents like teachers or policemen not only fail to exercise their paternal authority and responsibility but engage themselves in acts that are contrary to their professional duties and constitute a blunt breach of ethical standards. The ability to act as a role model has failed in their case too. Many elderly people complain that the younger generation does have bad manners, sitting around on the street, eating in trains, putting make up. As shown above it is not the young, who are to be blamed but in fact the adults who have a role model responsibility they do not fulfill. The new mobile phone subculture has itself contributed largely to the deterioration of social forms and manners. Teenagers and children have lost their ability to communicate and exchange meaningful conversations. The rate of internet/e-mail related cyber crimes has shocked many but is only a symptom of the deeper cultural malaise of being unable to express feelings and thoughts through verbal communication means. It is regrettable that language itself has lost its role as identity tool and that more and more crap vocabulary is integrated in the language. The speaking and writing ability among juveniles has diminished dramatically as a result.

The dangers of psychological self-negation

The term new religions is often used to refer either to fraudulent, bizarre or violent cults. Its original use was to categorize organized religions other than Christianity, Shinto and Buddhism. Most of these religions began as offshoots of the main organizations and adopted some of their elements. Two of the biggest existing lay organizations are associated with the *Nichiren* sect of Buddhism which used to be the former quasi official state religion under Tokugawa ruler ship: the *Soka Gakkai* or Creative Education Society in English, which has more than 17 million members and the *Rissho Koseikai* or Society for Establishment of Righteousness and Personal Perfection through Fellowship in English, with about 7 million members. *Soka Gakkai* has long been associated with the influential *Komeito* political party and supports the party financially as well as morally.

The Aum case

The cult that has received most attention since the mid 1990s is Aum Shinrikyo or Aum Supreme Truth in English, responsible for a series of kidnappings and murders that culminated in the sarin gas attack on a Tokyo subway in 1995 which killed 12 and injured over 5000 passengers. Cult members used truth drugs, sleep deprivation, kidnapping, murder and countless business fronts to keep followers in line and amass huge amounts of money. The activities and ideological foundations of the occult cult turned violent have been well documented (Murakami, 2002; Reader, 2000; Hardacre 2003; Clarke 2006; Maekawa 2001). In his study Clarke (2006) concludes that the cult, which counted 10 000 registered members in Japan as well as 30 000 overseas with a focus on Russia, attracted highly intelligent brilliant people who lacked however an intense emotional life, compassion and social skills. Maekawa (2001) observes that the offenders sentenced in the Aum trials had never shown any real remorse or repentance towards the victim's families. Their inability to feel pain or empathy with the victims makes them look as not belonging to the human family. One of the mysteries of Aum remains what made the members subject themselves voluntarily and blindly to somebody without thinking or reflecting on what they were asked to do. It is striking to observe the lack of common sense, life principles, norms or ethical standards that would act as a barrier or prevent people from doing morally and legally wrongful things. One of the attractions of the new religions is said to be the sense of community they give to people who lack the mental and spiritual support historically provided by the extended family, the local community, and the traditional religions. Sects do appeal to people because of their simplistic messages promising happiness and a meaningful life fulfillment. Such messages may be disguised as peace for the world, inner harmony or authentic self-transformation. Maekawa (2001) examines in her paper the quest for self-negation of Aum cult members that turned ultimately in anti-social behavior, violence and destruction. The de-humanization of the followers, who lived completely withdrawn in an artificial world, explains why it was possible for the cult to achieve such a high level of mind control and obedience. According to Maekawa (2001) all lives were regarded as nothing but "energy bodies", indistinct of personal features or characteristics from each other. Human relationships if existing at all were reduced to the technical or formal exchange of energy. She characterizes the guru-disciple relationship as it-it relationship to highlight the distance and alienation between humans. Maekawa (2001) cautions that the Aum problems reflects also on a society that created the conditions for such an evil cult to spread. Media, the state and the public at large had failed long before the outburst of violence in 1995 to take action against the morally and legally dubious methods employed by the cult to purchase land, attract new members, boost its public image or be incorporated as a religious body. The spiritual leader of the cult Chizuo Matsumoto has never accepted any personal guilt or responsibility for his murderous acts despite being sentenced to death and awaiting his execution since.

The social reaction to the illness of Princess Masako
   In 2007 a book published by an Australian journalist caused an unprecedented uproar in Japan because it asks and answers many questions which can never be raised in Japan because of the reverence in which the emperor and his family are held. The fuss made about the book gave it probably more publicity than it deserved based on its ungrounded speculations, pointless revelations and contents. Masako has been absent from most of her official duties for five years due to her alleged illness which was publicly announced as unspecified adjustment disorder. Others, including the Australian journalist, believe that she is suffering rather from a severe depression caused by various external stress factors such as the pressure to bear a male heir to the throne, be a good wife to the Crown Prince and wise mother to her daughter and the pressure to fulfill public duties and conform to the protocol.

One of the problems is that depression as an illness is very badly understood by normal Japanese. People see it, mistakenly, as something to fight hard to overcome, so any failure to do so is seen as a failure of the spirit. Regardless of the controversy regarding her accurate diagnosis, the Princess reappeared all smiles in the public again in late 2008 to meet and socialize with foreign dignitaries. The media who sympathized initially with her illness have in the meantime turned against her and accuse her of faking her condition and enjoying herself in private on the back of taxpayers. The Imperial Household Agency has been trying hard to keep it a low profile issue and divert the topic from the public eyes and ears. The secrecy that is upheld about her mental state of mind and wellbeing has spurred a very aggressive and feisty tabloid media campaign accusing the Imperial Household Agency of withholding the facts and misguiding the public.

In a column for the Mainichi Shimbun the psychiatrist Tamaki Saito pretends that the social reaction to the disorder of Princess Masako is grounded in the belief that members of the Imperial Family are not allowed to experience the same problems than ordinary human beings and that behind this belief lies a deep desire to project one's dependence on others. According to him it is no coincidence that the motives behind crushing the February 26 military rebellion and Coup d'état in 1936 have been as controversial as the secrecy that has been uphold around the problems of Princess Masako. Japanese children are taught at school that emperor Hirohito was personally a good willed emperor who was manipulated by the military caste (Crome, 1998). His image has however been tainted by his role and personal involvement in crushing down the rebellion of young officers as well as his other war related acts such as having personally approved the war brothels. In a note left behind by army officer Asaichi Isobe, who was executed for his commitment in the February 26 incident in 1936, he stated his honest loyalty to the same emperor. Isobe was one of the young imperial officers influenced by the rightist Ikki Kita who aimed at suspending the constitution; dissolve both houses of the Diet and place the entire nation under martial law.

The benign trust put forward in the person of the emperor was deceived by the same emperor who regarded the young officers as enemies of the state and gave the personal order to crush the rebellion with determination and in cold blood. His grave decision to evict the lives of misled and mistaken, immature young soldiers has been severely criticized later on when more facts came to be known. Mishima was greatly fascinated and expressed sympathy with the spirit of the rebellious officers. In 1966, he wrote the novel 'The voices of heroic dead' to denounce Hirohito for renouncing his divinity after the war and having betrayed the young rebellious officers. The voice he mentions in a passage is said to be that of Isobe's sprit who was in despair that the emperor had refuted their cause and wondered why the God-Emperor did descend himself to a mere human? The 'why did you become a mere human' resonates with the criticism against Crown Princess Masako that she were not permitted to become ill like anyone else, considering her position.

According to Saito the psychiatrist Hisao Nakai proposed the monarch-subject malignity complex in discussing emperor Showa. This concept shows how adoration toward the emperor transforms into hatred against his aides, just like disgust to one's father can easily transform into affection to one's grandfather. This sentiment is sometimes expressed in the form of criticism of the Imperial Household Agency, but it has once been a serious factor of political instability. The note of Asaichi Isobe can be said to be a typical monarch-subject malignity complex. The common tendency here is that they regard the emperor as if he were an immaculate and hollow being where they desire to project their own ideals. The same desire can be seen in Mishima. Just as Nakai used the word grandfather instead of god, the emperor has an amiable makeup as if he were a member of our family. That is why people experience some kind of narcissistic dependence. The domestic-violence-like nuance of the suicide of Mishima is not much different from this violence rooted in dependence. The illness of the Crown Princess reveals that there are still so many people who want the emperor to stand somewhere between god and human.

Chapter Three.

Ecological utopia

The chapter discusses and questions the technology solution oriented focus and voluntary commitment approach taken by Japan. Learning from ecological lifestyle and practices in the Edo period opens a path for alternatives to the current patterns of mass consumption and over affluence. The chapter argues that more vigorous public political involvement and participation from environmental NGOs and NPOs will open the doors for a new post-Kyoto ecological vision.

From the pre-Meiji discourse of peace with nature to the post-Meiji exploitation

Human life as we know it faces an environmental crises of monumental proportions. Clear evidence includes the complex and controversial effects of global warming, depletion of energy sources, soil contamination, pesticides and pollution by agricultural chemical fertilizers, pollution from asbestos and dioxin, sea land reclamation projects, dam, tunnel, road and bridge construction projects, crises in waste management, degradation in air quality, rampant deforestation, lack of safe drinking water, exploitation and extinction of animal species, rampant noise pollution and serious doubts regarding the preservation of a sufficient quality of life. The underlying causes for the environmental degradation of today are overconsumption and pollution grounded in human ill-behavior. Japan has undergone a radical transformation in its way of living from a basically pre-Meiji ecological ethical wisdom and nature protection to a post-Meiji utilitarian submission and exploitation of nature (Barrett, 2005; Schreurs, 2004; Palmer, 2001).

It is believed that originally the Japanese language had no word for nature because people considered themselves to be an intimate but integral part of nature that could not be separated from their being. The nature in Japan used to be regarded as a blessing and sacred encompassing forests, mountains, lakes or the sea. In Shinto most of the Gods are related to nature. Technology and science had a human face: one example is *wasan*, a type of mathematics developed in the Edo era that resembles more to art and play. Another example is the unique traditional technology for producing steel or agriculture without chemical fertilizers. The well-known painter Kai Higashiyama has eternalized the innocent wild beauty of nature in his acclaimed paintings.

Japanese used to respect and leave in peace with nature and the native religion Shinto is a kind of ritual to worship the wild beauty of nature. Later on the axial religions and philosophers such as Confucius and Buddha hailed an ap-

proach of living in peaceful coexistence with nature and environment. The hu-
man-nature analogues in the early Confucian texts compare natural elements and
good moral behavior (Tucker et al, 1998). Those who are wise are thought to be
similar to the natural flow of water and those who are good are thought to be
similar to a mountain. Nature and ethical thinking are seen as being identical and
this holistic view contrasts with western dual thinking. A dual concept of culture
versus nature or economy versus ecology could not manifest itself as it had done
in the West where nature has been subject to early radical human intervention
and remodeling. In Japan the boundaries between culture and nature have been
fluid and it is believed that nature and culture could not be clearly separated. The
traditional way of living has always been very natural in the sense that man and
nature coexisted side by side. In traditional thinking there is no symbolic or real
separation between man and nature.

During the closure of the country international trade was restricted and the
shogunate had to supply food, water and energy for thirty million inhabitants by
relying on domestic resources. Under those restricted conditions the population
was kept constant and a sustainable lifestyle could be achieved. Forests were
soundly managed to preserve woods as a renewable resource; sewage and night
soil were recycled into organic fertilizers for rice and vegetable fields. Paper,
clothes, ceramics were reused as well. Waste wax, oil and metals were collected
and reprocessed. Edo was a low or zero emission society and environmental
pollution incidents were at pre-industrial levels. Many of the Samurai used to
live simple, frugal and ascetic lives (Mishima, 1978).

During Japan's self chosen closure and isolation from the rest of the world
Confucian, Buddhist and Shinto thinkers excelled in environmentally sound
ethical thinking reflected in original theories and principles of moral behavior
towards nature. A shared theme that appeared in their thinking is the interaction
of nature and humans in a state of mutual reciprocity and not antagonism (Tucker et al, 1998). Kaibara Ekken (1630-1714) is believed to be one of the early
Confucian conservationists. His thought can be described as a naturalist religios-
ity rooted in profound reverence and gratitude toward Heaven as the source of
life and earth as the sustainer of life. He felt that by recognizing one's debt to
these great parents, human beings activated a cosmic filiality toward all living
things. This idea of filiality implied that one should preserve nature, not destroy
it. The highest form of filiality was humaneness called *jen or jin*, through which
humans formed an identity with all things. Baigan Ishida (1685-1744) proposed
a theory concerning frugality and how merchants should act. Kyoto was the
cradle of *Shingaku*, a code of practical ethics that in direct translation means
"the school or science of the heart". It was originally formulated as a theory of
moral education by Baigan Ishida. The name *Shingaku* was a happy choice, as it
carries the connotation of a respect for learning and a strong resonance with the
feeling and thought of the people. *Shingaku* was originally and essentially a
philosophy for merchants. It told merchants to make profits, with the under-

standing this will work to the benefit of the people and society. It told the merchants that they should think not only about their own gain; rather, the transaction must benefit both parties. Both must gain. The important premise is that continuation in business is essential for any accumulation of substantial profit. If a business is to continue to make profits, then its transactions must lead to profit for its customers as well as itself. *Shingaku* is simple and practical in concept. It does not attempt to impose ethical behavior by spiritual or moral strictures, but rather by the strictures of reality. Ando Shoeki (1703-1763), a philosopher and physician may be considered one of the early agrarian reformers who build his theory upon a belief in the ancient communal oneness of man and nature as embodied by the true way of Shinto. He advocated land reform, and required that the circulation of money be stopped. Finally, Norinaga Motoori (1730-1801), a Kyoto physician and scholar stressed the idea of *mononoaware* (to feel an empathy toward things), which expresses a Japanese view of nature. It is the capacity to experience the objective world in a direct and unmediated fashion, to understand sympathetically the objects and the natural world around one without resorting to language or other mediators. The Japanese could understand the world directly in identifying themselves with that world; in addition, the Japanese could use language to directly express that connection to the world.

The Meiji restoration changed the patterns of traditional lifestyle radically. Western utilitarianism and pragmatism replaced ecological, holistic thinking and meat consumption replaced the vegetarian food culture. Cars appeared on the street, railroads and streets were built and the electrification of the country was initiated. The crusade against Ainu culture and their forced assimilation from hunting and fishing to the Japanese lifestyle was the most symbolic act of giving absolute precedence to economy over ecology. According to Walker (2005) American expatriates introduced strychnine to Hokkaido to exterminate wolves so that horse breeding and other agricultural development could become feasible. The brown bear which is the ultimate symbol of ecological Ainu wisdom and culture became the preferred target of Japanese mainland colonization and modernization (Knight, 2003). Nature became more and more a commodity and means to an end instead of being preserved worshipped or simply enjoyed per se. The herring industry in Hokkaido is a good example of transformation of a natural dietary and abundant food resource and source of valuable protein into an artificial mass fertilizer for agricultural production increase. By 1955 the herring had been exterminated in Hokkaido due to overfishing and the industrial-commercial over usage. Another example is the replacement of natural virgin forests by timber forests. The gradual eradication of the black bear can be traced to excessive human timber forestry activity.

Historic phases of pollution

There are three distinctive phases of pollution: the first phase happened be-

tween 1880 and 1900 and can be traced back to the hazardous waste generated
by copper mining especially the notorious Ashio copper poison mass pollution
case dating back to 1878 when Japan attempted ruthlessly to catch up with and
copy Western style imperialism and militarism on the back of nature and human
health and safety. The disaster created a mass movement against private and governmental irresponsibility led by Japan's first ecological activist and thinker
Shozo Tanaka (1841-1913). In his desperation Shozo Tanaka had tried in 1901
to personally appeal to the emperor to bring the copper mine poisonings into
public view and stop operations in Ashio. To show his opposition to government
plans he moved to a village called Yanaka that was later to be destroyed to serve
as a huge water reservoir. Aritomo Yamagata, who aimed at the expansion of the
military-bureaucratic cliques, attempted to pass a tax increase bill in view of the
Russo-Japanese War. Instead, he passed a bill which allowed the Diet members
to receive 2.5 times of their annual salary. Shozo refused to receive the salary
and reaffirmed his determination to fight with the farmers. He also developed an
original ecological theory that was critical of modern industrialization and had
advanced ideas on an alternative constitution as well (George, 2005). The public
sphere and private interests prevailed finally in maintaining operations at Ashio
despite the massive and long-lasting heavy pollution impact on local farming
communities for the sake of national industrial development. It took the bureaucrats and the private mine owners almost 100 years to pay some credible compensation amounts for the huge damage caused to the local farmers. Nevertheless despite the formal settlement the long-lasting fallout of past mistakes will
create a risk hazard for decades to come. The long-term risks are still today real
as Shoji and Sugai notice in their study on the Ashio pollution:"(…) there exist
today very real possibilities of disaster should one or more of the slag accumulation basins collapse and be washed or moved into the river systems" (Shoji et al,
1992, p.61). The full restoration of natural surroundings in Ashio to its original
status before it was destroyed will be a huge task as well.

The second phase occurred between 1910 and 1920 when water pollution by
factories became a problem and the third phase covers the 1960s when Japan
underwent a rapid industrial economic growth. As a result of uncontrolled heavy
industrialization water, soil and air pollution became a large problem affecting
the health and even lives of citizens directly. The alienation between man and
nature reached a tragic peak with the Minamata disease in 1953 and it took a
ruling of the Supreme Court of Justice in 2004 to recognize the administrative
responsibility of the national government and the local prefecture for this unique
human disaster, the *Itai-Itai* disease outbreak and the asthma cases in Yokkaichi
city. At the same time commercial-industrial fishing led almost to the quasi ex-
termination of the world's fishing population. The enormous damage done by
industrial-commercial mass fishing to shrimps, salmon, whaling and blue tuna
reserves is well known. Due to the commercial mass fishing by Japanese industrial vessels blue tuna has almost disappeared from the world map. In the case of
whaling Japan has failed to acknowledge that the industrial-commercial mass

killing of whales amounts to an environmental crime and has nothing to do with preserving traditional food culture, which serves as a pretext to protect a specific lobby and industry (Hirata, 2005). By the way, the only ones who really deserve hunting and killing whales in limited numbers are the local coastal fishermen, who consume whale meat for their immediate self sufficiency needs. Local food self sufficiency does not require the industrial mass killing of thousands of mammal species in far and remote territories.

Despite the ongoing global ecological crisis economic expansion and industrial competitiveness have remained unchanged key drivers. The pollution that has occurred is a result of the priority placed on uncontrolled rapid industrial induced growth, the unwillingness to prevent or punish bad environmental behavior or give citizens effective rights to sue irresponsible governments or private corporations in civil courts and failing to implement minimum standards to protect citizen's health and safety.

What is new about the current environmental issues of global concern is that the pollution problem in the advanced economies has shifted from the tangible, direct industrial materials pollution to a more indirect, intangible and invisible emissions pollution and from private companies to private consumers. The carbon emissions problem is essentially an energy problem and the private car driver who carelessly consumes underpriced energy by fueling his car with fossil conventional gasoline not only contributes to the worsening of the national balance of emissions but also endangers the public health of his fellow citizens by causing accidents, noise pollution and emitting other toxic emissions or dust particles. It is a distinctive feature of energy consumption that the ratio of electricity consumption to the total primary energy supply has grown from 25% in 1970 to almost 50% over the last 38 years. This trend is expected to continue if no decisive action is taken. The millions of electrical appliances such as microwaves, color televisions and air conditioners do harm the environment and this problem cannot be solved by increasing the carbon productivity–the amount of GDP produced per ton of CO_2 equivalents emitted into the atmosphere.

The government, who has launched by itself the '3R' initiative standing for reuse, recycle, reduce, backs back when it comes to asking the public to reduce private electricity consumption radically. As a result of careless fossil, non-renewable and underpriced energy consumption patterns Japan's greenhouse gas emissions have persisted on a historically unprecedented very high stable level over the last 16 years. According to the latest data for fiscal 2007 through March 2008 the emissions amounted to a record 1.37 billion tons worth of carbon dioxide, 8.7% above the fiscal 1990 level of 1.27 billion tons, the benchmark year of the Kyoto Protocol, the Environment Ministry reported in November 2008.

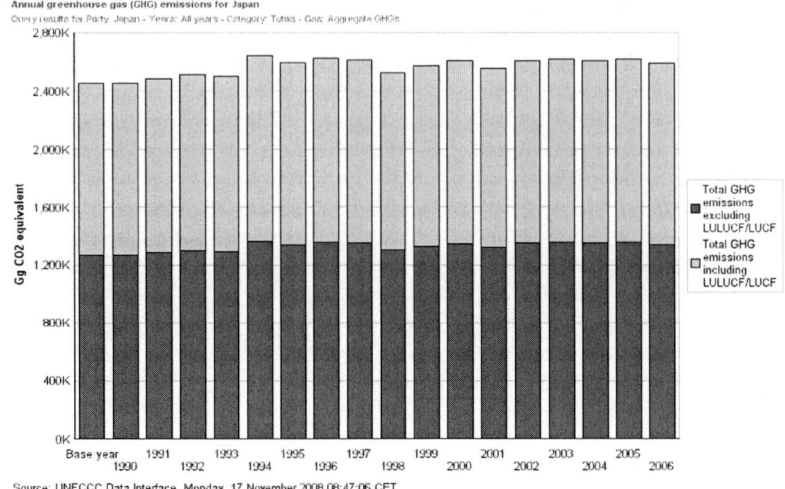

Source: UNFCCC Data Interface, Monday, 17 November 2008 08:47:06 CET

Graph 3-1: Japan's total greenhouse gas emissions from 1990 to 2006. Source: UN Framework Convention on Climate Change (UNFCCC) http://unfccc.int

In its environmental outlook to 2030 report the OECD has identified the "fears of impact on industrial competiveness" and "the under pricing of natural (non-renewable, PH) resources use and pollution" (OECD, 2008, p.11) as two among four of the major obstacles that have prevented radical change to more environmentally sustainable policies. Japan is no exception to pursuing a policy of under pricing fossil energies for the alleged sake of competiveness. In a semi-official document on energy issues to face the energy challenge the Energy Conservation Center of Japan recommends that Japan's high energy prices must be reduced to enhance the international competiveness of its industries. The future social and economic damage, burden and cost incurred by not taking drastic action for the environment now makes it imperative to review current ineffective policies according to the OECD:

> "We need forward-looking policies today to avoid the high costs of inaction or delayed action over the longer term" (OECD, 2008, p.8).

Japan has still not removed obstacles concurrent to irrational fear of loss of competitiveness, fully committed itself to setting and implementing targets, taken action to fully enforce the polluter pays principle and charge the total hidden social and ecological cost of nuclear power, private transport, land consumption or industrial growth.

The pricing or cost factoring of the damaging externalities of growth such as ozone depletion, global warming, transport damage to health and environment, fallout of agricultural pesticides, food disposal, forest depletion, species extinction, waste disposal, water or air pollution needs to appear in balance sheets and accounting registers. As long as the electricity tariff does not reflect the real cost impact on the environment in terms of carbon emissions consumption patterns will not change. As long as no carbon tax is levied on gasoline to reflect its impact on carbon emissions consumers will have no reason or incentive to change their lifestyle habits. It is up to the public sphere–especially NGOs and parliaments–to take decisive long-term action for the environment against the short-term thinking of private self-interests, unchanged consumer habits and government indecisiveness. Long-term, forward looking policies require huge changes in the way of thinking of modern societies and a review of basic economic concepts such as production, consumption, resource or productivity. Economists such E.F. Schumacher author of 'Small is beautiful' who defended a lifestyle based on self-sufficiency, J.K. Galbraith who in his book 'The affluent society' claims that modern economies because they rely on principles formulated in a pre-modern era of material poverty and scarcity continue relentlessly to produce more than can be consumed and Lewis Mumford who asserted that what matters about an economy is not the quantity of goods produced or consumed but the ratio of consumption to creativity with restriction of consumption being one of the preconditions for a more creative lifestyle. Alternatives have been worked out but Japan in concert with many OECD States still sticks to the old linear economic model of quantitative growth and more consumption for the sake of consumption.

The potentially future high costs of delayed action mentioned by the OECD are more than obvious in Japan's case: subsequent governments have ignored the potential of renewable energies for decades and therefore keeping the energy self-sufficiency at a very low level (4%) compared to other countries, refrained from creating public awareness for the scarcity of finite fossil energies such as oil, coal and natural gas and pushed relentlessly for the nuclear option. Policies to implement a strict polluter pays principle either in form of a carbon tax or as mandatory carbon trading system principle have been delayed as well; no radical action has been taken to reduce waste at its source or drastically reduce the huge per capita ecological footprint on nature and land. Omitting to take necessary action at the right time is as bad as taking wrong actions or insufficient actions.

The waste and packaging problem

The total output of waste has grown steadily since 1975 to 470 million tons in 2007 despite an array of environmental laws and regulations put into place starting as early as the 1950s. Japan lags behind when it comes to an ecologically viable resource protection and usage. The over usage of plastic and paper for packaging is one extreme example of resource and energy waste. Statistically packaging is a big business in Japan. According to the Japan Packaging Institute the shipment value of packaging materials in 2006 was almost 6 000 billion Yen, a slight increase over 2005. The industry accounts for 1.3% of Japan's GDP. More than 30 billion plastic bags are consumed a year. The 52.7 million tons (2005) of general waste respectively 421.7 million tons of industrial waste (2005) consumed each year do little to help keep landfills empty or waste incinerators at standstill. Due to lack of space 75% of the waste is burnt. Waste incineration occurs in highly populated areas and this adds to immediate health risks due to the emitting of toxins and furans and even chlorine that may cause gender related genetic changes. Public protest against building new municipal incinerators has been virulent. Plastic bags and disposable cup noodle pose a serious threat to wildlife in the seas. Besides plastics paper also plays a large role in the packaging process and while biodegradable and recyclable it is not without ecological implications. Paper bags require more energy not only to create but also to recycle than plastic and also contribute to the destruction of forests. In order to cut down the huge volume of waste a law promoting the recycling of containers and packaging came fully into force in 2000. In 2001 a law promoting green purchasing which makes it compulsory for the central government and related organizations to procure eco-friendly products and services went into effect. The scope of recycling has expanded with the introduction of laws such as the Household Electric Appliance Law (2001) which makes the recycling of televisions, refrigerators, washing machines and air conditioners obligatory; the Food Recycling Law (2001) to prevent food from being thrown away; the Construction materials Recycling Law (2002); the Personnel Computer Recycling Law (2003) and the Automobile Recycling Law (2005). In 2007 a law took effect that promotes the effective use of resources. It is also called the '3R' law. Japan has been very eager in making efforts towards garbage separation, recycling and reuse but when it comes to waste reduction and garbage prevention the balance sheet looks less impressive. Municipalities apply differing policies when it comes to garbage separation and garbage collection. Some require no separation at all. One recent trend among some local municipalities has consisted of applying the polluter pays principle to private households and oblige citizens to pay for recycled garbage bags. It is a step in the right direction.

Energy conservation and new energy

Japan is known to be largely behind its Kyoto emission curbing commitments and continues to rely on an overdue linear economic model of carbon emissions and overconsumption of natural and energy resources. Since the first oil crisis Japan has achieved significant breakthroughs in energy conservation technologies. The Energy Conservation Law came into force in 1979 providing the legal basis for energy conservation activities. The Energy Conservation Center, a governmental corporation, was established in 1978 to support and promote energy conservation measures. Despite ever-growing final energy consumption Japan regards itself -on the input side and in terms of primary energy supply per GDP- as very energy efficient country. That means that the running cost is kept low thanks to highly intelligent and efficient technical systems and technologies. The incentive for energy efficiency has been largely the economic payoff rather than ecological insight. In a country where shops operate 24 hours, air conditioners, vending machines and TVs run around the clock, everywhere and strong fluorescent bulbs illuminate every corner day and night energy efficiency ratios have to be maintained or increased in order to keep the current high standard of living.

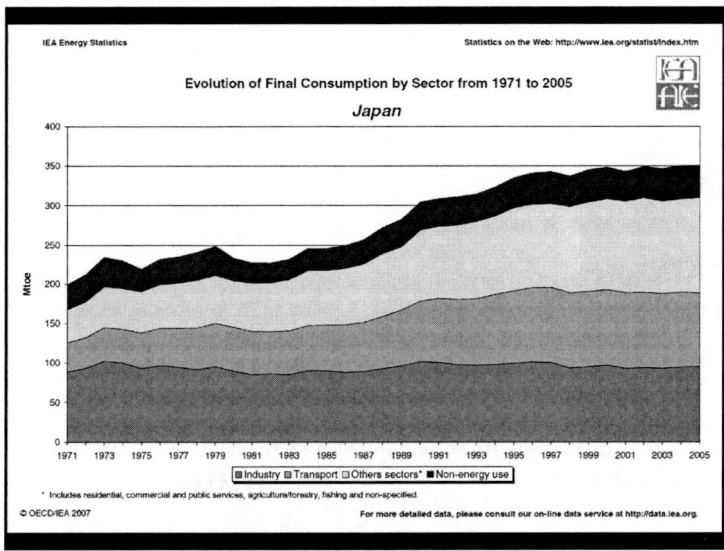

Graph 3-2: Evolution of final energy consumption by sector from 1971 to 2005 in Japan. (Source: http://www.iea.org/)

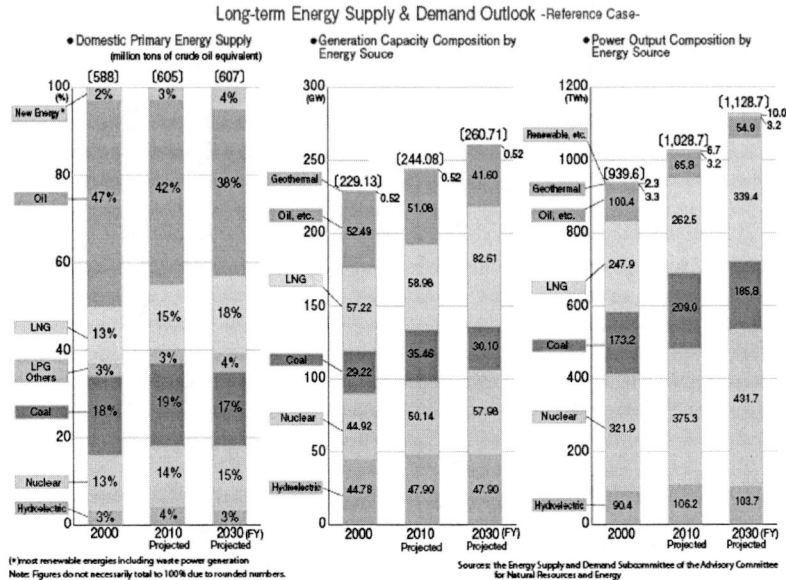

Graph 3-3: Long-term energy supply and demand outlook up to 2030 in Japan. (Source: Federation of Electric Power Companies of Japan http:// www. fepc. or. jp/english/index.html)

Energy consumption in Japan has risen to the highest levels ever and the 127 million Japanese consume a large part of fossil and non-fossil energy resources of the world. Japan's overall energy consumption has increased continuously and has reached a post war peak despite being a world leader in energy saving technology and energy efficiency.

Fossil fuel use is the main source of carbon dioxide emissions. It must be noted that almost 50% on the energy supply side in Japan is fossil petroleum. The energy efficiency gains rely basically on a non renewable energy model. Japan's final energy consumption has increased almost consistently since the mid-1980s. While energy consumption by the industrial sector has remained mostly level, growth in energy consumption by the commercial / residential sector and transport sector has risen sharply. The transport sector includes energy consumption for all transportation purposes, whether household or commercial. In the commercial / residential sector, energy consumption by the commercial sector especially has risen in recent years. This has been mainly caused by the rise in the total floor area of office buildings and large-scale retail stores; an increase in the amount of air conditioning equipment and lighting appliances used in those facilities; and the growth of office automation.

Our daily drives

Fossil powered transportation has become the biggest emitter of greenhouse gases in industrial countries. The logic behind transportation is moving and consuming: Trucks transport goods that are produced in Hokkaido to Okinawa for consumption, airplanes fly passengers to distant places for a one night stay trip at lowest fares, households own in average two or more cars, employees are transferred from one work location to another in frequent intervals and commute back home on weekends. On top of environmentally damaging behaviors energy prices are kept down and environmental taxes based on the polluter principle as well. The number of private cars owned by Japanese households came to 57 236 620 as of March 31 2007, up 0.7% from a year before as shown in data compiled by the Automobile Inspection & Registration Information Association. This means statistically one car is owned for every 2.2 people or per single household unit. By prefecture, Fukui ranked top in the number of cars per household with 1.7, followed by Toyama, Gunma, Gifu and Yamagata. In sharp contrast, Tokyo recorded the lowest number of 0.5, apparently due to the convenience of public transport systems, followed by Osaka, Kanagawa, Kyoto and Hyogo. The Ministry of the Environment has created a DVD entitled: Eco-driving: Money Saving Tips for Household Managers. This DVD introduces easy tips on how to drive a car wisely while saving on gas and reducing CO_2 emissions. CO_2 emitted from automobiles accounts for 30% of the total emission from the household sector. Also, when examined by sector, emissions from the transportation sector, including those from automobiles, have increased by 20% from the 1990 level. Therefore, reduction of CO_2 emissions from automobiles is a pressing issue. Eco-conscious driving is said to increase fuel efficiency by 10-20% compared to driving without environmental consciousness. Instead of convincing people not to buy a car, raising prices for fossil energy consumption or implement policies to reduce car driving habits by offering alternatives to conventional private transportation such as using a bicycle or maintaining a good public transportation network the government and private industry continue to support private car usage and moving for the sake of moving, build more roads and other public projects that have no long-term payback for the environment or quality of life and keep energy prices low.

In response to the recent changes of supply and demand structure and diversifying risks in the international energy market, the Ministry of Economy, Trade and Industry drafted the New National Energy Strategy in 2006. This presents Japan's long-term energy strategy centering on the reinforcement of energy security, and stipulates numerical targets such as improving energy efficiency by no less than 30% by 2030. Regarding nuclear energy, the goal is to maintain the share of power output from nuclear energy at the level at least 30% to 40% by 2030 and thereafter.

Japan has been calling for the halving of greenhouse gas emissions from present levels by 2050. In 2008 the Ministry of Economy, Trade and Industry announced the Cool Earth Energy Innovative Technology Plan to fulfill the long-term goal of a 50% reduction of greenhouse gas emissions by 2050 proposed in the government's Cool Earth 50 initiative in 2007. The plan selected 21 innovative technologies to be given high priority including solar energy and fuel cell vehicles. On an international level Japan will provide funds over the next five years to developing countries that are making efforts to reduce greenhouse gas emissions and achieve economic growth in a compatible way. Grant aid, technical assistance and aid through international organizations will be provided to address the needs in developing countries. A new scheme of grant aid, Environment Program Grant Aid, will be created as a component of this package. In the context of improved access to clean energy, feasibility study on rural electrification projects with geothermal energy and co-benefit projects that address climate change will be conducted. The Climate Change Japanese ODA Loan with preferential interest will be created to provide loans for the purpose of implementing programs to address global warming in developing countries.

More energy consumption means more profits for Japan's privately held power energy companies, packaging industry, food retail industry, transport industry or air-conditioning industry. The most powerful electricity company in the world Tokyo Electric Power (TEPCO) pursues contradictory policies when it comes to energy saving: one side the company wants to increase output and sell more volume on the other side offer cannot meet the ever-increasing demand. During peak consumption in the hot summer season of 2007 elevators had to be stopped, lights turned off and air conditioners turned off because supply could not meet demand. The all electrification house campaign of TEPCO which aims at selling more electricity to more households only worsened the problems on the supply side. Efforts had to be taken to secure the stable supply. To reassure the public TEPCO announced in a press release on its website:

"In case of ordinary summer, the supply would be enough to cover the demand. However, in case of the very severe lingering summer heat, the demand would exceed the supply. In order to avoid such a case and to secure stable supply, we will exercise the measures below.
(1) Continue to make efforts to get additional supply
(2) Try to secure the stable supply even after the summer peak
(3) Ask our customers to save electricity and try to reduce the demand in case of rapid increase of the demand." (Source: http://www.tepco.co.jp/en/index-e.html)

A good example might illustrate how inappropriate regulations and policies can be. Air-conditioning temperature control in buildings all over Japan is to be set between 28 degrees maximum and 17 degrees minimum whatever the ambient conditions are. Not much ecological commonsense is needed to imagine that in a well insulated building or house there is no need to run an air conditioner fulltime on a hot winter day or a cool summer day. Not running an air-conditioning device, not watching TV, not playing virtual games and not driving a car are definitely the most energy efficient ways. Not showing any readiness to abandon the current wasteful and over consumptive lifestyle is the reason why Japan has stayed one of largest emitters of absolute C02 emissions in the world in the past. As long as this trend continues the target to reduce C02 emissions by 50% by 2050 to limit the global temperature rise to 2 degrees cannot be achieved. In what looks like an increasingly difficult race to achieve its emissions-reductions targets and meet the Kyoto deadline the government has started in 2008 to buy emission offset rights from Eastern European countries. Carbon offsetting is seen as a convenient way to mitigate the impact of emissions and to claim carbon neutrality. But it should be just one part - the last part- of a national carbon reduction strategy otherwise it can be viewed as a quick fix which in itself can be of dubious worth because it is an external short-term solution that does not lead to required internal structural changes such as reducing fossil energy consumption radically, switching to new safe renewable energies, assessing the possibility of replacing carbon intensive production or manufacturing processes with more efficient alternatives or look for opportunities to cut emissions elsewhere.

The pitfalls of solar energy

Japan is one of the most blessed countries in the world with natural sunshine throughout the year. Compared to other energy providers such as uranium, gas or oil solar power is a limitless source of energy and a clean way to produce energy. Japan which has been active in the research and development of solar cells since 1975 has the potential to become the world's most advanced solar nation in terms of technological innovation and level of awareness. Japan used to be the world's frontrunner in terms of cumulative generation capacity until 2005 when a subsidy program for solar energy was abandoned. The initial subsidy of 900 000 Yen per kilowatt in 1994 when the program was started went down step by step to 20 000 Yen in 2004 before being stopped. The subsidy went down proportionally with the decrease in system price as more and more homes used solar energy the unit cost for solar energy panels came down. Until then the government had spent 130 billion Yen to support the private installation of rooftop solar cells. By 2005 more than 300 000 homes had been equipped with rooftop systems. With the end of subsidies came Japan's end as world leader for solar energy. In 2004 Germany bypassed Japan as world's leader of solar energy generation. A system of subsidized loans has also fostered purchases of solar installations for individual homes. Japan has fallen behind because a law based on Japan's Renewable Portfolio Standard (RPS) policy, which took effect in 2003, has failed to boost alternative energy generation. The law requires power utility to buy or produce a specified percentage of electricity from renewable but the standard is too low to make a difference.

Nevertheless Japan's aim is to regain the world's top position in solar power generation by increasing generation capacities drastically. The government has decided to again reintroduce the popular subsidy scheme for solar energy home use from fiscal 2009 which is expected however to cover not more than about 10% of the total system cost.

The nuclear power card

Japan possesses advanced technology in nuclear-power generation and if pluthermal and fast-breeder technologies can be commercialized as scheduled, it shall be able to recycle the nuclear fuel in a closed cycle as well. In 2006 several significant steps took place in the nuclear fuel recycling program: Japan Nuclear Fuel Co.'s reprocessing plant in Aomori prefecture started a test operation to extract plutonium from spent nuclear fuel with full operation to start in 2008; Kyushu Electric Power Co. obtained approval for its pluthermal project in Saga and Shikoku Electric Power Co. was given permission for a similar project in Ehime. In total the government has set aside 452 billion Yen in fiscal 2008 to develop nuclear energy. Japan relies on 55 reactors for about a third of its power generation needs, but aims to push this to 40% or 60 to 70 reactors within the next decade. At home, Japan's plans include an ambitious commercial fast-breeder program, and a huge and trouble-plagued new nuclear reprocessing plant at Rokkasho in the north of the country, which will make Japan one of the planet's largest producers of plutonium.

The Ministry of Economy, Trade and Industry is also expected to give the green light the construction of the world's first commercial thermal reactor to run exclusively on spent nuclear fuel, known as mixed-oxide. Nuclear power is fueled by uranium. After use the spent nuclear fuel stills contains elements that can be reprocessed and used again as fuel such as plutonium and uranium that has not undergone fission. The reprocessed fuel is used in light-water pluthermal reactors that have a history of more than 30 years of operation in France. In the future fast breeder reactors which create more plutonium that can be obtained from nuclear fission will increase efficiency. The development of fast breeder technologies is set to be commercially operational by 2050. The village of Rokkasho is ground zero for Japan's nuclear fuel recycling efforts. Along with the reprocessing plant are high/low level radioactive waste sites and a uranium enrichment plant. The reprocessing plant, which extracts plutonium and uranium from spent nuclear fuel, has been in the final phase of its trial operation. Part of the radioactive waste is disposed of at the disposal facility in Rokkasho. After the plutonium and uranium content is recovered from the spent fuel, the remaining high level radioactive waste is vitrified and stored underground for cooling for 30 to 50 years. The vitrified waste is then encased in thick metal and clay and disposed of more than 300 meters below the earth's surface.

The Japan Atomic Energy Agency, a government body, plans to dispose of highly radioactive nuclear waste in Hokkaido at various underground sites and is conducting tests at its Horonobe Underground Research Center in rural Teshio-gun.

According to the webpage of the center,

> "The basic national policy of Japan is to dispose high-level radioactive waste in the deep underground after extracting usable uranium and plutonium from spent fuel. The Horonobe Underground Research Center conducts research and development on geological disposal of high-level radioactive waste and geoscientific research to verify the technical reliability of geological disposal through testing and research conducted in actual deep geological environments." (Source: http://www.jaea.go.jp/english/04/ horonobe/index.html)

Japan supports also research activities into the controversial nuclear fusion technology known also as the ITER project.

Ecotaxes and carbon taxes

One important concept underlying environmental taxation is the polluter pays principle, which uses the tax leverage to bring within the polluter's own cost base the so called negative externalities associated with its activities; namely the costs that fall on the public, such as damage to the environment. Energy pricing that takes into account the full cost of carbon emissions is necessary. In its comprehensive outlook on environmental trends up to 2030 the OECD strongly recommends "long-term policy frameworks that allow environmental costs to be priced into economic activities to make green technologies cost competitive and provide business with the incentive to innovate" (OECD, 2008, p. 9). As DeWit (2008) stresses in his paper a carbon tax offers a neutral win-win situation for public health, employment and economy overall as it is a corrective to environmentally negative behavior rather than levied on income or profits. What is paradox about green taxes is that positive behavior leads to less taxation. The more successful green taxes become in changing people's behavior the less tax is levied and the less tax is generated for the state. Another side effect is that this tax income can be shifted to subsidize cleaner but more cost intensive renewable energies. DeWit concludes that "carbon taxes are the most efficient, least interventionist means of effectively controlling emissions and spurring the innovation needed to carry Japan, its cities and its countryside, out of the oil age and into the new economy" (DeWit, 2008, p. 25).

The Ministry of Environment announced that it plans to introduce a carbon tax by fiscal 2009. It has sought over the last four years to have an environmental tax implemented but so far to little avail. If the government does decide to introduce a tax for environmental causes, it will likely come in the form of funds set aside from so-called road-related tax revenues, which the government decided to ship on off to fund projects other than road construction. Up to date, the road-related taxes have been levied on gasoline and motorists for purchasing and owning cars and the proceeds have been earmarked mainly for road construction projects. With the diversion, the budget for road projects is expected to shrink from next fiscal year, and the government and the ruling coalition is seeking to keep the provisional surcharge on the gasoline tax, one of the road levies to secure funding for road construction. The extra levy on gasoline, despite being called temporary, has been in place for more than three decades and has doubled the original tax rate. The government and the ruling parties have found a new mantra–the environment–to try to convince the public about the use of road-related taxes for other purposes. As if to corroborate this line of thinking, the economic policy guidelines endorsed by the cabinet in mid 2008 mentioned an environmental tax for the first time, calling for an overall review of the tax code and studying the introduction of such a tax. Last year the ministry proposed charging levies of 665 Yen per ton of carbon dioxide emissions and 1580 Yen per ton of coal and setting a gasoline tax charge at 1.52 Yen per liter. The proposed tax system was projected to generate 360 billion Yen a year, which translates into a 2000 Yen levy per household. The proceeds were to be used to promote purchase of home-use, energy-saving equipment and fuel-efficient cars. Under the plan, the taxpayers' money would also be used to fund local authorities' projects aimed at combating global warming. The environmental tax plan has been put on hold in the face of stiff resistance from industry, which refuses to assume an additional tax burden, saying it would hurt Japanese companies' competitiveness in the global marketplace. Automakers, oil companies and motorists, meanwhile, are digging in their heels to block the ministry's environmental tax plan. Environmental groups also voice their concerns about the ministry's plan from a different perspective and are calling for more robust measures. The Carbon Tax Research Group, which comprises nongovernmental organizations and various researchers, says revamping road taxes alone is not enough and that the government should consider raising other energy-related taxes as well.

Emissions Trading Schemes (ETS)

Market mechanisms such as carbon emissions trading can provide pricings signals and have the economic potential to deliver economic incentives to the private sector. The EU introduced an emissions trading system in 2005. The scheme targets sector specific industrial plants that account for about 50% of C02 emissions. Kimura and Tuerk (2008) observe that "rather than taking leadership by implementing a mandatory ETS early on, Japan has carefully followed international developments"(Kimura and Tuerk, 2008, p.1). On a private level the powerful Japan Business Federation Keidanren proposed a voluntary industry by industry action plan in 1997 even before Japan had ratified the Kyoto protocol (2002). In 2005 Japan introduced a voluntary emission trading scheme based on absolute reduction targets. This scheme was not a success. In 2008 the government shifted its attention to a mandatory emissions trading system that will only become fully mandatory after 2013 and include absolute reduction targets only. Japan's discussions regarding the post-2012 framework will be led by the Council on the Global Warming Issue, and this government council is expected to promote discussions about effective climate change measures from a comprehensive perspective. The Keidanren had been staunchly opposed to such a mandatory system. As a first step a voluntary test phase has been introduced since fall 2008 on a national and local basis. The companies will be allowed to set not only total or absolute emission targets but also intensity based emission targets. Intensity targets can only measure the C02 efficiency improvement on the input side whereas absolute targets measure the real nominal output reduction. This has been criticized because greenhouse-gas emissions won't fall if firms increase production while limiting per-production emissions to a set level. This is similarly true for the high energy efficiency, high consumption dilemma: energy consumption has increased in absolute terms despite high energy efficiency or intensity. Environmental groups have urged the government to introduce an emissions trading system in which the government imposes mandatory reduction targets and company participation. By making the targets intensity based–by setting a certain amount of C02 emissions per unit of production output–the transition scheme aims to get a larger number of initial participant companies. The intensity based method would also be designed to have credit allocations reflect progressive improvements in energy efficiency over the years. Any company wishing to increase emissions above its self-allotted level is required to buy carbon credits from companies that are generating emissions below their own self-set levels. In Europe and in parts of the United States, authorities are responsible for capping emissions and issuing carbon credits to big companies.

The Tokyo metropolitan government has opted for a mandatory ETS that will start to become compulsory in 2010. The limit for each business establishment will be calculated by taking into consideration past emission performances and the reduction rate for each of various industries to be determined by the metropolitan government in fiscal 2008. Businesses that fail to meet their emission goals will have to pay a penalty charge of 500 000 Yen. Carbon trading will also be introduced. Those that fail to meet the emission goals can buy carbon credits from enterprises whose reductions exceed the goals. If businesses purchase electricity from renewable sources such as wind power and solar batteries, the purchase will be counted as an emission reduction. The metropolitan government hopes to reduce emissions by 15% to 20% by fiscal 2020 from the average emission level of the past three years. DeWit (2008) asserts that carbon trading is the second best solution to having a carbon tax because trading requires more time consuming implementation related regulatory steps.

Despite Japan being the world leader in registered environmental 14001 ISO certifications there is no proof up to date that ISO certification has had any impact on the reduction of carbons emissions.

Biodiversity

Between 1960 and 2000 the human population of the world has doubled whereas during the same period animal populations have declined by 30%. An ecological footprint is a measure of the demands put on the land and sea by humans. This is calculated by taking into account all the built-on land, cropland, grazing land, forest and fishing ground used by a country, as well as their nuclear energy and carbon emissions. To keep the world within a sustainable limit 1.8 global hectares per capita or less if taking into account the needs of wild species are desirable. According to Schreurs (2004) Japan gets bad scores when it comes to sustainability performance measurements. There are several international available indexes to compare individual countries against each other's and the ecological footprint is one of the most descriptive and authoritative. According to the latest data available Japanese citizens consume a little less than 5 hectares per capita per year. This is far above the sustainability limit of 1.8 hectares. Taking into account that the size of the country is statistically too small to support the high affluence level it is assumed that Japan consumes large amounts of foreign land and sea for domestic purpose and as a result the aggregated footprint almost doubles. The disposable chopsticks made of imported timber consumed in Japan are a good example to illustrate the fallout of domestic consumption on foreign natural resources.

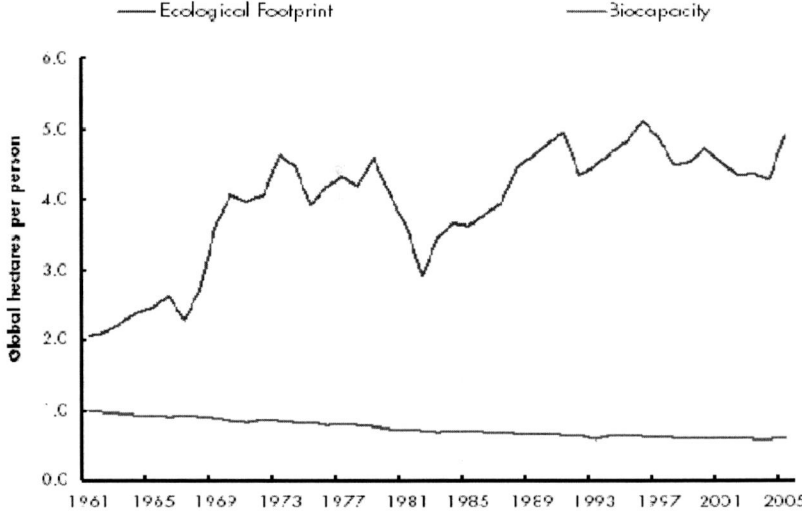

Graph 3-4: The ecological footprint of Japan. Source: Global Footprint Network http://www.footprintnetwork. org/en/ index.php/GFN/

The graph 3-4 tracks, in absolute terms, the average per person resource demand (Ecological Footprint) and per person resource supply (Biocapacity) in Japan since 1961. Biocapacity varies each year with ecosystem management, agricultural practices (such as fertilizer use and irrigation), ecosystem degradation, and weather.

The failure to coexist with nature and respect the boundaries between man and nature have taken their toll on biodiversity and wildlife as exemplified by the extinction or threatened extinction of bears, the wild stork, the ibis or the wolf in Japan (Walker, 2005; Knight, 2003; Miyaoka, 2004).

Storks for example used to be observed everywhere in Japan including Toyooka in the Tajima region in the northern part of Hyogo prefecture. Storks inhabit rural habitats and require a fully intact ecosystem to survive. In order to preserve the species the local retainer lord banned the hunting and capture of stocks during the Edo era. However the population of wild storks decreased rapidly after 1930 and eventually the last wild stork died in Toyooka in 1971. The main causes of the extinction have been identified as lifting of the hunting ban in the Meiji era, the loss and deterioration of feeding habitats through land and river works, health degradation caused by agricultural pesticides containing poisonous mercury in addition to the deforestation of the pine trees that the stocks used as nesting sites. Since 1999 efforts have been underway to aim for the reintroduction of captive storks to the wild by 2010 onwards.

The cost of human development: Towards the extinction of the black bear and brown bear

Whereas the relationship of the indigenous Ainu people with the brown bear of Hokkaido has been well documented, particularly by anthropologists and ethnologists, the relationship of the Japanese with the Asiatic black bear has not attracted much scholarly interest. Perhaps this is because it does not fit neatly with common preconceptions of what constitutes Japanese nature.

Nevertheless, the bear is a part of Japan's nature, and one that is increasingly difficult to ignore. This once elusive creature is becoming a frequent visitor to Japan's upland villages and towns, where it damages crops, breaks into chicken coups, and occasionally injures or kills people. In 2004 and 2005, the bear-problem led to unprecedented media coverage and countless symposia, as people grappled for answers to the recent upsurge in bear incidents. The Japanese approach towards solving the human - wildlife conflict, a problem facing many societies in the world today, has been commented in critical terms. The Japanese black bear is the largest mammal of Japan's three major islands Honshu, Kyushu, and Shikoku. After World War II, a large portion of their habitat in the mountains was converted from indigenous deciduous or mixed forests to afforested coniferous forests for timber production.

This course of action drastically reduced the availability of food, forcing the bears to come down to human residential or farm areas. Various public works such as dams and roads separate their habitats, which interferes with their movements and isolates them from neighboring populations. The population of Japanese black bears has been split into several smaller groups. Within these groups there are further sub-populations from each other by cities, express roads, railways and dam lakes. One population, in Kyushu, is already extinct and another, in Shikoku is critically endangered. The bears in the Western part of Honshu are isolated into few small sub-populations. Only numbers in the Eastern Honshu are considered healthy but they are also facing numerous problems, including hunting, city encroachment, and construction of express roads, dams, and golf and ski resorts. Working in close collaboration with local groups and individuals, a World Wildlife Fund (WWF) project has aimed to set up a conservation plan for the Shikoku population based on the findings of an ecological survey. It will also create a co-existence model in Nagano, central Japan to reduce human-bear conflict. Each year, a large number of bears are caught or killed by commercial hunting and eradication programs to protect local agriculture, forestry and human life. Without effective management to address the threats, Japan may lose this species in the future. The black bear is one of the key indigenous species and its survival depends on the restoration of indigenous ecosystems. WWF Japan has supported surveys and land purchase for a national trust and established collaborations with individuals and organizations concerned with the conservation of the black bear.

Hokkaido- the lost dream

The Hokkaido region case documents the impact of human intervention on local eco- systems. The population of Hokkaido was only 50 000 when its development began in full scale. The wilderness was reclaimed under an elaborate colonization plan developed by the Colonization Commission. In the 130 years following that, Hokkaido turned into an agricultural land with a population of over 5.7 million. Meanwhile, the Ainu were being driven from their traditional homes as the mountains and plains that had been their hunting and fishing grounds came under the control of the government. The Colonial Department banned many traditional customs, forced the Ainu to use the Japanese language and take Japanese names, and encouraged them to engage in agriculture. The Ainu culture was being rapidly eroded. Expectance to Hokkaido in the land development work in those days was reflected, and emphasis was put for the increased production of food, the development of electric power resources, the land improvement of the traffic, the development work of the underground resources. Hokkaido hosted the G8 summit in 2008 to boost its image and appeal to foreign visitors and investors.

A hundred years ago the Meiji government decided to colonize the northern region, bring in immigrants from the main island and develop it economically and assimilate culturally its native inhabitants called Ainu. Hokkaido delivers a stunning example of cultural mainland arrogance, economic failure and mismanagement. The biggest mistake done by the central government was to settle the island with immigrants knowing that the self sustaining and self viable economy of Hokkaido could not offer many opportunities to new immigrants apart from abundant nature. In theory only the fittest could have been able to make a living on their own or survive under the harsh conditions. The government just stepped ahead with its blunt policy of forced development and decided to ignore the basic ecological and natural requirements and living conditions of Hokkaido. No other prefecture has been so much subsidized with taxpayer money and artificially been kept alive as Hokkaido has been over the past 100 years.

The simple logic was to pour people to Hokkaido and give them work to support their survival and living expenses. The pouring in of people and money from Tokyo was not primarily aimed at keeping and maintaining a balance between a fragile ecology and a self sustaining local economy. The sole purpose was to spend money on building and maintaining public work projects such as road or dam constructions. There have never been any attempts to look at investment paybacks, long-term benefits or incorporate ecological risk assessments. The spectacular bankruptcy of the city of Yubari is perhaps the most striking example of failure of the economic development model conceived by the central government for Hokkaido. Instead of learning from its mistakes the government continues its economic policy of seeking investors, developing eco-tourism as a source of income, building new renewable energy supplies, attracting tourists from abroad and dumping radioactive fallout waste into the deep undergrounds. The self proclaimed leadership with regard to environmental respect and thinking does not make sense at all if one looks at the reality of unproductive and unsustainable mass subsidizing. Automobiles for examples are a particularly essential means of transportation in the harsh winter. In vast depopulated Hokkaido, there are 6 291 km of national highway. To maintain the road infrastructure in winter huge investments are needed. Because Hokkaido plays a vital role in Japan's national prosperity, its public projects are given a higher rate of national subsidy than those in other prefectures. In 2001 the budget was 942 billion Yen and 34% went into road improvement. Today one of the biggest employers besides local municipalities in the region is the army.

The government has created national parks not only to protect species, but also to attract eco-tourists and vitalize the local economy. Eco-tourism has become a hit among travel agencies who seek to develop new markets. The ever-increasing flow of eco-tourists into nature reserves such as Ogasawara, Yakushima, Shirakami Sanchi or Shiretokko is damaging the biodiversity, contributes to waste increase and is invasive. A huge road construction project in the northern Okinawa region of Yanbaru is another example illustrating the ecological disaster caused by reckless economic development.

Organic farming and food self-sufficiency

According to estimates from the Ministry of Agriculture, Forestry and Fisheries the food self-sufficiency rate in Japan has remained at dramatically low levels of 40% in comparison with Australia's 237%, US'128%, France's 122%,
Germany's 84% and UK's 70%. The government has decided to increase the rate
to 45% by 2015, but the situation remains gloomy because of the smaller intake
of rice due to changed westernized dietary habits and the deterioration of agriculture and fisheries. The safety of imported food had been a problem before,
such as BSE (Bovine spongiform encephalopathy) and bird flu, but despite a series of domestic scandals involving manipulated expiry dates, preference for
domestic products has once again swung back after a food-poisoning case involving frozen dumplings imported from China. Furthermore, the soaring cost of
grain which became conspicuous from late 2006 and the restrictions on tuna
catches are indicative of global competition for limited food resources.

Food self-sufficiency is not only a matter of trade and import ratios but also
related to food quality, nutritional balance and impact on the environment. The
high demand for meat contributes to global warming and CO_2 emissions and
causes obesity and health problems, the use of pesticides in agriculture leads to
negative changes in biodiversity and endangers human health. More and more
Japanese have come to realize that organic food production and supply without
pesticides, hormones and antibiotics can help to improve their health and quality
of life and they are ready to pay for the difference in price. Organic farmers do
not rely on conventional methods to fertilize the soil, control weeds and pests or
prevent disease in livestock. Compared to European countries, Japanese organic
farming is still behind. To clarify, there are only a few public institutions that are
doing the research on organic farming in Japan. The percentage of land used for
organic farming is only 0.13%. Only 0.17 % of all produce grown in 2006 was
certified as organic under Japan Agricultural Standards and the NPO Jona. Jona
is a non profit, non-governmental organization approved as a legal entity following the new NPO Law implemented in 1999. It is a third party certification
body to certify organic products that has been approved as the registered certification body by the Minister of Agriculture, Forestry and Fishery in August 2000
to certify organic products under JAS organic regulations. Producers, family
farmers, farmers group, farmers cooperative can apply for certification of agricultural products, agricultural processed food or livestock and feed. Crops har-
vested on organic field in the third year can be certified as organic. Processed
products in which over 95% of ingredients are certified as organic that are used
and processed organically can be certified as organic. Organic farmers face several challenges: consumers dislike fruits or vegetables which do not live up to a
certain norm and form and do not want to share the higher cost. Given the proportion of the area per farm hectares, Japan is using the greatest amount of
agrochemicals in the world. Again the long-term damage done to eco-systems in
case of agro-pesticides necessitates further scientific investigation and research.

After a recent series of food safety scandals more and more consumers ask for pesticide free food supplies and this new health trend will create further demand for organically certified food. There are organic cooperatives that promote and distribute their products directly to end-users. There are several private experimental farms in Japan, for example, International Nature Farming Research Center, which is conducting the research on the EM or Effective Microorganisms technology. However, there are no public experimental farms specialized in organic farming like in the European countries. Things started changing in December 2006 when the new Law on Promotion of Organic Agriculture was enacted. In April 2007, the Ministry of Agriculture and Fisheries released a set of five-year guidelines from fiscal 2007 to 2011 for the comprehensive and systematic promotion of organic farming.

Environmental NGOs: the fight of David against Goliath

Citizens' Nuclear Information Center (CNIC)

Citizens' Nuclear Information Center is an anti-nuclear public interest organization dedicated to securing a safe, nuclear-free world. The Center was formed to provide reliable information and public education on all aspects of nuclear power to ultimately realize this goal. Data gathered, compiled, and analyzed by the Center are condensed into forms useful to the media, citizens' groups, policy makers, and the general public. The Center is independent from government and industry and is supported by membership fees, donations, and sales of publications. The CNIC was established in 1975 in Tokyo to collect and analyze information related to nuclear energy including safety, economic, and proliferation issues and to conduct studies and research on such issues. During 1995-97, the center spearheaded an independent study on mixed uranium-plutonium oxide (MOX) fuel with a number of prominent researchers from Europe, the U.S. , and Japan. The Research Director of the International MOX Assessment (IMA) project, Dr. Jinzaburo Takagi, together with the Research Sub-Director, Mycle Schneider, received the Right Livelihood Award for this study and activities relating to plutonium issues. In September 1999, CNIC was certified by the government of Tokyo as a Specified Nonprofit Corporation, and thus acquired legal corporate status. Information is central to CNIC's purpose. The Center gathers its information from many sources including the internet, newspaper and journal clippings, government and industry publications, raw data from accidents and incidents and scientific reports and theses. CNIC collates and analyses this information to produce an understandable overview of the nuclear industry and the government's policies in Japan. With these analyses CNIC tries to present a balanced view of nuclear power and helps local citizens' groups make informed decisions about the nuclear issues that affect their lives.

Institute for Sustainable Energy Policies (ISEP)

ISEP is a small but influential NGO lobbying for political change towards a more sustainable energy supply for Japan. The institute is an independent, non-profit research organization, founded in 2000 by energy experts and climate change campaigners. Through its work it aims to provide resources and services to realize sustainable energy policies. Main areas include promotion of renewable energy, improvement of energy efficiency, and restructuring the energy market. It engages itself in a wide range of programs and activities by providing policy recommendations with regard to renewable energy and energy efficiency to the Japanese government, guidance and advice to local municipalities, conducting events such as international conferences and symposiums. It also closely liaises with many organizations in Europe, the United States and Asia to promote exchange and introduce updated information on sustainable energy policies. In addition, it has implemented community winds and solar power projects through Citizens' Fund and Green Energy Com which is the relevant body for project implementation. ISEP is a third party organization independent from government and industry, aiming at the realization of sustainable energy policies. ISEP was founded by environmentalists and professionals who are experts in the area of global warming and energy issues.

KIKO Network

Kiko Network is a non-governmental organization supported by individuals, organizations and regional networks from all over Japan. The goal is the practical implementation of the Kyoto Protocol and the prevention of dangerous climate change. It's five objectives are as follows: 6 % reduction of greenhouse gases emissions by drastic domestic measures; construction of environmentally sound socio-economical systems; promoting climate change prevention under leadership of citizens and communities; citizen participation and information disclosure into the policy-making process and cooperation among NGOs in developed and in developing countries to achieve global justice.

Japan Center for a Sustainable Environment and Society

The Japan Center for a Sustainable Environment and Society is an independent NGO think thank established in 1993 with the following objectives. To analyze and evaluate Japanese environmental policy and provide information on the environment and relevant policy movements in Japan. To monitor and assess Japanese Official Development Assistance (ODA) and international financial institutions in terms of environmental and social impacts. To monitor decision-making procedures at the Earth Summit (UN Conference on Environment and Development) in 1992 and encourage the participation and cooperation of citizens and citizen groups in the process of UNCED follow-up. Currently research is done in the areas of water conservation, green tax reform, ecological footprint and an environmental framework for ODA.

Japan for Sustainability (JFS)

Japan for Sustainability (JFS), established in 2002, is a non-profit organization providing information on developments and activities in Japan that lead towards sustainability. During the past years, JFS released over 1800 news articles and 200 feature articles in both English and in Japanese, on topics ranging from sustainable lifestyles and wisdom in Japanese traditions to the current state of the environment in Japan and new technologies, regulations and practices in citizen movements and business to promote sustainability today.

Destruction of cultural heritage

The real-estate developers are the forerunners of cultural asset destruction in Japan. Wood used for long to be the primary natural construction material before steel constructions and concrete put their footprint on landscapes. The destruction pace of cultural properties such as wooden houses or stone buildings is unprecedented. Golf courses, leisure parks, large hotel complexes, road construction and dam projects have disfigured the country sides. The replacement of wooden one-story houses with mansions and high rise buildings is destroying neighborhood communities that are rooted in mutual help and assistance. The construction of roads and pushing of public building projects in the countryside puts at risk the very foundations of Japanese culture in a large sense for the sake of increasing tourism revenue, a non-sustainable selfish lifestyle. The massive urbanization and indiscriminate land use takes its toll on the local environment and local communities. The disrespect for nature has reached a level that is unprecedented: ancestors used to worship the gods in the sacred mountains and installed a *tori* to symbolically demonstrate their bounds with the gods. Nowadays corrupt mayors waste tax payer money on public projects that do not benefit the local community long-term. The bankruptcy of the city of Yubari in Hokkaido has demonstrated the dramatic consequences of wrong investment policies. Once the nature has been destroyed for good ecological damage will be irreversible and long-lasting. It is more costly to spend for corrective actions once the damage has occurred than to invest in long-term prevention policies. In his study on urbanization and city planning Sorensen (2002) concludes that economic development has not led to a significant improvement of the quality of life as might have been expected following the radical growth period. In Japan the quantitative public wealth accumulated has failed to translate into a higher quality of life in terms of nearby green zones or forests to recover, absence of air, water or soil pollution, safe food, short travel times from work to home, intact mutual aid and convivial neighborhoods.

Learning from the ecological wisdom of Germany

Germany and Japan share lots of experiences with addressing the challenge posed by pollution and environmental effective policies (Széll et al, 2004; Schreurs, 2003). Similar to Germany environmental extra parliamentary protest against pollution and environmental destruction in Japan started already in the early 1970s (Hasegawa, 2004; Foltjany-Jost, 2005; Sasaki-Uemura, 2001). Local citizen groups formed protest against Narita airport construction, construction of second *Tomei* highway, construction of new tunnels and garbage incinerators. Opposition to nuclear energy was one of the main issues that led to the founding of the Greens in Germany. What differentiates Germany from Japan is that the NGOs in Germany succeeded with their protests to initiate a nationwide public debate on nuclear power and energy supply. Furthermore the German NGOs succeeded in having elected environmentalists in local and national parliaments. The extra-parliamentary movements had understood that the only way to undertake a radical change in energy policy was to channel protest into political legislative actions and get the buy in and understanding of the public and media. The participation of the Greens in the national government coalition was a key event that led to the decision of abandoning nuclear power.

In Japan neither the Chernobyl disaster of 1986, nor the Tokaimura accident in 1999, nor the fatal accident at Mihama's plant in Fukui prefecture, nor the shutdown of the Kashiwazaki-Kariwa Nuclear Power Plant after the 2007 Niigata earthquake triggered a controversial policy debate on energy supply issues. Other differences that may explain why German NGOs have been so active is their sometimes extreme radicalism when it comes to protecting nature. NGOs can become very confrontational when perceived vital threats to life are at stake such as the protest against a nuclear waste disposal or against the construction of a new airport runway extension. Sometimes activists become overly sentimental or emotional when it comes to save trees threatened by acid rain or animals subject to inhuman treatment. Another reason that explains the strong activism of German NGOs is their financial and organizational strength embedded in European wide networks.

Since they left the national government the Greens have become less influential on a national level. There are two reasons for this: The established political parties have become greener and taken away voters from the Greens and some NGOs have distanced themselves from the Greens perceived to have become too mainstream or established. The current generation of new Greens has a more pragmatic stance towards ecology than their forefathers. The newly chosen approach is less confrontational than in the past and values the economic payoffs of ecological investments highlighted under the popular slogan "Ecological modernization creates jobs". In order to realize a complete ecological modernization of society, the Greens have set challenging goals for both climate and energy policies. They believe an intelligent mix of market instruments, incentive programs and legal regulations can reach these aims. It has been Germany's high environmental standards that have made it the global market leader for environmental technologies. German companies' share of the global environmental technology market, at just under 19%, makes them world leaders in the field. Additionally, about 23% of the patents registered annually for environmental technologies come from Germany, evidence that stringent environmental standards encourage innovation. Chief beneficiaries of these developments have been German workers, 1.5 million of whom were employed in the environmental sector in 2006. And that figure continues to increase. An additional success during the Green participation in government was the implementation of the ecology tax, which made the wasteful use of natural resources more expensive while lowering non-wage labor costs.

The representation of the Greens in parliament led to dramatic changes in state policies and priority setting. The decision to opt out of the nuclear option was a long-term strategic decision against short-term economic interests based on risk impact assessment such as the unsolved problem of how to safely deposit radioactive waste permanently or the limited remaining amount of global uranium reserves.

Energy policy has always been a key priority of the Greens' legislative efforts in Germany. Since the early 80s, the Green parliamentary group pointed out possible effects of global warming and developed strategies to combat climate change. From the beginning, the party's parliamentary group supported the expansion of renewable energy and a decentralized energy supply. The Green parliamentary group put together an ambitious yet realistic energy strategy for Germany preparing for a drastic restructuring of the country's energy supplies. The concept addresses the entire energy sector: electricity, heating and cooling as well as transportation. The future of all three fields will be marked by greater energy efficiency, energy conservation and the use of renewable energy. The scenario for fossil energy is bleak. From the International Energy Agency to the Energy Watch Group, experts conclude that oil production will peak between now and 2020. There is a broad agreement that the age of seemingly limitless oil is over. The green-red coalition issued to this effect its revised Renewable Energy Sources Act that has become a model to many other countries who have copied the German example. Under the so called feed-in tariff system viewed as the cornerstone of German climate policy it is required that power utility firms to buy all electricity produced by solar and other renewable plants at fixed prices, even though the power costs more than fossil-fuel generated electricity. The law has been very effective. From 2000 to 2004 the volume of electricity generated from renewable energies supported by this Act more than doubled. During the same period the Act resulted in the volume of electricity generated from wind and biomass more than doubling, and brought about a nine-fold increase in electricity generated from photovoltaic systems in Germany. The law is very efficient, because the costs for renewable energies hinge largely on investment security. If an investment is high risk, banks demand high interest rates for the loan and the investors demand high-risk mark-ups. Since the structure of the law guarantees a particularly high investment security, credit interest rates and risk mark-ups are low compared with other instruments. Furthermore, the lowering of fees as laid down in the law for installations commissioned at a later date ensures further price reductions. This regression has already had an impact: the costs for installing photovoltaic systems dropped by 25% between 1999 and 2004; for wind turbines, costs were reduced by 30% between 1993 and 2003. Each citizen, company and municipality is encouraged to produce renewable energy by themselves and feed in the public power circuit. The share of renewable energy has been increased since to 14 % of total energy supply. Germany has pledged to increase the share further to between 25% and 30% by 2020. Internationally more than 47 states have copied the German model up to date.

Japan is also talking about promoting new energy sources but with less ambitious intentions and less impressive results. The revised law concerning the promotion of new energy, which came into force in 2002, stipulates 14 new energy sources such as solar, wind power and biomass. Because of the alleged high cost and low power generation new energy accounts for less than 3% of the total primary energy supply.
Carbon capture and storage

It is becoming apparent that the use of carbon capture and storage (CCS) technologies at coal-fired power plants won't be available before 2020. It remains questionable if CCS will ever be effective. Although coal supplies are not scarce, prices will increase as demand, particularly in China and India grows and other fossil energy resources are used up. Storage of CO_2 raises several environmental policy questions. That is why the Greens strongly object to building new coal power plants in the near future before the industry's touted CO_2-free coal plants are technically feasible as well as ecologically and economically sound.

Emission trading ensures that measures against climate change are implemented where it is most affordable. By backing the legislation for renewable energy, the Greens have created economic incentives to battle the greenhouse effect. Germany's eco-tax has helped encourage energy conservation while lowering non-wage labor costs. In order to limit increase of global temperatures to a maximum of 2 degrees, industrialized countries must cut their greenhouse gas emissions 40 % by 2020 and 80 % by 2050. With government backing, wind energy generation is expanding, and wind turbines are growing into a strong export industry. Germany now has more capacity of generating solar energy than Japan does. Germany's drastic goal is to increase the level of renewable energies to 20% of the entire electricity supply, and reduce greenhouse gas emissions by 40 % from 1990 levels.

The OECD outlook up to 2030 (2008) has prioritized four key sectors where action is needed to prevent massive environmental damage: the energy sector, transport, agriculture and fisheries. Omitting to take action will reduce the chances for preventing irreversible future damage. If a no new policy prevails for example in the energy sector CO_2 emissions are to increase by 52% ; similarly if no action is taken to reflect the costs of environmental damage caused by private cars CO_2 emissions are projected to raise by 58%; if no action is taken to stop the conversion of natural land to farm land and stop the usage of farmland for the production of crops for bio fuel more bio species will be lost and the reservoirs of drinking water will become threatened; if no action is taken with regard to preserving the world's fisheries the marine environment as a whole will be threatened.

Environmental education

The importance of environmental education was globally acknowledged at the United Nations Conference on the Human Environment (UNCHE) held in Stockholm in 1972. UNCHE was followed by numerous international conferences and symposiums on environmental education hosted by such organizations as UNESCO and UNEP. In 1992, Agenda 21, an action program for sustainable development, was adopted at the United Nations Conference on Environment and Development (UNCED) held in Rio de Janeiro. This action program stresses the importance of promoting environmental education for young people. Environmental education aims to help students and citizens understand the environment, acquire necessary skills, contribute to environmental conservation, develop their own values and create an alternative lifestyle. Environmental education is an essential endeavor for the re-evaluation of contemporary society, thereby helping us in the transition to a sustainable society. It emphasizes comprehensive understanding of the environment and learning through experience. It is essentially interdisciplinary, involving a wide spectrum of disciplines from the natural sciences to the social sciences and the humanities. It deals not only with environmental issues such as acid rain, climate change and loss of biodiversity, and related issues such as population, energy and food issues, but also with various problems related to local communities, historical and ethnic cultures, primary industries such as agriculture and forestry, and the necessities of life. In Japan environmental education originated in anti-pollution education and education for nature preservation during the period of high economic growth in the 1960s. In the latter half of the 1980s as the threat of environmental problems was becoming globally acknowledged and conservation issues were attracting more attention, the importance of environmental education became increasingly recognized by foresighted educators, researchers and policy makers. In response to this heightening environmental awareness, the Japanese Society of Environmental Education, an academic organization, was founded in 1989. In cooperation with other educational associations founded at that time and with many environmental NPOs/NGOs, the Japanese Society of Environmental Education helped in many kinds of environmental education programs and projects in Japan. A diversity of educational activities was established during the 1990s. The Ministry of Education, Science, Sports and Culture established a guideline for environmental education in 1991 leading to the introduction of environmental education in schools throughout the country. Environmental education is now becoming more common in schools, and environmental in-service training programs for teachers have begun. Information exchange networks connecting schools have been enhanced and expanded. Formal education in Japan has been attaching a great importance to environmental education. Schools are expected to correspond to this theme by referring to variety of activities and promoting participation of the local community. Environmental education is considered to connect to daily educational activities at school through every subject and extra-curriculum, for example, social studies, science, moral education and special activities. The Ministry of Education assumes the responsibility of educational administration at the national level. It prescribes guidelines for the curriculum, the courses, and credit requirements from kindergartens through high schools. Curricular standards for elementary and secondary schools are described in the courses of study produced by Ministry of Education. It is also responsible for authorizing textbooks for elementary and secondary schools. The problem of the environmental education curriculum is that it is not clearly located in the curricular activities of environmental education. It is the Ministry of Education that has strong authority over schooling. However, it is a problem that these policies are not adopted as part of education courses. The Ministry of Education has not actively adopted environmental education at the curricular level. Each school can make their own curriculum based on the course of study. However, the Ministry of Education has the authority to develop the course of study, which is the core of the curriculum, and authorizes textbooks based on this course of study. Therefore, as long as the Ministry of Education does not take positive action environmental education will not be formally incorporated in the curriculum. Currently in Japan many initiatives on environmental education come from Ministry of the Environment, Ministry of Land, Infrastructure, and Transport, and the Ministry of Agriculture, Forestry and Fishers, not from Ministry of Education. The lack of strong involvement of Ministry of Education has tended to marginalize environmental education from the mainstream and this has resulted in a lack of coherent plans, for progression in school education. It would be preferable if the Ministry of Education and Ministry of the Environment worked together to develop integrated governmental policies on environmental education, not just an isolated plan of each ministry.

The power of the consumer

Due to the urgency of the worldwide environmental degradation any public or private program has to address the issue of consumer motivation and change of habits like driving short distances by car or by plane, using plastic bags when shopping, or running electrical appliances all day long. In principle it does still pay off–so far–not to be environmentally friendly in Japan; for the atomic lobby it pays off to put the burden for risks and costs of nuclear power on the back of the taxpayer; for the ordinary citizen it pays off to drive cars and ride planes without caring about the ecological and social damage caused; for the national Diet it pays off to omit enacting laws enforcing the strict application of the polluter pays principle. So far neither the private nor the public sector have succeeded in changing the attitudes or habits of consumers in a significant way and this is largely due to the fact that the invisible and intangible real cost of environmental damage has not been cost factored or made transparent in a drastic way to citizens.

The fact that carbon emissions raised in 2007 due to a technical defect in a major nuclear reactor has not helped to shift the discussion to a new radical ecological paradigm towards renewable energies as in Germany. Instead of questioning the safety and reliability of nuclear reactors Japan continues to make consumers believe that renewable energies are costly and low performing whereas nuclear power is deemed costly but clean, safe and high performing. How one defines a given problem often determines the solution one is looking for. Government and private business have continued for decades to make people falsely believe that linear economic growth and welfare can be maintained on a high level just by increasing the technical energy efficiency or recycling. This belief has proven wrong as the increase in waste output, carbon emissions and global warming shows.

In Japan many initiatives have been taken in the recent past to address the problem of global warming such as the '3R' initiative, the warm/cool biz initiative, ISO 14001, green purchasing, eco-tourism, eco-driving, eco-architecture, energy saving and eco-fairs. However the basic stance taken in Japan is to address the problem of global warming technically and on a private or state induced voluntary basis (Pizer et al, 2007). However, energy efficiency increases alone and voluntary acts alone will not solve the problems. To reduce carbons emissions one would need to increase the efficiency ratio by a factor of four or five based on the current already very high standards of efficiency in Japan: this is technically a mission impossible and even the most powerful car maker will have to acknowledge that technology and green purchasing will not solve the most urgent problem human mankind faces. The assumption that the environment can be saved with technology whilst maintaining the same current standards of mass consumption is not only refuted by NGO activists and critical scientists. In the simulative study on environmental trends up to 2030 even the cautious intergovernmental body OECD warns that technical efficiency gains will not be effective to counter the negative fallout of economic growth: " (...) in most cases the increasing pressures on the environment from population and economic growth have out-paced the benefits of any efficiency gains" (OECD, 2008, p.6). As critically observed by Professor Ryoichi Yamamoto from the University of Tokyo, one of the leading experts for green purchasing, a sense of urgency and the willingness to take drastic and radical measures among business leaders, academia, consumers and government authorities is missing. Continuing to offer the same solutions to problems which have been caused by these solutions is not realistic. Switching on an air conditioner in summer to cool down the room temperature will only increase the heat island effect and carbon emissions. Using an air conditioner to combat air pollution or make the air cleaner will only worsen the negative impact on the climate balance. It should not be forgotten that even energy efficient cars and energy efficient convenience stores, shopping malls, vending machines contribute to land destruction, congested roads, car accidents, garbage increase and noise pollution. As long as the quantitative economic gains are getting bigger attention than qualitative gains in terms of children friendly environments, high quality of living, slow life, green zones or community based conviviality a paradigm change is unlikely to happen.

The power of court justice

Several landmark decisions by courts have helped to enforce the polluter pays principle in the early 1970s. Six petrochemical companies in Yokkaichi were ordered in 1972 to jointly pay 88 million Yen to the victims of air pollution; the Mitsui Mining and Smelting Company was ordered in 1971 to pay 2.3 billion Yen in compensation for 489 victims of the so called 'Itai-Itai' disease caused by dumping cadmium into water used for irrigation of rice fields; the notorious Chisso corporation was ordered in 1973 by the district court of Kyushu to pay 930 million Yen in compensation to the victims of the 'Minamata' mercury poisoning. These lawsuits set precedents for subsequent rulings related to environmental pollution. The burden of proof was shifted on the polluter, who had to proof that he had not caused the pollution rather than the plaintiff needing to proof the contrary; new standards were set for proof and scientific evidence: a direct causal root cause effect was not anymore a strict requirement but it sufficed that there was statistical evidence for the damage allegations; finally the principle was established that industries have a joint and collective liability for pollution so plaintiffs could sue a single corporation rather than being obliged to take action against the whole industry.

A Japanese court has ordered the government to pay damages to 17 workers including eight who have died since who contracted lung diseases through exposure to asbestos on U.S. naval vessels. In a ruling from 2002 the Yokohama District Court said the government had failed to protect the safety of former employees of the Yokosuka naval base, who contracted cancer and pneumoconiosis. In 2004 Japan's Supreme Court had upheld a ruling that the state shares responsibility for the mercury poisoning at Minamata. The court in his decision ordered the national government and Kumamoto prefecture to pay 71.5 million Yen to 37 victims in compensation. The case that reached the high court was brought by victims who did not recognize a 1995 settlement, seeking instead a ruling that would support their claim that the government shared responsibility for Japan's worst environmental disaster.

In mid 2008 the Saga District Court ordered the government to open the floodgates of the Isahaya Bay dike in Nagasaki Prefecture, ruling in favor of some 2 500 fishermen who claimed the state project to fill in the bay has damaged the seawater environment in the area and hurt their business. "A substantial degree of evidence has been established that the closure of the floodgates has caused damage to the inside of the bay and the nearby fishing grounds," the presiding Judge said. But the judge declined to recognize a correlation between the floodgates' closure and damage in the entire Ariake Sea, citing insufficient verifiable evidence. The judge ruled that the government should leave the dike open for five years as a research period. The government has a three-year moratorium on the opening of the dike. The government has so far refused to open the floodgates, citing the huge costs of such an operation. The fishermen from four prefectures along the bay - Fukuoka, Saga, Nagasaki and Kumamoto - claimed the current in the Ariake Sea has weakened since the bay was closed by the 7 km dike in 1997, resulting in red tides and doldrums for their business. The government authorized the 250 billion Yen land fill project, designed to create farmland as well as to prevent floods, in 1986, creating controversy over the costs and benefits of the project and its environmental impact. The fishermen filed their first lawsuit seeking an injunction against the project in November 2002. The court granted their demand in August 2004 and fill work was halted. But the Fukuoka High Court authorized the resumption of the project and the Supreme Court upheld the decision in September 2005, prompting the plaintiffs to file a lawsuit eventually to demand that the government remove the dike and open the floodgates.

The Naha District Court in November 2008 supported about 600 residents' demands and ordered local governments to not use public funds to continue reclaiming Awase Tideland in Okinawa City. The ruling pointed out that it cannot recognize the economic rationality of the reclamation of development of the Awase district promoted by the local governments of Okinawa Prefecture and Okinawa City. The national and prefectural governments have promoted the reclamation of the Awase Tideland and surrounding area of 178 hectares. Okinawa City has planned to construct resort facilities there after jointly footing the bill of 7.4 billion Yen with the prefectural government to buy the reclaimed land.

The litigation against the under-construction of a road tunnel at Mount *Takao*, a declared quasi-national park, has been going on for the last two decades. The completion of the tunnel is critical for connecting the new 300 km long ring expressway the *Ken-o* expressway that stretches from Yokohama to Chiba area and aims to reduce traffic congestion. Since 2000 environmental opponents have filed four lawsuits against the government to stop construction of the planned tunnel. Activists also bought a plot land within the planned construction site but the government plans to expropriate landowners anyhow.

Product safety, malpractice litigation, information disclosure suits and environmental suits are key public rights of civilian society. Unfortunately most environmental litigation cases involve criminal or offensive behaviors that caused physical damage or permanent injuries and even death to the victims. The justice has a responsive or restorative function because environmental laws did not exist, had been violated or ignored, were not strict enough or had not been implemented. In Japan as in many others countries courts are the last resort for the citizens to have their victim status confirmed, to clarify guilt, accountabilities and responsibilities, to obtain compensation for incurred damage or seek financial redress or simply to draw public attention to their case. Unfortunately litigation cases are time consuming, cost a lot of money and have no preventive mecanism.Courts will only intervene when damage has been caused and when a victim represented by a lawyer brings up a case.

Recent large scale projects financed largely by taxpayer's money such as the newly built Shizuoka and Ibaraki airports or the second *Tomei* expressway have been pushed ahead by government and private industry despite their huge negative impact on the local environments for generations to come. Even though an environmental impact risk assessment law exists the state and the private industry have always given priority to the short-term economic gains before they consider long-term environmental concerns. They were irresponsible and did nothing until the court ordered them instead of taking proactive action to establish environmental responsibilities and awareness prevent pollution to happen or take appropriate measures to monitor and contain pollution at its source.

Opposition from prefectural governments against large scale projects that benefit only a few, offer no longterm social or qualitative payback or increase in quality of living for the local community is growing day by day. There is a hope that a new post Kyoto vision called *mottomenai* meaning literally not to buy, wish or desire things will eventually attract more followers and believers. There are many examples of citizens in Japan consuming only what they need, being aware of the longterm damage caused by unhealthy lifestyles, trying to predict and foresee the longterm environmental impact of their behavior and helping the community to preserve nature and the common heritage.

Conclusion and outlook

Japan needs a radical, inspiring refocus and reorientation rooted in its humanistic pre-Meiji traditions. Spiritual values such as ethical individualism, moral judgment, compassion, respect, tolerance, relative equality and justice that underpin the positive side of globalization need to be nurtured and fostered. There is a hope that a new political culture of global responsibility will help to instill positive social change and strengthen civil society further but for the time being the huge gender gap, the antagonism of childlessness versus over aging of society, severe mental distress among the general population, interpersonal alienation, ruthless private for profit thinking, low quality of life in terms of work life balance, natural resource overconsumption and unsolved social disparity problems keep Japan stuck in a spiritual and psychological no-man's-land under the heading "change without purpose".

The wish and desire for qualitative change may be there but reality talks a different language. The many grass root groups and NPOs that operate for the sake of a more just, equitable and fair society in Japan lack financial resources and institutional organization which might be viewed as a strength on one side as it means flexibility and spontaneous initiative but is also its weakness: to be long-term efficient NPOs need to voice their political agenda and lobby for their cause either through being represented in local, prefectural and national parliaments or through direct legislative participation in form of local, prefectural or national plebiscites.

The current social tensions and problems created by the limitations of the current economic model of over affluence and working for consuming call for a more child and family friendly environment, a better work-life balance, a higher quality of life, more support for family and community networks, better equal working opportunities, a higher representation of women in public functions and offices and more investments in long-term sustainable projects without putting a financial burden or health hazard on future generations. Some of the below recommendations may sound utopian and reflect wishful, idealistic thinking rather than reality. It is however hoped that citizens will exercise their influence either through NGOs or at the voting ballot to convince politicians, private industry leaders and top civil servants that it is more than overdue to correct and counterbalance the negative side of unilateral economic globalization by deeply reforming and improving the domestic social and public sectors.

Twenty changes citizens can believe in:

1. Abolish the lifetime employment privileges of civil servants, slash their

numbers radically, and open the civil service to foreigners. Compulsory volunteer community services for civil servants to be implemented.

2. Purge all the graduates with a degree from the Law Department of Tokyo University from the public or semi-public service and treat the ongoing *amakudari* practice as criminal and punishable act.

3. Allocate the active and passive voting rights to permanent foreign residents.

4. A political institutionalized class of civil servants and private industry representatives has been dominating public life for the last 100 years. To destroy the iron triangle politicians will not be permitted to be re-elected for more than two parliamentary terms and family members will not be permitted to succeed to a vacant constituency seat on national, prefectural and local levels. A 50% quota of parliamentary seats will be reserved exclusively to women. All parliamentary bills must come from the floor and must be discussed in public (public hearing) before being submitted to voting. Actively promote legislative referendums (plebiscites) initiated by citizens and give full access to information (information disclosure) and equal access to public media.

5. To improve the quality of family life in general it is necessary to take measures to radically reduce the anti-social male fulltime work ethos and change the role identity of male job earners. Promote measures to radically reduce male work time, implement new job sharing schemes, introduce work from home schemes, expand public day care center network, and give financial and social incentives for males to take a three year child care or parental leave and do the entire housework for that period. Increase male nurses and male social care workers. Promote active job reintegration measures and legislation to facilitate the return to work life for housewives as part of the workforce and reduce thereby the labor shortage. Radically increase wages and salaries for qualified women (equal pay for equal work)

6. Sustainable and grass root change will be driven mainly by women, who have been excluded from the public sphere for centuries. Reserve a quota of 50% for all government senior positions and private board of director appointments to qualified woman.

7. Food self-sufficiency rate to be brought back to a reasonable level. Public support and subsidies for organic food production. Production and use of pesticides and food additives to be strictly restricted and regulated.

8. The problem in Japan is not the lack of energy but the overconsumption of energy. The phasing out of nuclear energy has to go hand in hand with massive investments into renewable energies and a radical cut of energy consumption among households and in the transport and commercial sectors.

Implement a 100% price and tax hike on fossil energy use and gasoline for conventional cars. Increase the highway road taxes. Use the additional tax revenue generated to support investments and employment in the renewable energies sector. Expand public transport services in rural areas.

9. Implement a human rights ombudsman system. Treat mobbing and bullying as a criminal and punishable act. Promote diversity, ethnic tolerance and anti racism education in schools.

10. A right to Japanese nationality for every child born in Japan.

11. Promote bilingual curricula, mother language education and secure employment of foreign teachers for mixed children in public schools.

12. Abolish entrance exams and replace by graduation exams. Slash the tuition fees. Moral civil education, diversity education, non-violence and human rights education and environmental subjects to become the cornerstone of basic elementary education. Tax subsidies for schools who promote new global minded, ecological, less competitive and more convivial approaches to education.

13. The long-term ecological risks assessment of large public and private projects is ineffective despite the existing environmental legislation. This is due to the lack of effective citizen legal defense mechanisms against unviable and non sustainable projects. Establish a constitutional right to clean land/soil, air and water access and allow every citizen to file lawsuits against the state/private companies/individual polluters and ask for compensation. Lawyers shall be provided free of charge to plaintiffs. Strict application of the polluter pays principle.

14. The problem of public finance in Japan is not the lack of tax funds but the inequitable distribution and waste of taxpayers' money by civil servants respectively tax evasion by the wealthy. To combat growing social disparity local withholding taxes will be channeled to create an anti-poverty pension fund. Every unemployed, homeless, poor, foreigner, old aged or disabled citizen to be entitled to receive a minimum pension to ensure his own and/or dependent physical survival. The monthly lump sum is set at 100 000 Yen per person aged 18. The pension will be tax-free and set off against any other incomes to prevent abuse. Everybody can qualify for receiving the survival pension. The local Hello work office will be made accountable and responsible for paying out the pension, secure free housing upon request, provide free of charge job skills qualification training and find suitable employment to those receiving the pension. Once job stability and housing are secured pension payout will stop.

15. Too much attention and support is given to criminal offenders. Develop and employ thousands of new public mental health counselors to support victims and survivors of bullying, domestic violence, child abuse, substance abuse, crime and disaster victims. Establish a public education and support program against anti-social behavior of juveniles. Child care centers to give special support to young abusive parents. The prefectural mental health care centers need to be radically upgraded with resources, funds and qualified personnel.

16. Replace the institutionalized army by a volunteer corps and radically reduce its numbers. Restrict the role of the military to natural disaster intervention. No overseas dispatches to armed or non-humanitarian missions and no changes to the spirit and text of article 9. Overseas humanitarian SDF missions shall only be allowed and mandated by the UN Security Council.

17. Investments to extend natural parks and reserves and enforcement of strict protection of species and wildlife. No land development projects or business activity allowed near natural parks or in protected zones.

18. The members of the Japanese Packaging Association who accounts for most of the garbage and waste generated have to invest a certain percentage of their profits into environmental cleanup activities. Industries that pose a health hazard such as the artificial food additives industry or the pesticide producing industry have to finance public health campaigns.

19. Enable taxpayers to allocate 10% of their tax burden such as the income tax or resident tax to specific charity projects or NGO activities. Allow for all the 36 000 established NGOs to receive tax free donations from citizens.

20. War memories must be made open and transparent and preserved to prevent history from repeating itself. Mourning and remembering the memory of the civilian victims of Japanese aggression helps to overcome guilt and shame. The biographies of Asian war victims are to be documented and preserved in a national documentation center; the war crimes of Japanese against civilians are to be exhibited nationwide in museums; a national war memorial for the Asian victims of war to be built; slave laborers and comfort women to be morally and financially compensated; domestic history textbooks of world war II to be reviewed and approved by an international expert commission; a public agency of civic education to be founded under the auspices of UNESCO and publish free of charge studies about the war responsibility of the emperor and the war atrocities committed by Japanese soldiers in Asia such as the Nanking massacre, the experiments of Unit 731, the officially sanctioned rape of comfort women, the forced suicide of civilians in Okinawa, the secret killings of slave laborers and state abduction of citizens. Promote the study of joint war history by cross border school exchange initiatives and

create joint cross border cultural institutes for the prevention of war and study of peace in Asia. Take the German after war reconciliation efforts as best practice example.

Appendix A:

Full text of briefing by Minister of Environment Dr. Ichiro Kamoshita on May 21 2008 to the Foreign Press on the anti global warming policy of Japan.(Source Foreign Press Center of Japan)

(...) Please have a look at your materials. Item 1 is a scenic view of Toyako, and I will begin my discussion from item 2. The pie graph on the left shows major CO_2 emitting countries. About 27.1 billion tons of CO_2 is emitted every year, of which about 1.1.4 billion tons is absorbed by forests and oceans. Simply put, the planet is able to absorb no more than half of the CO_2 that we produce. The remainder accumulates in the atmosphere, and what to do about this excess CO_2 is an issue of the gravest importance for the people of this planet. As you are already aware, emissions by country—and bear in mind that these figures are for 2005 and therefore somewhat different at present—is 21% for the US, 18.8% for China, 12% for the 15 nations of the EU, 5.7% for Russia, and 4.5% for Japan.

More importantly, the graph on the right shows that emissions for the advanced countries between now and 2100 will for the most part peak and then gradually decline while emissions for developing countries will dramatically increase if they continue at their present pace. I don't think anyone disputes the scientific validity of the IPCC Fourth Assessment Report and what I've just presented. Therefore, constructing a framework for the period following the Kyoto Protocol requires that every country formulate a policy for taking part in such a framework and also requires that they overcome their different positions and viewpoints and make a real effort to achieving its goals. As I observed a moment ago, that we are emitting twice as much CO_2 than the planet is able to absorb is a fact that needs to be taken seriously.

Last December I attended the United Nations Framework Convention on Climate Change (COP13) at Bali. At the initial conference developing, newly industrialized, and advanced countries asserted their respective views and a chaotic debate ensued. Nonetheless, fearing the consequences of failing to bring their views together, in the end representatives of the various countries put together the Bali Action Plan. The Bali Action Plan is significant in that it puts every nation on a common course for dealing with a common issue. I think this represents a historic and splendid step forward for humankind. There is now tremendous debate over the specific items contained in the Action Plan leading up to next year's COP15, and reaching agreement is expected to be quite difficult. But I ask all of you to reflect deeply on the significance of the IPCC receiving the Nobel Peace Prize last year. Even now, countries in the South Pacific such as Tuvalu are on the verge of disappearing under rising sea levels. As glaciers in the Himalayas melt water builds up, causing pressure that threatens to give way in the form of floods and landslides. These developments mean that we must succeed in implementing the Bali Action Plan at COP15 next year in Copenhagen. Therefore, as the host country of this year's G8 Summit, Japan should take the lead in maintaining and building on the momentum for dealing with these environmental problems - climate change especially - and including issues concerning international opinion and science and technology.

Item 3 shows the upcoming international conference schedule. COP15 in 2009 is one of the schedule's goals. The Toyako Summit is positioned midway between COP13 and COP15. I think the Summit will address how active a role the advanced countries—G8 countries especially—will take and how they can assist the Group of 77 developing countries. Since both developing and advanced countries will take part in COP15, the G8 Summit will address how and to what extent the advanced countries can help along the developing countries, including issues concerning the transfer of technology and capital mechanisms. Also important is whether the G8 countries can take the initiative by coming to an agreement concerning their own emissions reductions because that will determine how much cohesion they have on the issue ahead of COP15.

As the schedule shows, the G8 Environment Ministers' Meeting will be held in Kobe this weekend from the 24th through the 26th. Item 4 shows the meeting's agenda. One of the objectives of the meeting, of course, is to engage in a substantive discussion and obtain agreements from each country prior to the G8 Toyako Summit. Another item is to deliberate on the framework to be put in place starting in 2013. There is considerable interest as to what extent the position of the Environment Ministers' Meeting at the mid-point in the schedule can contribute to the process. A specific topic will be how to manage the transition from our current fossil fuel-dependent carbon society to a low-carbon society to ensure that we achieve our long-term emission targets. I want to see deliberations on the specific nature of a vision for achieving these long-term goals. There will also be discussion on how to maintain international research partnerships. These partnerships are presently bilateral in form, and I would like to see efforts toward achieving a more solid framework. I also think we need an exchange of views about the system and policy needed to make the transition to a low-carbon society.

The second topic is the issue of cooperation between developed and developing countries. As you may already know, Japan has exchanged memorandums of agreement with countries in Asia—China and India, for instance—for cooperation in the form of a bilateral "co-benefit approach". Put simply, the co-benefit approach entails working closely with countries that face the same air, water, and other pollution issues Japan faced when it was industrializing decades ago. This is called a "co-benefit approach" because working seriously on pollution produces a second benefit of preventing global warming.

The discussion on developed-developing country cooperation will focus on how to implement appropriate policies and how to form a cooperative framework for capital aid and human resource training.

I think the final topic, "the next framework", will entail substantial debate at the Environment Ministers' Meeting in Kobe. One item is reduction levels leading up to the peak emissions period. Prime Minister Fukuda announced at the Davos Conference in January that Japan will take the initiative in implementing the second item, the "sectoral approach", which uses scientific data to establish fair national targets. There will also be discussion on how developing countries can achieve reductions. Finally—and as you are probably already aware of from news reports—I understand that discussion on the major country dialogue process will focus on how to keep the Gleneagles G20 Dialogue moving forward.

I will now turn to item 5, Japan's effort to establish quantified national targets under the Cool Earth concept. As I mentioned a moment ago, Prime Minister Fukuda presented this concept at the Davos Conference. The IPCC has warned that targets in any post-Kyoto Protocol framework must have global greenhouse gas emissions peak within the next 10 to 20 years and reduce them at least by half by 2050. The IPCC has also requested that the UN study policy alternatives to achieve this, and Japan on its part has announced its support of quantifiable national targets to accompany efforts to reduce greenhouse gases by major emitting countries. Crucial to formulating these targets is a bottom-up approach that sets the potential amount that can be reduced and ensures fair reduction targets. The second item is the Cool Earth Partnership, a framework for international environmental cooperation that entails building a new capital mechanism in the 10 billion ton range for assisting the global warming efforts of developing countries. The third item is innovation. Developing innovative technology and making the transition to a low-carbon society is crucial, and over the next five years around 30 billion dollars of capital will fund research and development in the environmental and energy fields.

Now please look at item 6. The relationship between gross targets by country and the sectoral approach is often misunderstood, so I want everyone to have a proper grasp of the relationship. I noted that Japan advocates gross targets by country as the way to reach a global emissions peak in the next 10 to 20 years and halve emissions by 2050. Setting national gross emissions entails a scientific approach to ensure that potential reductions for a given sector are fair and involve the application of technology. To promote effective emissions reductions on a worldwide basis requires the participation of every major emitting country. For instance, when we look at specific sectors such as steel, electricity, or cement, it is evident that potential reductions can be derived based on a fair formula and then aggregated to determine the gross amount.

I want us to take the initiative to introduce the sectoral approach to the international community, and I intend to thoroughly discuss the issue at this weekend's Environment Ministers' Meeting.

Now we turn to item 7 and the topic of Asian and global partnerships and cooperation. Explosive economic growth is occurring all over the world and in Asian countries especially. Greenhouse gas emissions are expected to increase and in fact this is already happening. Pollution and waste problems are clearly evident. It is crucial to find comprehensive solutions to the environmental and climate change issues accompanying regional growth and achieve sustainable development. A solution depends on the rapid transfer of pollution prevention and energy conservation technologies refined by the experience of advanced countries. That is, it is necessary to simultaneously promote solutions in the form of a "co-benefit policy" aimed at fostering low-carbon, resource recycling sustainable societies. As the diagram illustrates, how developed countries assist developing countries is crucial to achieving the fundamental objective of enabling the latter to take advantage of the lessons already learned by developed countries and "leapfrog" directly to the low-carbon society stage. I want to work toward achieving a "clean Asia initiative" by discussing this issue in greater detail at the Environment Ministers' Meeting this weekend and at the East Asian Summit Environment Ministers' Meeting in October.

Now, I'll take a look at Japan's own efforts to deal with global warming. Japan must work to become a low-carbon society. Item 8 shows current CO2 emission trends by sector. The industrial sector, which includes factories and that kind of place, accounts for most emissions but also shows a slight downward trend. In contrast, compared with 1990 levels, emissions for things like office buildings that make up the commercial sector and the residential sector have significantly increased. If Japan is to exercise leadership as the host country of the G8 Summit, it must meet its Kyoto Protocol target of a 6% reduction. The industrial sector needs to formulate Voluntary Action Plans that are more far-reaching and work harder to achieve them. Unfortunately, the commercial and residential sectors have yet to make a sufficient effort in this regard. The Kyoto Protocol Target Attainment Plan was revised in March, but I think progress will need to be very closely monitored. The Law Concerning Measures to Cope with Global Warming and the Law Concerning the Rational Use of Energy, which are currently under debate in the Diet, both need to be revised to ensure that Japan's global warming measures make steady progress. If the state of progress doesn't improve, it may be necessary to introduce additional administrative measures over the next two years. Japan has made an international commitment to reduce emissions by 6%, and I am confident that an effort by every citizen can achieve this first commitment period target. But it may be difficult for Japan to achieve the mid-term and 2050 long-term reduction targets needed to achieve a low-carbon society relying only on the Voluntary Action

Plans of the industrial sector. But this is only my personal opinion.

Item 9 summarizes the various issues that Japan needs to work on. The left side lists the "supply of energy conservation technologies" that will be needed and the right side "demand for low-carbon goods and services" as well as "lifestyle innovation". I think everyone is aware that Japan is a world leader in the area of energy conservation technology innovation. In addition to innovation, Japan will need to make a shift in energy use. Achieving a low-carbon society will require increasing the use of nuclear power generation. We will also need to use as much renewable energy as possible, especially solar and small hydropower and biomass. In addition, Japan needs to consider finding ways to apply carbon capture and storage, though I don't know the specifics about the potential of this technology. Concerning lifestyle innovation on the right side, I think it very important that Japan's citizens change their lifestyles through environmentally conscious working and living.

For instance, today I am speaking to all of you in person, but all one needs is an IT terminal to take part in a meeting like this at home, thus eliminating the CO_2 emissions generated by the transportation used to get here. Indeed, about half of the work we all do can be done at home as long as there is a networked computer. Working to conserve energy through incentives that apply only to the purchase of environmentally conscious products will foster business style innovation by stimulating demand for low-carbon products and services. Another goal is "compact cities" in which people can get around on foot and which already exist in EU countries. I think this will involve revitalizing areas around train stations and building mass transit and infrastructure. I am convinced that smoothly combining these policies and moving quickly to implement them can achieve a low-carbon society. Carbon pricing through emissions trading and environment taxes—which links the supply of energy conservation technologies on the left and the demand for low-carbon goods and services on the right—provides even more incentive to reduce emissions. Since a menu of these incentives already exists, how fast they are incorporated into the social system will be a factor in a political solution to the problem.

Now, I'll go over the current state of deliberations on emissions credits in Japan. The Policy Strategy Working Group of the Council on the Global Warming Issue out of the Prime Minister's office has started to discuss emissions trading. The Ministry of the Environment, which has already implemented a voluntary domestic emissions trading system, has issued an interim report detailing the specifics of a domestic emissions trading system minus the "voluntary" component. The Ministry of Economy, Trade and Industry is increasingly working on this issue and I have heard that the Tokyo Stock Exchange has started researching it as well. For its part, the Ministry of the Environment wants to formulate a plan for a complete system and present it to the public and experts for detailed debate as early as possible. (...)

Questions & Answers

Q: Concerning your discussion of incentives, I often hear people involved in wind generated electricity in Japan complain that they receive no government assistance whatsoever. Likewise, those involved in solar power talk about the fact that the feed-in-tariff has been abolished. Do you think these incentives will be revived or that the situation will change?

A: To promote the efficient use of renewable energy, solar energy especially benefited from subsidies and its use spread rapidly as a result. Since the use of solar energy has become common the decision was to eliminate subsidies for the time being—though this was not the Ministry of the Environment's decision. But now that we are in the first commitment period for the Kyoto Protocol and need to reduce emissions by 6%, there is once again debate within the government over creating incentive mechanisms.

Q: In Japan, I think the industry that has the most potential for more efficient energy use is construction. As everyone here is well aware, homes in Japan are cold in the winter and hot in the summer and require air conditioning year round. What do you think about requiring the construction industry to build homes of the same sturdy construction as in the US and Europe?

A: Prime Minister Fukuda has talked about "200 year housing", and the government has started discussing the need for a durable housing stock to replace the "scrap and build" method. Prime Minister Fukuda proposed this very early on and I think policy will move in that direction. But there is room to question whether US and European housing is really suitable to Japan. Traditional Japanese rooms are well ventilated to resist humidity, and so I think one approach would be to review the characteristics of the traditional Japanese home.

Q: As Minister, you have sent the message to the industrial sector that Japan must reduce emissions by 6%. But you also seem pessimistic as to whether the industrial sector can actually achieve this. You mentioned the possibility of additional administrative measures, so what specifically are you referring to?

A: I think the emissions credits that I discussed at the end are the most effective alternative. The industrial sector has indicated that it can achieve the 6% reduction included in the recent revision of the Kyoto Protocol Target Attainment Plan, so we will want to carefully watch how things develop for a while. But failing to reach targets by the 2010 mid-point will make it very unlikely that the targets will be attained by 2012. Therefore, at this stage we are already talking about strictly managing progress and adopting an even more extensive policy as early as we can.

Q: What views did you exchange with China's environmental policy leaders during your recent trip to China to attend the Boao Forum for Asia?

A: I was invited to attend China's Boao Forum for Asia, which I thought was a quite magnificent and substantial conference. For environmental issues especially, I am thoroughly convinced that China is becoming more deeply engaged and is enthusiastic about assuming a responsible role in the international community. Moreover, deliberations among the various participants included the exchange of information as well as discussion about coordinating policy, especially concerning the increasing problem of cross-border pollution, yellow sand, and oxidant pollution. I also think the Chinese understood my position that "common but differentiated responsibility" is the underlying principle of the sectoral approach. In any event, I left the conference convinced that China and Japan are important partners when it comes to dealing with the environment.

Q: In order for Japan to halve emissions by 2050 you say it may not be enough to rely on the industrial sector to regulate itself and that it may be necessary to impose various requirements. If voluntary regulation is insufficient, what kind of mandatory reduction targets might be imposed on the industrial sector?

A: This issue has to be considered in two parts. The first commitment period of the Kyoto Protocol honors the Voluntary Action Plan approach. Nonetheless, I also think that Voluntary Action Plans are incapable of achieving the 25% to 40% reductions that are part of the post-Kyoto framework that follows. Therefore, we need to introduce incentives to the reduction effort in the form of policy and economic measures, and in this regard I think a cap-and-trade system is the first choice. I also think that the industrial sector is gradually becoming aware of this possibility for the post-Kyoto phase. I am confident that the 6% reduction will be achieved for the first commitment period, but we are giving careful consideration to introducing an environmental tax or cap-and-trade system, depending on the situation, as a means for quickly reaching the targets in the event that it should appear otherwise.

Q: The G8 Environmental Ministers' Meeting is coming up, so what is the position on the sectoral approach of the other G8 countries? Are any countries especially opposed? And do you think all countries will have reached agreement by the end of the G8 Summit this summer?

A: On May 8 during the Bali Conference the sectoral approach was discussed at a workshop attended by many scholars and policy officials. One view at this gathering expressed concern that developing countries cannot achieve reduction targets via the sectoral approach alone. On the other hand, I think advanced countries agreed that accumulating results by sector is a very scientific approach. I observed earlier that reaching gross national targets by aggregating sectors is one approach to attaining emissions targets.

Therefore, one approach is aggregating results by sector using a scientific approach. Ultimately, there needs to be some kind of national gross target, however. I observed earlier that developing, newly industrialized, and advanced countries have different approaches and that the sectoral approach under the principle of "common but differentiated responsibility" is one of these. I think the validity of this approach is universally understood and so I believe that we will obtain the agreement of the other countries at the G8 Environmental Ministers' Meeting."

Appendix B:

Interview conducted by P.Hein with Mr Marutei Tsurunen, member of the
House of Councilors of Japan for the Democratic Party. Published by P. Hein in
'Japan Magazin', 2005, Vol 16, No 6, pp 12-13

Questions to Mr. Tsurunen:

1. Why is Prime Minister Koizumi himself and his politics so popular among
    Japanese voters?

Answer: Koizumi focused in the latest election only on the topic of postal
privatization. His core message was: either you vote for against postal privatization. He repeated this same message all again during his campaign. The mass
media also rallied behind him and was against the "Democratic Party". Voters
and mass media seem him as a strong leader but for us he is a dictator who does
not listen to anyone. He really thinks people are behind him and therefore he is
arrogant too.

2. Why has your party been so weak in the elections?

Answer: I do not agree with the term "weak". The reason why we lost so
many seats is because our election program formulated in our political manifest
did not reach the people. Again the mass media did not introduce our ideas to the
voters. Another reason for our defeat was that we did not have a clear counter-
proposal for postal privatization- due to the strong influence of the postal labor
union in the party our approach was to implement postal privatization little by
little. Finally the timing was bad: the election came too soon to convince voters.
In previous elections our manifests succeeded well. Looking however at the total
number of opposition votes obtained it is important to know that the opposition
had one million more votes than the ruling party in proportional districts but
those votes were divided within the three main opposition parties- the social
democratic; the communist and the Democratic Party and therefore the opposition could not gain constituency seats.

3. Why are so many LDP members so keen to visit the Yasukuni shrine again
    and again and provoke thereby the international community?

Answer: Because of the strong nationalism among the leaders of the LDP. In
their mind the war against Asia was not an invasion but aimed to help Asia. So
in their thinking the military officers who have been punished in 1945 are not to
be looked upon as criminals but as a kind of war leaders. Before Koizumi became prime minister he promised to the influential organization of victims of the
war which counts seven millions members and constitutes a big support organization to the LDP to visit the shrine and pray for the victims. So he is probably

honest when he says that he only wants to pray to all the victims of war. The newly appointed ministers among them the possible new Prime Minister Aso have promised to Koizumi that they will continue those visits. Another LDP member, Fukuda, who opposed the visits has not been given a minister post as a consequence.

4. The LDP wants to alter the Japanese peace constitution and abolish article 9. How do you evaluate this development as a member of the Constitution parliamentary committee?

Answer: The LDP actually wants to add new changes and not really abolish article 9. The LDP mentions the Self Defense Forces for the first time in the Constitution and wants to allow Japan to defend itself, to send SDF units overseas if the UN asks for help and to allow them to take in part in collective security activities to support the Allies. Any changes to the Constitution need to be approved by a two third majority of both houses and a national referendum and so we need not be worried about too big changes.

5. How do Japanese look at long-term resident foreigners like you? Why is it not possible for foreigners to get equal political rights?

Answer: Unfortunately foreigners are considered as outsiders here. Japanese only accept us on their terms and expect us not to get involved too much into politics. Our party and the Buddhist ruling coalition party 'Komeito' favor more political rights for foreigners, the LDP is against because they fear that if foreigners would be elected as local mayors or even prefectural governors they would control Japan. It is still a long way to equal political rights for foreigners in Japan.

6. How can Japan contribute to the Irak?

Answer: We should not keep SDF units in the Irak. The only reason they are there is to show the world that Japan supports the USA. The few Japanese there can do very little. It would make more sense to help the Irak by helping the local people to help themselves. If the US quit Irak Japan will do the same. Koizumi listens too much to the USA.

7. The abduction issue of Japanese citizens to North Korea is a hot spot issue. Why is Japan not opting for economic sanctions against the dictator Kim Ill Sung?

Answer: Economic sanctions should not be decided by Japan alone but done in concert with the USA, China, South Korea and Russia. Moreover the USA has more interest in solving first the nuclear weapons issue. Personally I think-

and there I am in disagreement with most Japanese- that the abduction issue should not be politically highlighted too much for two reasons: Japan did more terrible things during the war to Koreans and North Korea has abducted far more people from South Korea without leading to a political stir. Of course it remains a crime and the abductees should get back.

8. The relaxed education policy of the Education Ministry has failed. What needs to be done to improve the education system in Japan?

Answer: I think that the *yutori* concept in itself has not been wrong. 'Yutori' means that pupils have school free on Saturdays, have a less compulsory curriculum with more free time and can focus on more selective topics. What is wrong is that there is too much competition in education. Parents send their children to special afterschool cram schools to prepare them for tough school entry exams. A relaxed approach to education will only be possible if the competition is reduced and if it is made easier to enter university like in Finland for example. Also I believe strongly education should be free of charge.

9. Japan is behind its targets to reduce C02 emissions. What is your evaluation of environmental policy in Japan?

Answer: Much more should be done. The new environmental tax plan is a good reform but it is not enough. New energies and not nuclear energy which is dangerous have to be much more promoted. Among the new energies hydrogen is the most promising. Iceland for example gains plenty of energy from hydrogen I am personally very active to promote organic farming in Japan and reduce environmental poisonous substances like asbestos or pesticides. This is becoming a big problem in Japan.

10. Do you think that Japanese have become more global, international and global minded over the last 20 years or so?

Answer: To this question I have to reply: yes and no. Yes if you consider the intensity of international exchange with Japanese and the influence of Japanese culture abroad but open-minded: no.

Even if Japanese know much more about the world than before they are still very close minded and conservative, especially old people. It is their conviction that Westerners cannot understand the Japanese mind. Even in my case it happens to me that my parliamentary colleagues ask me during a conversation in Japanese: do you really understand us? And then I get angry because I really want to understand even if I am an outsider.

Appendix C:

Interview conducted by P.Hein with Ms Yukiko Koike, member of the governmental LDP party and previous Minister of the Environment of Japan. Published by P.Hein on 18 February 2005 in 'Letzeburger Land', p 7

Q: Kyoto protocol: Japan is far behind its targets to achieve the legally required 6% reductions. What actions you intend to take in 2005 to reduce greenhouse gases (Climate Change) dramatically?

Answer :

According to the latest data of the Ministry of Environment greenhouse gases have increased by 8% in 2003.The Kyoto target is 6% reductions based on the 1990 levels. So the total level of reductions to be achieved in the period from 2008 to 2012 amounts to 14%. At this stage the Government is assessing and reviewing its "Climate Change Policy Program" to identify necessary additional effort to reach the target. The Central Environment Council (A Council of environmental authorities) has recommended additional measures: among them 1. A "Mandatory Greenhouse Gas Accounting and Reporting System" for private companies; 2. A "Voluntary trading emissions scheme" similar to the EU Emission Trading Scheme and 3. A "carbon or energy tax" discussed currently in the public.

To mark the worldwide validation of the Kyoto protocol an international event hosted by the Ministry of Environment will take place in Kyoto on 16 February. What is however most important is to change the mindset of the people living in Japan. Reducing the emission of greenhouse gases is finally good for the future of our children.

Q:Japan is far behind Europe when it comes to investments in renewable energies. What are your planned actions to increase its percentage? Do you plan to stop nuclear energy production like in Germany?

Answer:

I recently visited Denmark to visit wind power stations. Denmark is advanced in the use of wind power. However, I hear they may import cheap electricity generated by nuclear power plant in Germany due to liberalization of energy supply market. Japan plans to increase the use of wind power; for solar energy Japan is already number 1 producer in the world. Regarding solar energy technology Japanese companies like Sharp are world leaders and export their technology even to Europe. Japan plans to produce 4820000 kW solar electricity and 3000000kW wind energy by 2010. To achieve these targets, a law requires power suppliers to buy electricity generated by renewable energy.

Furthermore, experimental "renewable energy model areas" in various parts in Japan are planned. It is also planned to expand the use of solar energy for private housing.

Nuclear power does not contribute to global warming and is considered an important energy supply source. Reprocessing and disposal of nuclear waste is planned in Rokkasho (Northern Japan). Making the safe and cost-efficient use of nuclear power possible will be a key issue.

Q:Japan's final energy consumption and C02 emissions grows year by year. The national consumption grows steadily. What laws do you intend to introduce to drastically reduce energy consumption like in Europe? Will there be higher taxes on fuel energy consumption?

Answer:

Energy efficiency of Japan is internationally high due to huge effort for energy saving in the past responding to the oil crises in 70s and 80s. CO2 efficiency for the iron and steel sector and cement industry which account for high amount of emissions is higher in Japan than in Europe.   Yet national energy consumption and C02 emissions in particular have been increasing since 1990 but for greenhouse gases overall the emission record has improved in recent times. Especially for transport sector, private sector and private/public offices an increase in C02 emissions has been noticed. Now the government is working to strengthen the Climate Change Policy Law and the Energy Saving Law. A new "carbon/energy tax" which has been proposed by the Ministry and is currently under discussion will be effective for the private and transport sector...

China should not pollute the world. The total energy balance for China calculated in tons of oil exceeds Japan by far (570 Mio ton versus 342 in 2001). C02 emissions in Japan are less than half of China. Japan has been making big effort in environmental cooperation with China. Overall it can be said that changing the mindset of people like using bicycles instead of car can contribute to achieve the targets.

Q:Garbage production is a big problem in Japan. What actions you plan to take to reduce garbage production and pollution of the environment? Will you continue to build artificial islands in the sea from garbage?

Answer:

Due to economic development production of waste has increased and amounts to 1.1kg per person per day. To tackle this challenge the government has introduced in 2000 the "Fundamental law for establishing a sound material-cycle society". This law aims to change the lifestyle of people by promoting recycling and more efficient use of resources. Laws have been introduced for the recycling of food, home electronics, construction materials and cars. As of today recycling ratios for pet bottles (61%); aluminum can (81%) and steel cans (87.5%) is already high in Japan.

The target of better use of resources is to improve and raise efficiency (in terms of resource input per produced economic value) by 40% in 2010 compared to 2000. Non-recyclable waste is burned and only the residue (ash) is land filled. The dioxin emissions have been reduced by 98% thanks to tighter regulations and new technology used in waste incinerators. Landfill of waste in the sea has been reduced to 29 locations (1.4% of all waste locations).

In April this year the G8 environmental ministers will meet in Japan to launching the 3R initiative. 3R stands for Reduce, reuse, recycle. 3R initiative was agreed on at the G8 Summit last year based on a proposal by Japan.

Q:It appears to foreigners that compared to Europe big Japanese famous industrial companies/groups are only interested in "ecology/environment" if it serves their business interests. NPOs seem to have little influence in Japan. Do you intend to better control the big companies (tax incentives) and also do you intend to give more –financial-support to NPOs?

Answer:

Japan is not behind Europe: Japan is leading the hit list of ISO14001 awarded companies in the world with almost 17,000 companies registered. More than 700 companies issue environmental annual reports. The Prius hybrid car from Toyota is a bestseller worldwide. Tax wise companies can make an extraordinary depreciation for environmental investments. The planned carbon tax takes into consideration total activities of a company in the field of global warming. As for NPOs they play an active part in legislation in Japan: a "Japan Fund for Global Environment" has been created to support NPOs active in the field of environmental protection financially.

Q:What important environment improvements have you achieved since you became minister under Koizumi?

Answer:

I have launched an initiative called "HERB" standing for healthy; ecology and economy; rich (material and spiritual) and beautiful. It is a vision for the environment for the year up to 2025. We work also on Ecotourism projects to promote sustainable tourism based on local natural resource and intend to appoint "100 000 Ministers of Environment in a family" among the citizens in Japan who contribute to increase environmental consciousness. Everybody contributing to the environment by his actions can apply through the internet.

Regarding environmental education, environmental education is incorporated in the curriculum at school. Internationally we work closely together with Korea and China to promote environmental education.

References

Abe, Chikara (2002) Impurity and death. A Japanese perspective, Publisher.com

Adachi, Nobuko ed. (2006) Japanese diasporas: unsung pasts, conflicting presents, and uncertain futures, NY and London: Routledge

Akira, Kawasaki (2007). Article 9's global impact. Foreign Policy In Focus, Washington DC, retrieved on April 18, 2008 from the internet address http://fpif.org/fpiftxt/4426

Alomes, Stephen ed. (2005) Islands in the stream: Australia and Japan face globalization, Hawthorn: Maribyrnong Press

Amemiya, Koji and Macer, Darryl (1999) Environmental education and environmental behavior in Japanese students, Eubios Journal of Asian and International Bioethics, 9, pp 109-115

Amino, Yoshihiko (1987) Muen, kugai, raku: freedom and peace in middle age Japan (in Japanese) Heibonsha, Zoho edition

_____(1992) Deconstructing Japan, East Asian History, 3, pp 121-142

_____(1996) Emperor, rice and commoners in: Donald Denoon, Markavan Hudson, Gavan McCormack, Tessa Morris-Suzuki eds. (1996) Multicultural Japan: Palaeolithic to Postmodern, pp 235-244, Cambridge University Press

_____(2001) Commerce and finance in the middle ages: the beginnings of capitalism, Acta Asiatica 81, pp 1-19

_____(2007) Medieval Japanese constructions of peace and liberty: muen, kugai and raku, International Journal of Asian Studies, Vol, No 2, pp 161-172

Ansart, Olivier (2007) Loyality in seventeenth and eighteencentury samurai discourse, Japanese studies, Vol 27, No 2, pp 139-154

Aoki, Hideo (2006) Japan's underclass: day labourers and the homeless, Melbourne: Trans Pacific Press

Arase, David (1995) Buying power.The political economy of Japan's foreign aid, Boulder Colorada: Lienne Rieler

Arase, David ed (2005) Japan's foreign aid: old continuities and new directions,

Oxon and New York: Routledge

Arendt, Hannah (1958) The human condition, University of Chicago Press

_____(2005) Promise of politics, Westminster: Knopf Publishing Group

_____(2007) The great tradition I: law and power, Social Research, Vol 74, No 3, pp 713-726

_____(2007) The great tradition II: ruling and being Ruled, Social Research, Vol 74, No 4, pp 941-954

Baerwald, Hans H (1974) Japan's parliament: an introduction, London: Cambridge University Press

Befu, Harumi (2001) Hegemony of homogeneity: an anthropological analysis of "Nihonjinron", Melbourne: Trans Pacific Press

Benedict, Ruth (1989) The Chrysanthemum and the sword: patterns of Japanese culture, Boston: Houghton Mifflin Company

Bernstein, Gail Lee et al (2005) Public spheres, private lives in modern Japan 1600-1950. Essays in Honor of Albert Craig, Harvard Monographs Series

Barrett, Brendan F. D (2005) Ecological modernisation and Japan, Routledge

Burgess, Chris (2004) (Re)constructing identities: international marriage migrants as potential agents of social change in a globalising Japan, Asian Studies Review, Volume 28, Issue 3, pp 223-242

Burkman, Thomas W. (1990) Nitobe Inazo : from world order to regional order in: Rimer, J.Th., Culture and Identity : Japanese intellectuals during the interwar years, Princeton University Press

_____(2008) Japan and the league of nations, Honolulu: University of Hawai Press

Buruma, Ian (1994) The wages of guilt: memories of war in Japan and Germany, New York: Farrar, Straus, Giroux

Calichman, Richard F. Ed. (2005) Contemporary Japanese thought, New York: Columbia University Press

Chan, Jennifer (2008) Another Japan is possible: new social movements and global citizenship education, Stanford University Press

Chang, Gordon (2006) Nuclear showdown: North Korea takes on the world, New York: Random House Inc.

Chiba, Shin (1995) Hannah Arendt on love and the political: love, friendship, and citizenship, The Review of Politics, Vol. 57, No. 3, pp 505-535

_____(2006) Hannah Arendt, the nation state and federalism - beyond the Sovereign System?, The Journal of Social Sciences, 57 COE, Special Issues, pp 5-36

Chun, Jayson Makoto (2006) A Nation of a hundred million idiots? A social history of Japanese television, 1953 – 1973, London: Routledge

Clammer, John (2001) Japan and its others: globalization, difference and the critique of modernity, Melbourne: Trans Pacific Press

Clarke, Peter B. (2006) New religions in global perspective, New York : Routledge

Conduit, Anne & Andy (1996) Educating Andy. The experiences of a foreign family in the Japanese elementary school system, Tokyo: Kodansha

Crome, Peter (1988) The Tenno. Japan behind the chrysanthemum curtain (in German), Koeln: Kiepenheuer und Witsch

Dale, Peter N (1998) The myth of Japanese uniqueness, London: Routledge

Delanty, Gerard (2004) An interview with S.N. Eisenstadt: Pluralism and the multiple forms of modernity, European Journal of Social Theory, 7 (3), pp 391-404

Denoon, Donald et al eds. (2001) Multicultural Japan: palaeolithic to postmodern, Cambridge: Cambridge University Press.

DeWit, Andrew (2008) Mediating externalities: energy and environmental risks in Japan, paper retrieved on 1 November 2008 from the internet address http:// www.rikkyo.ac.jp /eco/research /paper /no061.html

Doi, Takeo (2004) Understanding *amae*: the Japanese concept of need-love, Honolulu: University of Hawai Press

Doi, Takeo (1992) On the concept of *amae*, Infant Mental Health Journal, 13, 7–11

American Psychiatric Association (2000) Diagnostic and Statistical Manual of Mental Disorders DSM-IV-TR Fourth Edition, American Psychiatric Publishing, Inc

Duerckheim, Karlfried Graf (2003) Hara, Otto Wilhelm Barth Verlag (in German)

Eades, J.S., Gill, Tom and Befu, Harumi eds. (2000) Globalization and social change in contemporary Japan, Melbourne: Trans Pacific Press.

Eisenstadt, Samuel N. (1971) Political sociology: a reader, New York: Basic Books

_____(1996) Japanese civilization: a comparative review, University of Chicago Press

_____(2003) Comparative civilizations and multiple modernities : a collection of essays, Brill, N.H.E.J., N.V. Koninklijke, Boekhandel en Drukkerij

Feldman, Eric A. (2000) Ritual of rights in Japan: law, society and health policy, New York: Cambridge University Press

Field, Norma (1993) In the realm of a dying Emperor: Japan at century's end, New York: Vintage Books.

Foljanty-Jost, Gesine (2005) NGOs in environmental networks in Germany and Japan: the question of power and influence, Social Science Japan Journal, 8: pp 103-117

Foreign Press Center (2008) Inside-Out. A mini-encyclopeadia of Japanese culture, Tokyo

Frankl, E. Viktor (2006) Man's search for meaning, Beacon Press

Friday, Karl (2004) Samurai, warfare, and the state in early Japan, Routledge

Fujiwara, Masahiko (2007) The dignity of the nation, Tokyo: IBC publishing

George, Timothy S. (2005) Tanaka Shozo's vision of an alternative constitution-al modernity for Japan, pp 89-116 in: Bernstein, Gail Lee et al, Public spheres, private lives in modern Japan 1600-1950. Essays in Honor of Albert Craig, Harvard Monographs Series

Georgeou, Nichole (2006) Tense relations. The tradition of *hoshi* and emergence of *borantia* in Japan, University of Wollongong thesis retrieved on 15 october 2008 from the internet address http://www.library. uow.edu.au/ adt-NWU/uploads/approved/.../public/02Whole.pdf

Galbraith, John K. (1958) The affluent society, New American Library

Goodman, Roger (2001) Children of the Japanese state: the changing role of child protection institutions in contemporary Japan, Oxford University Press

_____(2002) Family and social policy in Japan, Cambridge University Press

Goodman, Roger and Philipps, David (2003) Can the Japanese change their education system? (Oxford Studies in Comparative Education), Symposium Books

Gordon, Andrew ed. (1993) Postwar Japan as history, Berkeley and Los Angeles, California: University of California Press

Griffiths, Kathleen M. et al (2006) Stigma in response to mental disorders: a comparison of Australia and Japan. BMC Psychiatry 6:21, retrieved on 17 October 2007 from the internet address http://www.pubmed central.nih. gov/ articlerender.fcgi?artid=1525161

Habermas,Juergen (1983) Hannah Arendt: on the concept of power: in philo-sophical-political profiles, London: Heinemann

Haddad, Marie A. (2007) Politics and volunteering in Japan: a global perspective, Cambridge University Press

Hara, Kimie and Jukes, Geoffrey eds. (2007) New initiatives for solving the northern territories issue between Japan and Russia: an inspiration from the Aland islands, retrieved on 10 october 2008 from the internet address www.csis.org/media/csis/pubs/issues insights_v07n04

Hardacre, Helen (2003) After Aum: religion and civil society in Japan in: The state of civil society in Japan, Edited by Frank J. Schwartz and Susan J. Pharr, Cambridge and New York: Cambridge University Press

Hasegawa, Koichi (2004) Constructing civil society in Japan: voices of environmental movements, Melbourne: Transpacific Press

Hasegawa, Mike (2006) "We Are Not Garbage!": the homeless movement in Tokyo, 1994-2002, London: Routledge

Hashimoto, Akiko (1999) Japanese and German projects of moral recovery: toward a new understanding of war memories in defeated nations, Harvard University Edwin O. Reischauer Institute of Japanese Studies Occasional Papers in Japanese Studies Number 1999-01

Hayashi, Sachiko et al (1998) Client-centered therapy in Japan, Journal of Humanistic Psychology, Vol 38, No 2, pp 103-124

Hein, Laura ed. (2000) Censoring history: citizenship and memory in Japan, Germany and the United States, East Gate Book

Hein, Laura E. (2004) Reasonable men, powerful words : political culture and expertise in twentieth-century Japan, University of California Press

Hein, Patrick (1990) Politically explosive ritual (in German), Tagesspiegel, 11 November issue

_____(1992) The Japanese plutonium program. The strictest controls in the world (in German), Japan Magazin 2, 6, pp21-22

_____(1999) More yutori to solve the educational crisis? (in German), Japan Magazin 10, 10, p 7

_____(1999) The last shogun (in German), Japan Magazin, 10,12, pp 31-32

_____(1999) Out of touch with reality: legalisation of national flag and anathem (in German), Japan Magazin, 10, 9, pp 7-8

_____(2000) The slave laborer compensation issue in Germany and the Green party (written in Japanese), Mirai, 405, pp 1-5

_____(2000) The neoconservative stagnation (in German), Japan Magazin 11,1,pp 11-13

_____(2001) No comfort for comfort women (in German) Japan Magazin 12,2,pp 8-9

_____(2002) At 45 in a deadend (in German), Japan Magazin 13,4, pp 10-11

_____(2003) Youth violence (in German), Japan Magazin, 14,5, pp 5-7

_____(2003) Japan's nuclear industry. Are nuclear power reactors safe? (in German) ,Japan Magazin, 14,1, pp 45-46

_____(2004) Saigo Takamori. The last true samurai (in German), Japan Magazin, 15,6, pp 38-39

_____(2004) TV Drama Oshin (in German), Japan Magazin 15,2, pp 8-9

Hendry, Joy (1986) Becoming Japanese: the world of the pre-school child, Honolulu: University of Hawaii Press

_____(2004) Understanding Japanese society, London: Taylor & Francis

Hillsborough, Romulus (1999) Ryoma: life of a renaissance Samurai, Ridgeback Press

Hirata, Keiko (2002) Civil society in Japan: the growing role of NGOs in Tokyo's aid and development Policy, New York: St. Martin's Press.

_____(2004) Civil society and Japan's dysfunctional democracy, Journal of Developing Societies, 20(1-2), pp 107-124

_____(2005) Why Japan supports whaling, Journal of International Wildlife Law & Policy, 8, pp 1-21

Hongo, Jun (2007) Falling off the educational ladder. Brazilian schools have it all for students -except accreditation, Japan Times online edition, Feb. 17, 2007

Hook, Glenn D. and Takeda, Hiroko (2007) Self-responsibility and the nature of the post-war Japanese state: risk through the looking glass, Journal of Japanese Studies, Vol. 33, No. 1, pp. 93-123

Hook, Glenn D. and Hasegawa, Harukyo eds. (2006) Japanese responses to globalization, Houndmills, Basingstoke, Hampshire: Palgrave MacMillan

Hook, Glenn. D (2001) Political economy of Japanese globalization, Routledge

Hoston, G. A. (2005) Civil Society and the Public Sphere in the Construction of 'Modernity' in Japanese Political Thought Paper presented at the annual meeting of the American Political Science Association, Washington, DC

Howes, John F. ed. (1995) Nitobe Inazo: Japan's Bridge Across the Pacific, Boulder, San Francisco, Oxford: Westview Press

Howes, John F. (2003) Who was Nitobe Inazo?, Tokyo: Japan Echo, December issue, pp 48-54

Iokibe, Makoto (1999) Japan's civil society: an historical overview in: Yamamoto, Tadashi ed., Deciding the Public Good: Governance and Civil society in Japan, Japan Center for International Exchange, Tokyo

Iida, Yumiko (2002) Rethinking identity in modern Japan: nationalism as aesthetics, London: Routledge

Ikegami, Eiko (1995) The taming of the Samurai: honorific individualism and the making of modern Japan, Harvard University Press

_____(2003) Shame and the Samurai: institutions, trustworthiness and autonomy in the elite honor culture, Social Research, Vol 70, No 4, pp 1351-1378

_____(2005) Bonds of civility: aesthetic networks and political origins of Japanese culture, Cambridge University Press

_____(2007) My sociological practices and commuting identites in: Deflem Matthieu ed., Sociologists in a global age, pp 203-218, Ashgate Publishing

Imura, Hidefumi & Schreurs, Miranda A. eds. (2005) Environmental policy in Japan, Cheltenham, UK and Northampton, MA: Edward Elgar

Inoue, Masamichi S. (2007) Okinawa and the U.S. military: identity making in the age of globalization, Columbia University Press

Ishikawa, Eisuke (1996) Edo volunteerism (in Japanese), Tokyo: Kodansha Publishing, English excerpts retrieved on 28 September 2007 from the internet address http://www.japanfs.org/en/column/ishikawa 01.html#ishikawa

Ito, Hiroto and Lloyd, I. Sederer (1999) Mental health services reform in Japan, Harvard Review of Psychiatry, Vol 7, No 4, pp 208-215

Ito, Kimio (1998) The invention of *wa* and the transformation of the image of Prince Shotoku in modern Japan, pp 37-47 in: Vlastos, Stephen, ed. Mirror of modernity: Invented traditions of modern Japan, Berkeley and Los Angeles: University of California Press

Itoh, Mayumi (2000) Globalization of Japan: japanese sakoku mentality and U.S. efforts to open Japan, New York: Palgrave Macmillan

Iwabuchi, Koichi (2002) Recentering globalization: popular culture and Japanese transnationalism, Durham and London: Duke University Press.

Iwasaki, Michiko (2005) Mental health and counselling in Japan: a path toward societal transformation. Journal of Mental Health Counselling. 27, 2, pp 129-141

Jansen, Marius B. (1995) Warrior rule in Japan, Cambridge, England: Cambridge University Press

_____(2002) The making of modern Japan, Harvard University Press

Jaspers, Karl (1962) Socrates, Buddha, Confucius, Jesus, Harcourt & Brace

Japan Labor Review (2008) Disparity, poverty and labor, Vol 5, Number 4

Japan Labor Review (2009) The gender gap in the Japanese labor market , Vol 1, Number 1

Johnson, Chalmers (1995) omote (Explicit) and ura (Implicit): translating Japanese political terms, Chapter 8 in C. Johnson, Japan: Who Governs?: The Rise of the Developmental State, New York: Norton

_____(2003) Looting of Asia, retrieved on 28 August 2007 from the internet address http://www.lrb.co.uk/v25/n22/john04_.html

Johnson, David T. (2002) The Japanese way of justice. Prosecuting crime in Japan, Oxford University Press

_____(2005) The vanishing killer: Japan's postwar homicide decline, Social Science Japan Journal, 9, pp 73-90

_____(2006) Where the state kills in secret, Punishment & Society, Vol. 8, No. 3, pp 251-285

Jolivet, Muriel (1997) The childless society, Routledge

Jugon, Jean-Claude (1998) Social phobias in Japan (in French), Esf Editeur

Kagohashi, Teruko (2004) Childcare quality of Japanese approved daycare centers, retrieved on 10 July 2007 from the internet address http://www.childresearch.net/RESEARCH/MJ/MJ0004.HTM#7

Kato, Hideki (2002) Breaking ths state monopoly on public affairs in : Mann, Thomas E. and Sakaki, Takeshi eds., Governance for a new century: Japanese challenges, American Experience, Tokyo: Japan Center for International Exchange

Kamibeppu, Kiyoko (2005) Reconsideration of motherhood in contemporary Japan. The American Journal of Psychoanalysis, 65, 1, pp 13-29

Kaneko, Sachiko (1994) The struggle for legal rights and reforms: a historical view, pp 3-15 in: Fujimura-Fanselow, Kumiko and Kameda, Atsuko eds., Japanese Women. New Feminist Perspectives on the Past, Present and Future.

Kanno, Toshiko (2007) Act on the welfare of workers who take care of children or other family members including child care and family leave in: Japan Labor Law Review, Vol 4, Issue 3, p 29-53

Kawai, Hayao (1995) Dreams, mythys and fairy tales in Japan, Einsiedeln: Daimon

_____(1999) Individualism in the Japanese cultural context. Asia-Pacific Review, Vol 2, Number 2, pp 12-23

Kawasaki, Osamu (2006) Hannah Arendt and political studies in Japan (in Japanese), The Japanese Journal of Political Thought, No. 6, pp. 82-109

Kerr, Alex (2001) Dogs and demons: the fall of modern Japan, Penguin Books

Kyu, Hyun Kim (2008) The age of visions and arguments. Parliamentarianism and the national public sphere in early Meiji Japan, Massachusetts: Harvard University Press

Kimura, Hitomi and Tuerk, Andreas (2008) Emerging Japanese emissions trading schemes and prospects for linking. Working Paper 5. 22. Publisher: Climate Strategies, retrieved on 14 November 2008 from the internet address http://www.joanneum.at/ climate/ linking/index.html

Kodama, Shigeo (2003) Rethinking Hannah Arendt in the context of politics in the 1990s Japan - focusing on Arendt's critique on Karl Marx, retrieved on 20 July 2008 from the internet address http://hdl.handle.net/10083/762

Kingston, Jeff (2004) Japan's quiet transformation: social change and civil society in the 21st century, Routledge Curzon Press

Knight, John (2003) Waiting for wolves in Japan: an anthropological study of people-wildlife relations, Oxford University Press

Kobayashi, Nobuhisa et al (2003) The effect of paroxetine on Taijinkyofusho: a report of three cases, Psychiatry 66 (3) , pp 262-267

Krauss, Ellis et al eds. (1984) Conflict in Japan, Honolulu: University of Hawaii Press

Krauss, Ellis S. (2003) TV news in Japan: reporting on politics or shaping it? Broadcasting politics in Japan: NHK and television news , Ithaca, NY: Cornell University Press. Available online at http://www. ojr.org / japan /media /1 054281719.php

LeBlanc, Robin M. (1999) Bicycle citizens: the political world of the Japanese housewife, University of Berkeley Press

Lebra, Takie (2007) Identity, gender and status in Japan, Honolulu: University of Hawai Press

Lee, Soo Im; Murphy-Shigematsu, Stephen; Befu, Harumi (2006) Japan's diversity dilemmas: ethnicity, citizenship, and education, iUniverse Inc.

Leonardsen, Dag (2004) Japan as a low-crime nation, New York: Palgrave Macmillan

Lie, John (2001) Multiethnic Japan, Cambridge: Harvard University Press

Maekawa, Michiko (2001) The dilemma of authentic self-ideology in contemporary Japan, International Journal of Japanese Sociology, Volume 10, pp 16-28

Martinez, Dolores P. (2007) Modern Japanese culture and society, London and New York: Routledge

Maruyama, Masao and Morris, Ivan eds. (1969) Thought and behavior in modern Japanese politics, Tokyo, Oxford, New York: Oxford University Press

McVeigh, Brian (2002) Aisatsu: ritualized politeness as sociopolitical and economic management in Japan in: Donahue, Ray T ed., Exploring Japaneseness, London: Ablex Publishing

McCormack, Gavan (2001) The emptiness of Japanese affluence, New York: M.E. Sharpe

McCormack, Noah (2005) From alien to backward: reconceptualizing difference in modern Japan, paper retrieved on 30 october 2008 from www.ritsumei.ac.jp/acd/re/k-rsc/lcs/kiyou/17-3/17-3MCCORMACK.pdf,pp 209-222

Minato, Akiko (2003) Remembering a great educator and pacifist,Japan Echo, December issue, Tokyo, pp 44-46

Mishima, Yukio (1966) The Voices of the heroic dead (in Japanese) Tokyo: Kawade Shobo

_____(1978) The Samurai ethic and modern Japan, Tokyo : Charles E. Tuttle

Mitscherlich, Alexander and Margarete (1975) The inability to mourn: principles of collective behaviour, New York: Beverley R. Placzek

Mitscherlich, Alexander (1963) On the road towards a fatherless society (in German), Munich: Piper

Mitsumoto, Sato (2006) Renaming schizophrenia: a Japanese perspective, World Psychiatry, February , 5(1), pp 53–55

Miyamoto, Tsuneichi /Irish, Jeffrey Publisher (2009) The forgotten Japanese: encounters with rural life and folklore, California: Stone Bridge Press

Miyamoto, Masao (1994) Straightjacket society. An insider's irreverent view of bureaucratic Japan, Tokyo, Kodansha

Miyaoka, Isao (2004) Legitimacy in international society. Japan's reaction to global wildlife preservation, New York: Palgrave Macmillan

Mizuko, Ito et al (2005) Personal, portable, pedestrian: mobile phones in Japanese life, MIT Press

Ministry of Foreign Affairs of Japan (2004), ODA & NGO, Tokyo

Moriarty, Elizabeth (1972) The communitarian aspect of Shinto matsuri, Asian Folklore Studies, Vol. 31, No. 2, pp 91-140

Morris-Suzuki, Tessa (1997) Re-inventing Japan: time, space and nation, New York: M.E.Sharpe

Morris-Suzuki, Tessa ed. (2008) Contradictions of globalization- democracy, culture, and public sphere, Tokyo: IHouse Press

Morris, Ivan (1960) Nationalism and the right wing in Japan, London: Oxford University Press

_____(1975) The apotheosis of Saigo the great in: the nobility of failure: tragic heroes in the history of Japan, Holt, Rinehart & Winston

Morita, Masatake et al (1998) Morita therapy and the true nature of anxiety-based disorders (*Shinkeishitsu*), State University of New York Press

Motohashi, Yutaka et al (2004) Community-based suicide prevention program in Japan using a health promotion approach, Environmental Health and Preventive Medicine, 9, pp 3-8

Mumford, Lewis (1958) The transformations of man, New York: Harper and Brothers

Murakami, Haruki (2002) Underground: the Tokyo gas attack and the Japanese psyche, London: Vintage

Murphy-Shigematsu, Stephen (2000) Cultural psychiatry and minority identities in Japan: a constructivist narrative approach to therapy, Psychiatry, 63, 4, pp 371-384

_____(2007) Expanding the borders of the nation: ethnic diversity and citizenship education in Japan in: Banks, James A. Diversity and citizenship education: global perspectives, Jossey-bass

Nagera, Humberto (2005) The Oedipus complex revisited: suggestions for its amplifications and its role in later malignant acting out and conflicts, retrieved on 15 December 2008 from the internet address www.thecjc.org /pdf/ OEDIPUS_COMPLEX_REVISITED.pdf

Najita, Tetsuo and Harootunian, Harry (1988) Japanese revolt against the West: political and cultural criticism in the twentieth century in : Hall, John W et al , eds. The Cambridge History of Japan. Volume 6. The Twentieth Century, Cambridge University Press, pp 711-774

Najita, Tetsuo (1998) Visions of virtue in Tokugawa Japan, Honolulu: University of Hawaii Press

Najita, Tetsuo and Koschmann Victor J. eds. (2005) Conflict in modern Japanese history: the neglected tradition, Cornell East Asia Series

Nakada, Makoto et al (2005) Japanese conceptions of privacy: An intercultural perspective, Ethics and Information Technology, Volume 7, Number 1 , pp 27-36

Nakane, Chie (1970) Japanese society. California: University of California Press

Nakano, Yoshiaki (2003) Counseling systems as a means of preventing delinquency in: Foljanty-Jost, Gesine ed., Juvenile delinquency in Japan: Reconsidering the Crisis, Leiden:Brill

Nakano, Lynne Y. (2003) Community volunteers in Japan: everyday stories of social change, Curzon Press

Nakamura, Megumi and Watanabe-Muraoka, Agnes (2006) Gobal social responsibility: developing a scale for senior high school students in Japan. International Journal for the Advancement of Counseling. Vol 28,3, pp 213-226

Nathan, John (2004) Japan unbound: a volatile nation's quest for pride and purpose, Houghton : Mifflin

Ng, Chee (2008) Study visit on community mental health in Japan, retrieved on 23 october 2008 from the internet address http://www.nc np.go.jp/nimh/keikaku/vision/index_e.html

Nishizono, Masahisa (2005) Culture, psychopathology and psychotherapy: changes observed in Japan, pp 40-54 in: Weng-Shing, Tseng et al eds., Asian culture and psychotherapy, Honolulu: University of Hawai Press

Nitobe, Inazo (2007) Bushido. The soul of Japan, IBC Publishing Tokyo

Nitta, Mayumi (1999) Higashiyama Kaii. An artist for whom painting was a form of prayer, The East, 1999, 35:2

Nomiya, Daishiro (2004) Japan and Asia in a globalizing world. International Journal of Japanese Sociology, Number 13, pp 2-6

OECD (2007) Income inequality, poverty and social spending in Japan, retrieved on 21 August 2007 from the internet address http://www.olis. oecd.org /olis/2007doc.nsf/43bb6130e5e86e5fc12569fa005d004c/7cc992fec98ebdc0 c12572fe004811cd/$FILE/JT03228959.PDF

OECD (2008) Education at a glance 2008. OECD briefing note for Japan, re- trieved on 26 December 2008 from the internet address www. oecd. org/ edu/ eag2008

OECD (2008), Environmental outlook to 2030, Summary retrieved on 10 June 2008 from the internet address www.oecd.org/ dataoecd/29 /33/40200582.pdf

Oe, Kenzaburo (1999) On politics and literature. Two lectures by Kenzaburo Oe, Occasional Papers on the Doreen B. Townsend Center for the Humanities, No 18

Okano, Kaori H. (2006) The global-local interface in multicultural education policies in Japan. Comparative Education, 42, 4, pp 473-491

Okuda, Yasuhiro (2003) The United Nations convention on the rights of the child and Japan's international family law including nationality law. Hokudai Hogaku Ronshu, 54, 1, 456, pp 87-110

Ohnuki-Tierney, Emiko (2005) Japanese monarchy in historical and comparative perspective, pp 209-232 in : Quigley, Declan ed. , The character of kinship, Oxford & NY: Berg

Orr , James J. (2001) The victim as hero: ideologies of peace and national identity in postwar Japan, Honolulu: University of Hawaii Press

Oshima et al (2007) How many long-stay schizophrenia patients can be discharged in Japan, Psychiatry and Clinical Neurosciences, 61, pp 71-77

Palmer, Joy A. ed. (2001) Fifty key thinkers on the environment, Routledge

Pekkanen, R (2001) Japan's new politics: the case of the NPO law. Journal of Japanese studies, 26(1), pp 111-148

Pike, Kathleen M. and Amy, Borovoy (2004) The rise of eating disorders in Japan: issues of culture and limitations of the model of "westernization", Culture, Medicine and Psychiatry, Vol. 28, Iss. 4; pp 493-531

Pizer, William A and Morgenstern, Richard D. (2007) Reality check: the nature and performance of voluntary environmental programs in the United States, Europe and Japan, RFF Press

Preston, Ted M. (2003) The stoic Samurai, Asian Philosophy, Vol. 13, No 1, pp 39-52

Ravina, Mark (2004)The life and battles of Saigo Takamori, Hoboken. John Wiley & Sons

Reader, Ian (2000) Religious violence in contemporary Japan: the case of Aum Shinrikyo, Honolulu: University of Hawaii Press

Rebick, Marcus and Takenaka, Ayumi (2006) The changing Japanese family, Routledge, Contemporary Japan

Reischauer, E.O. & Jansen, M.B. (2004) Japanese today: change and continuity, Belknap Press

Riesman, David (1950) The lonely crowd, New Haven

Riordan, Brian (2005) Language policy for linguistic minority students in Japanese public schools and prospects for bilingualism: the Nikkei Brazilian case, retrieved on 25 May 2008 from the internet address www. indiana. edu /~iulcwp/pdfs/05-riordan.pdf

Roberson, James E. and Suzuki, Nobue eds. (2003) Men and masculinities in contemporary Japan. Dislocating the salary man Doxa, London: Routledge Curzon

Robertson, Jennifer ed. (2005) A companion to the anthropology of Japan, Blackwell Publishing Ltd

_____(2002) Blood talks. Eugenic modernity and the creation of new Japanese, History and Anthropology, Vol 13 (3), pp 191-216

Rogers, Carl (1995) What understanding and acceptance mean to me, Journal of Humanistic Psychology, Vol 35 No.4, pp 7-22

Saaler, Sven and Schwentker, Wolfgang eds. (2008) The Power of memory in modern Japan, Folkestone: Global Oriental

Sakamoto, Rumi (2001) Dream of a modern subject: Maruyama Masao, Fuku-zawa Yukichi, and 'Asia' as the limit of Ideology Critique, Japanese Studies, Vol 2, No2, pp 137-153

Sato, Iwao (2002) Autonomy and mobilization. Two faces of Japan's civil socie-ty, paper presented at the annual meeting for Social Science Research on Ja-pan on November 21-24, pp 197-210

Sato, Hiroaki (1995) Legends of the Samurai.Woodstock, NY: The Overlook Press

Sato, Mitsumoto (2006) Renaming schizophrenia: a Japanese perspective, World psychiatry, Vol 5, No 1. , pp 53-55

Sasaki, Masamichi (2004) Globalization and national identity in Japan, Interna-tional Journal of Japanese Sociology 13 (1), pp 69–87

Satow, Ernest (2000) A Diplomat in Japan, NY and Tokyo:ICG Muse

Semba, T. (2006) Present issues in mental health and welfare services in Japan, The Japanese Bulletin of Social Psychiatry; 14: pp 44-48

Seraphim, Franziska (2006) War memory and social politics in Japan, 1945–2005, Cambridge, Mass.: Harvard University Press

Schaede, Ulrike & Grimes, William eds. (2003) Japan's managed globalization : adapting to the Twenty-first Century, New York: M.E.Sharpe

Schoppa, Leonard J. (2006) Race for the exits: the unraveling of Japan's system of social protection, Cornell University Press

Schreurs, Miranda A. (2003), Environmental politics in Japan, Germany and the United States, Cambrige University Press

Schreurs, Miranda A. (2004) Assessing Japan's role as a global environmental leader,

Policy and Society, 2004 Vol. 23, No. 1, pp 88-110

Schulz, Kathryn (2004) Did anti-depressants depress Japan?,The New York Times online edition August 22

Schwartz Frank J. and Pharr Susan J. eds.(2003) The state of civil society in Japan. Cambridge: Cambridge University Press

Shiba, Ryotaro (1998) The last shogun, Tokyo: Kodansha

Shipper, Apichai (2002) The political construction of foreign workers in Japan, Critical Asian Studies, Vol. 34, No. 1, pp 41-68

Skov, Lise and Moeran, Brian eds. (1996) Women, media, and consumption in Japan, Honolulu: University of Hawaii Press

Soerensen, Andre (2002) Making of urban Japan: cities and planning from Edo to the 21 century, Routledge

Smith, David (2008) The killing of children by children as a symptom of national crisis: reactions in Britain and Japan (with Kiyoko Sueda), Criminology and Criminal Justice, 8, 1, pp 5-25

Sugimoto, Yoshio (2003) An introduction to Japanese society, Cambridge: Cambridge University Press

Sasaki-Uemura, W. M. (2001) Organizing the spontaneous: citizen protest in postwar Japan, Honolulu: University of Hawaii Press

Shoji, Kichiro et al (1992) The Ashio copper mine pollution case: the origins of environmental destruction, pp 18-62 in: Ui, Jun ed (1992) Industrial Pollution in Japan, The United Nations University Press Tokyo retrieved on 18 october 2008 from the internet address http://www.unu.edu /unu press /unup books /uu35ie/uu35ie00.htm#Contents

Strunkel, Kenneth et al (1976) The economic superpowers and the environment: the United States, the Soviet Union, and Japan, W.H. Freeman

Suzuki, S. (2005) A case about a boy with selective mutism: an attempt to give his mother the role of co-therapist. Japanese Journal of Counseling Science, 37, pp 54-63

Széll, György and Tominaga, Ken'ichi eds. (2004) The environmental challenges for Japan and Germany, Peter Lang Publishers

Tachikawa, Akira (2007) Education and democracy in Japan: historical and contemporary perspectives, pp 167-192 in: Cam, Philip ed. Volume 4: Philosophy, Democracy and Education, The University of New South Wales Sydney Australia

Tamotsu, Aoki (2002) Aspects of globalization in contemporary Japan in: Berger, Peter L. and Huntington, Samuel eds., Many Globalizations. Cultural Diversity in the Contemporary World, Oxford : Oxford University Press, pp 68-88

Tamotsu, Aoki (2004) Globalization, cultural diversity and Japanese culture: for the development of a multicultural world in: Proceedings of the International Symposium. Cultural Diversity and Globalization. The Arab-Japanese Experience and Cross-Regional Dialogue, Paris Unesco, pp 89-94

Tamura, Takeshi (2001) The development of family therapy and the experience of fatherhood in Japanese context, paper presented at the 13th International Family Therapy Congress, November 14, 2001, Porto Alegre, Brazil retrieved on 17 december 2007 from the internet address http://www. u-gakugei. ac.jp/~tam/research/culture/Brazil.html

Tanaka, Yasuhiro et al (2003) The media representation of 'Okinawa' and US/Japan hegemony, Inter-Asia Cultural Studies, Volume 4, Issue 3, pp

419-432

Tanaka, Yuki (2002) Japan's comfort women: sexual slavery and prostitution during World War II and US occupation, London: Routledge

_____(1996) Hidden Horrors: Japanese war crimes in World War II. Colorado: Westview Press

Terajima, Toshio (2006) The theory of Hannah Arendt: the quest for human centered politics (in Japanese), Kyoto: Minerubashobo

Tonaki, Yotetsu (2008) The reception of Hannah Arendt in Japan (in French), in: Hannah Arendt abroad. Lectures du Monde, in: Revue Tumultes, No. 30, pp 67-80

Tsuchiya, Kenji J. and Takei, Nori (2004) Focus on psychiatry in Japan, British Journal of Psychiatry, 184, pp 88-92

Tsunematsu, Naomi (2004) Gender power under female leadership: a local woman's association of Japan, Japanese Studies, Vol 24, No 1, pp 97-114

Tsunemoto, Yamamoto (1979) Hagakure. The book of the Samurai, Tokyo: Kodansha International

Tucker, Mary E. and Berthrong, John Eds. (1998) Confucianism and ecology: the interrelation of heaven, earth, and humans, Cambridge, MA: Harvard University Press

Upham, F. (1987) Law and social change in postwar Japan, Cambridge, MA: Harvard University Press

Ueno, Chizuko et al (2004) Nationalism and gender, Melbourne: Trans Pacific Press

Ueno Chizuko (2001) Modern patriarchy and the formation of the Japanese nation state, pp 213-223, in: Denoon, Hudson, McCormack and Morris-Suzuki eds. : Multicultural Japan, Cambridge University Press

Proceedings of the UNESCO globalization conferences hold in Japan can be accessed at the internet address http:// portal.unesco. org/en/ev.php-URL _ID=36914&URL_DO=DO_TOPIC&URL_SECTION=201.htm

Uno, Kathleen S. (1999) Passages to modernity : motherhood, childhood and social reform in early twentieth century Japan, Honolulu: University of Hawaii Press

Van Wolferen, Karel (1989) The enigma of Japanese power: people and politics in a stateless Nation, London : Macmillan

Vlastos, Stephen ed. (1997) Mirror of modernity: invented traditions of modern Japan, Berkeley: University of California Press

Walker, Brett L. (2005) The lost wolves of Japan, Seattle: University of Washington Press

Waswo, Anne (1996) Modern Japanese society 1868-1994, Oxford University Press

Watanabe, Hisako (1992) Difficulties in *amae*: a clinical perspective, Infant Mental Health Journal, Vol 13, No 1 , pp 26-33

White, Merry (2002) Perfectly Japanese: making families in an era of upheaval, University of California

Weng-Shing, Tseng et al (2005) Asian culture and psychotherapy, Honolulu: University of Hawaii Press

West, Mark D. (1997) Legal rules and social norms in Japan's secret world of Sumo, The Journal of Legal Studies, Vol. 26, No. 1, pp. 165-201

Wright, Leonore J. (2005) Plato's Socrates and Soseki's sensei: living the sovereign life, Asia Philosophy, Vol 15, No 1, pp 61-76

Yates, Charles L. (1995) Saigo Takamori. The man behind the myth, London; New York: Kegan Paul International

Yoda, Tomiko and Harootunian, Harry D. (2006) Japan after Japan, Duke University Press

Yoneyama, Shoko (1999) Japanese high school: silence and resistance, Routledge

Yoshino, Kosaku (1992) Cultural nationalism in contemporary Japan London: Routledge

Zeilenziger, Michael (2006) Shutting out the sun: how Japan created its own lost generation, Vintage Books

Zhou, Yanfei et al (2003) Childcare system in Japan, Journal of Population and Social Security, Supplement to Volume 1, pp 1-30

Index